The Periodicals of American Transcendentalism

BY
CLARENCE L. F. GOHDES

DURHAM · NORTH CAROLINA
DUKE UNIVERSITY PRESS
1931

PREFACE

The present volume undertakes a study of the periodicals which were conducted or controlled by people who were known in their day as transcendentalists. An exception is the last chapter, dealing with *The Index*, a journal which throws so much light upon the later history of transcendentalism that the writer felt that it should not be omitted from his study.

This book does not presume to be a general treatise on transcendentalism, and it takes for granted a knowledge of such investigations as have been made by O. B. Frothingham and H. C. Goddard.

In making the present study the writer has profited by the assistance and suggestions of a number of gentlemen to whom he would express his gratitude: Professors K. B. Murdock and Bliss Perry, of Harvard University; J. B. Hubbell, of Duke University; and A. H. Thorndike, H. Schneider, E. E. Neff, and R. L. Rusk, of Columbia University. For his generous aid and kindly direction the author owes an especial debt to Professor Rusk, under whose supervision this work was written as a Columbia doctoral dissertation.

The chapter dealing with "*The Western Messenger* and *The Dial*" is reprinted with few changes from *Studies in Philology* for January, 1929.

CLARENCE GOHDES

Duke University
April, 1931

CONTENTS

	PAGE
Chapter I—Introduction	3
Chapter II—*The Western Messenger* and *The Dial*	17
Chapter III—Orestes A. Brownson and *The Boston Quarterly Review*	38
Chapter IV—*The Present*	83
Chapter V—*The Harbinger*	101
Chapter VI—*The Spirit of the Age*	132
Chapter VII—Elizabeth Peabody and Her *Æsthetic Papers*	143
Chapter VIII—*The Massachusetts Quarterly Review*	152
Chapter IX—*The Dial* (Cincinnati)	194
Chapter X—*The Radical*	210
Chapter XI—*The Index*	229
Appendix—Two Uncollected Emerson Items	255
Index	257

THE PERIODICALS OF AMERICAN TRANSCENDENTALISM

Chapter I
INTRODUCTION

American transcendentalism, an eddy in the current of Romanticism, has never been satisfactorily defined. It has been variously regarded as a distinct philosophical system, a mere "faith," a recrudescence of the Puritan spirit in an age of developing national consciousness, a reaction against the dominion of Locke and the Scotch theologians, pantheism with a peculiar admixture of skepticism, and so on. Most of the important students of the transcendental movement have commented upon the various foreign influences which have shaped its course. The writings of Plato, Kant, Schelling, Coleridge, Carlyle, Cousin, Constant, and even the Orientals have been mentioned as possible sources. There has also been suggested the importance of the spirit of individualism fostered by the Congregational churches in New England since the days of the Mathers, or the survival of an intellectual restlessness which was the aftermath of the war with England.

The failure of later treatments of transcendentalism to be explicit and definite is, of course, inherent in the very nature of the subject. Religion, philosophy, and, to a less extent, sociology and literature are all involved. Moreover, like every phase of idealistic philosophy in the nineteenth century, it was eclectic. Indeed, should a new variety of idealism be discovered among the tribes of Africa, it would probably bear some of the earmarks of transcendentalism, for the characteristics of a "high Platonic mysticism," so much in evidence in the writings of Emerson and his friends, are practically the same wherever manifested. Jacob Boehme, Swedenborg, Saint Francis of Assisi, the youthful Jonathan Edwards, Alcott —all have much in common with the Hindu seer contemplating the word "Om." East and West will always meet when mysticism is involved.

One may further recognize the futility of later attempts to define transcendentalism if one undertakes to study the utterances made on the subject by its exponents and their contemporaries. In 1842 there appeared in Boston a tract of one hundred and four pages calculated to explain the matter. Its author, possibly Charles Mayo Ellis, wrote:

> This, then, is the doctrine of Transcendentalism—the substantive, independent existence of the soul of man, the reality of conscience, the religious sense, the inner light, of man's religious affections, his knowledge of right and truth, his sense of duty, the *honestem* [sic] apart from the *utile*—his love for beauty and holiness, his religious aspirations—with this it starts as something not dependent on education, custom, command, or anything beyond man himself.[1]

One is reminded of Plotinus's definition of mysticism: "the flight of the alone to the alone."

In 1865 a student at Williams College asked Emerson what transcendentalism was. His remarks, as recorded by his questioner, included these words:

> It isn't, I suppose, a commodity or 'Plan of Salvation,' or anything concrete; not, surely, an 'established church'; rather, unestablished; not even bread, perhaps, but a leaven hidden.
>
> If we will only see that which is about us, we shall see also above. Is God far from any of us? There is an equality of the human spirit to the world's phenomena. We look neither up to the universe nor down to it, but confront it. . . . The Transcendentalist sees everything as idealist. That is, all events, objects, etc., seen, are images to the consciousness. It is the thought of them only one sees. You shall find God in the unchanged essence of the universe, the air, the river, the leaf; and in the subjective

---

[1] *An Essay on Transcendentalism*, Boston, Crocker and Ruggles, 1842, p. 19. The work is anonymous. T. W. Higginson thought that Ellis was the author (*Harvard University Library Letters*, MSS., LXII, 133). A copy in the Boston Public Library is classified under Ellis's name.

unfolding of your nature, the determination of the private spirit, everything of religion. As for the name, no one knows who first applied the name.[2]

Emerson, still identifying transcendentalism with Platonic idealism, scarcely bettered the definition of one of his neighbors, who had told him years before, that the word simply meant "a little beyond."[3]

In 1840, Christopher P. Cranch received a letter from his father which exhibited great concern for his spiritual welfare, since a rumor had reached his home that he had been led astray by German speculative thought. In reply the son protested his ignorance of the philosophical writings of Kant and his German followers, and expressed an interest in the doctrines of Victor Cousin. He further attempted to assuage parental anxiety by an explanation of the word "transcendentalist":

> But somehow the name "Transcendentalist" has become a nickname here for all who have broken away from the material philosophy of Locke, and the old theology of many of the early Unitarians, and who yearn for something more satisfying to the soul. It has almost become a synonym for one who, in whatever way, preaches the spirit rather than the letter.
> The name has been more particularly applied to Mr. Emerson, or those who believe in or sympathize with him. Mr. Emerson has been said to have imported his doctrine from Germany. But the fact is, that no man starts more independently of other minds than he does. He seems to me very far from Kant or Fichte. His writings breathe the very spirit of religion and faith. Whatever his speculations may be, there is nothing in anything he says, which is inconsistent with Christianity. . . .
> It is convenient to have a name which may cover all those who contend for perfect freedom, who look for progress in philosophy and theology, and who sympathize with each other in the hope that the future will not always be as the past. The name

[2] Charles J. Woodbury, *Talks with Ralph Waldo Emerson*, New York, n.d. (1890), pp. 108-109.
[3] Emerson's *Journals*, IV, 114 (1836).

"Transcendentalist" seems to be thus fixed upon all who profess to be on the movement side, however they may differ among themselves. But union in sympathy differs from union in belief. Since we cannot avoid names, I prefer the term "New School" to the other long name. This could comprehend all free seekers after truth, however their opinions differ.[4]

Transcendentalism had the quickened zest of mystery. Even Dickens attempted to find out what had occasioned the excitement in the intellectual circles of Boston during his stay there.

The fruits of this earth have their growth in corruption. Out of the rottenness of these things, there has sprung up, in Boston, a sect of philosophers known as Transcendentalists. On inquiring what this appellation might be supposed to signify, I was given to understand that whatever was unintelligible would be certainly transcendental. Not deriving much comfort from this elucidation, I pursued the inquiry still farther, and found that the Transcendentalists are followers of my friend Mr. Carlyle, or, I should rather say, of a follower of his, Mr. R. W. Emerson. This gentleman has written a volume of Essays, in which, among much that is dreamy and fanciful (if he will pardon me for saying so), there is much more that is true and manly, honest and bold. Transcendentalism has its occasional vagaries (what school has not?) but it has good healthful qualities in spite of them; not least among the number a hearty disgust of cant, and an aptitude to detect her in all the million varieties of her everlasting wardrobe. And therefore if I were a Bostonian, I think I would be a Transcendentalist.[5]

The attempt of Dickens to explain transcendentalism reflects a certain attitude among many Americans who made the term a byword for obscure nonsense. For example, *Brother Jonathan,* a New York weekly, of importance largely because of its connection with one of Cooper's quarrels, in its issue for March 26, 1842, contained a bur-

---
[4] L. C. Scott, *The Life and Letters of Christopher Pearse Cranch,* Boston and New York, 1917, pp. 49-51.
[5] *American Notes,* 1842, cap. III.

Introduction

lesque account of a "Boz Dinner" in which a letter "from a transcendentalist" figured.

Sundial Ave. Feb. 1, 1842

Gentlemen of the Committee:

The wonder-sign of Great Goslington's furibundity is world-absorbing. Quozdom yawns abysmal. Liontzed humanity, ephemeral though, floats upon the time-stream of newspapers, and peradventure may avoid fuliginous obliviscity. . . .

On the time-trodden subject of old shoes, what metaphysics have been expended! Erebus-like, nevertheless, it frowns repellent; leaving respectable humanity to go barefoot or "toe the mark" in coricaceous integuments. Since calf-skin was made into knapsacks, cobblers have gone in leather aprons. But to Quozdom what avails this? Gentlemen, I incline not dinner-wise. And why?—I have dined already. *Pransi;*—enough.

I remain, gentlemen,

Moonshine Wilkywater

In his *Oak Openings* Cooper tried to portray his bee-hunter as a rather poetic follower of his craft, but hastened to assure his readers that he had "nothing of the transcendental folly that usually accompanies the sentimentalism of the exaggerated."[6] Convers Francis joked about Theodore Parker's "transcendental chirography," and, on December 30, 1843, wrote to him:

Exchanged [pulpits] last Sunday with Allen; and Dr. Gray (clarum et venerabile nomen) told me—would you believe it—about the wicked transcendentalists. I asked, "Do you know what the word means?" "Yes," was the reply. "Then you are lucky; what is it?" "A transcendentalist is an enemy of the institution of Christianity."[7]

The Reverend John Pierce, who held a record of having attended forty-six consecutive commencements at Harvard, observed in his notes on the proceedings for 1839:

[6] Cap. IV.
[7] Parker MSS. deposited by F. B. Sanborn in the library of the Massachusetts Historical Society.

For the Master's degree Robert Bartlett gave an oration of thirty-six minutes on "No Good that is possible, but shall one day be real." This I suppose to be the Transcendentalism which is captivating to a few irregular genius's. But to me it was like the tale of an idiot, full of sound and fury, signifying nothing.[8]

Another divine, after a trip to Concord, from which much was expected, opened his next service with the hymn "Thou first great cause, least understood," and preached on the text: "I saw an altar with this inscription, To an Unknown God." A Baltimore clergyman described transcendentalism as "a new philosophy which has risen, maintaining that nothing is everything in general, and everything is nothing in particular."[9] Akin to this definition is the more celebrated one delivered by a teacher who was traveling on a Mississippi River steamboat: "See the holes made in the bank yonder by the swallows. Take away the bank, and leave the apertures, and this is Transcendentalism."

When Holmes's Autocrat speaks of "relations with truth as I understand truth," the old gentleman across the table sniffs, and remarks that he talks like a "transcendentalist." Much better in its humor, of course, is Hawthorne's description of his substitute for Bunyan's monsters:

He is a German by birth, and is called Giant Transcendentalist; but as to his form, his features, his substance, and his nature generally, it is the chief peculiarity of this huge miscreant that neither he for himself nor anybody for him has ever been able to describe them. . . . He shouted after us, but in so strange a phraseology that we knew not what he meant, nor whether to be encouraged or affrighted.[10]

[8] *Proc. Mass. Hist. Soc.*, second series, V, 227.
[9] Moncure Conway, *Emerson at Home and Abroad*, Boston, 1882, pp. 187-188.
[10] "The Celestial Railroad," originally published at Boston in 1843, and later included in *Mosses from an Old Manse*.

Introduction 9

Although contemporaries of the movement were not able to say what transcendentalism was, they knew who the transcendentalists were. There is a tendency at present to include among their number such literary figures as Melville and Whitman, who assuredly did not regard themselves as transcendentalists.[11] In the theology of certain sects sanctification is treated in a two-fold manner: in a broader and in a narrower sense. For historical purposes a similar dichotomy might be made in a discussion of transcendentalism. In the broader sense one may include the philosophical notions of Whitman and Melville if circumstances seem to warrant. Of the exponents of transcendentalism in the narrow sense only those who were actually regarded by their contemporaries as such ought to be mentioned. These, of course, were practically all Unitarians at one time or another.[12] Upon considering the names of the narrower group, one finds that again two divisions seem desirable: the earlier and the later transcendentalists. The better known of the earlier transcendentalists in the narrower sense were: Dr. Channing, Emerson, Alcott, Orestes Brownson, Parker, Ripley, Convers Francis, W. H. Channing, F. H. Hedge, James Freeman Clarke, W. H. Furness, John S. Dwight, C. P. Cranch, Elizabeth Peabody, and, possibly, Margaret Fuller.

[11] Whitman once qualified a transcendentalist as "a writer of sunbeams and moonbeams, a strange and unapproachable person" (*The Complete Prose Works of Walt Whitman*, Putnams', Boston and New York, 1902, VI, 160). It was not until 1888 that he really understood what the transcendentalists believed (*With Walt Whitman in Camden*, New York, 1915, I, 125-126). In *Pierre* Melville made many remarks derogatory of transcendentalism (Constable, London, 1923, pp. 365-366), and referred to its exponents as "Muggletonian Scots and Yankees, whose vile brogue still the more bestreaks the stripedness of their Greek or German Neoplatonical originals" (*ibid.*, p. 290). In 1849 he wrote that he did not "oscillate in Emerson's rainbow" (*Some Personal Letters of Herman Melville*, ed. Meade Minnigerode, New York, 1922, p. 32).

[12] The more progressive Unitarian churches were often referred to as "Transcendental Unitarian" (cf., for example, H. F. Brownson, *Orestes A. Brownson's Early Life*, Detroit, 1898, p. 229). One of the earliest historians of transcendentalism, James Murdock, stressed the connection of the movement with Unitarianism (*Sketches of Modern Philosophy, especially among the Germans*, Edinburgh, 1843, p. 105).

Of the later ones, T. W. Higginson, Samuel Johnson, John Weiss, David A. Wasson, Samuel Longfellow, O. B. Frothingham, C. A. Bartol, and Moncure Conway should be mentioned. Bartol and Weiss are included in the second group because their chief activities in connection with transcendentalism belong to the later history of the New School.

When one undertakes to determine the reason why these men and women were known to their day as transcendentalists, the problem becomes very similar to that confronting the student of the New Humanism. A clear-cut analysis is hindered not only by the ramifications of the subject into almost every field of human thought, but by the absence of a definite set of principles with which to deal. Hence it is that a study of transcendentalism involves an interpretation rather than an exposition.

In the opinion of the present writer, transcendentalism was not primarily a philosophy or a reform movement: it was a mental and spiritual attitude. Essentially, it sought to find the source of all truth within the nature of man. Where the intellect failed to supply the necessary grounds for knowledge, "the soul," or spiritual intuition, came to the rescue. Although there was a considerable variation in the degree to which the transcendentalists exalted intuition over sense, all of them were potentially mystics. The chief manifestation of transcendentalism was in the sphere of religion. Indeed, transcendentalism in the narrower sense might be defined as Unitarianism in the process of "getting religion."

The origin of transcendentalism can be explained in a number of ways. It may have arisen as a natural reaction against the empirical philosophy of Locke, which dominated the religious opinions of the earlier Unitarians. Its fundamental principle, a belief in the infallibility of intuition, may have owed much to the writings of the Quakers, of Cudworth and Henry More, and the earlier works of Jonathan Edwards—all of which formed a part of the background of New England thought. But certainly when the transcendentalists began to express themselves in print they borrowed from the terminology of foreign Romantic doctrines retailed to America principally by Coleridge and Victor Cousin.

Interesting as the study of the sources of the transcendental movement may be, its history is more important for present purposes, and, accordingly, a brief survey of its course seems desirable. Although many of the younger followers of Dr. Channing, such as Emerson, Ripley, Hedge, Furness, and Brownson, had expressed their transcendental beliefs in print before 1838, it was not until that year that transcendentalism really began to attract public attention. Emerson's *Divinity School Address* precipitated such a conflict in the religious and intellectual circles of Boston that the press immediately undertook to satisfy public curiosity about the issues involved. For the time being Emerson took the place of Dr. Channing as the leader in the attack upon American Fundamentalism. But Emerson's unwillingness to sacrifice his art for his convictions led him to retire from the scene of controversy, and Theodore Parker assumed the mantle of Elijah. Until his death in 1850 Parker was in reality the chief transcendentalist in the narrower sense.

With the death of Parker the transcendentalists suffered a severe loss, for they had no leader to enunciate their principles. Moreover, their interest had turned into channels other than religion. The establishment of Brook Farm in 1841 had split them into two parties, and the growing importance of the abolition movement made nugatory any attempt to arouse wide interest in religious controversy. The force of transcendentalism as a moulder of public thought had long been dissipated by the pronounced individualism of its adherents, and even before the Civil War it was occasionally spoken of in the past tense.

But after the clamor of the war died away, the transcendentalists sought to rehabilitate their religious position by opposing the conservatism of the Unitarian church. Particularly active were the men who have been designated as the later group of transcendentalists, most of whom had not as yet left the ranks of the ministry. But with the desertion of various individuals from the cause, and the reluctance of many of the older transcendentalists to abandon their private intellectual pursuits, the more active rebels found it desirable to join forces with a constantly increasing number of materialists, whose ideas were based upon the philosophy of "Realism." With the growing popularity of evolution among the intelligentsia of the United States, the transcendentalists found themselves faced by a liberalism more liberal than their own. The result was inevitable, and transcendentalism passed from the American scene—to live on in the hearts of its surviving adherents, but never to attract public attention again.

In attempting a study of the transcendental movement through the analysis of a manifestation of coöperative activity among its exponents, the student is perplexed by a pronounced element of individualism. Then, too, there were undoubtedly various phases of the movement.[13] The so-called Transcendental Club was too informal an assemblage to be considered a practical demonstration of coöperation among its members. Its nature was somewhat that of an open forum.[14] The Concord School of Philosophy

---

[13] Cf. Marjorie H. Nicolson, "James Marsh and the Vermont Transcendentalists," *The Philosophical Review*, XXXIV, 29.

[14] Theodore Parker to G. E. Ellis, May 27, 1838: "There is a little society of good fellows such as Francis, Stetson, Ripley, Emerson, Alcott, Hedge and three

Introduction 13

had only a "local and reminiscent" interest in transcendentalism, according to its latest historian.[15] Its secretary maintained that "from the first, three quite distinct currents of philosophy flowed together in its teachings—of which only one was what is usually termed 'New England Transcendentalism'."[16] Brook Farm is often considered to have been a product of the movement, but the opposition to its principles manifested by a number of the leading transcendentalists indicates only too well the very lack of coöperation which led to its early failure. After a "private experiment," to use Ripley's own words, the West Roxbury community tested the theories of Fourier, and finally became a Phalanx based upon the doctrines of the French socialist as modified by Albert Brisbane.[17]

In his history of the movement in New England, O. B. Frothingham observes:

> The transcendental faith found expression in magazines and newspapers, which it called into existence, and which no longer survive. Its elaborate compositions were, from the nature of the case, few; its intellectual occupancy was too brief for the creation of a permanent literature.[18]

Accordingly, so far as literature is concerned, the closest approximation to concerted activity upon the part of the people who were known as transcendentalists in their own day, was the attempt to bring their views before the public by means of periodicals. The importance, then, of such a study as is undertaken in the present volume should be apparent.

---

or four more of us young striplings who meet when Hedge or Clarke are in this vicinity" (Parker MSS. in the library of the Mass. Hist. Soc.).

[15] Austin Warren, "The Concord School of Philosophy," *The New England Quarterly*, II, 230.

[16] F. B. Sanborn, *Recollections of Seventy Years*, Boston, 1909, II, 497.

[17] See "A Brook Farm Labor Record," by the present writer, *American Literature*, I, 297-303.

[18] *Transcendentalism in New England*, New York, 1876, p. 383.

When one realizes that when the New School began to express itself the leading journals of the country were all controlled by the conservatives, and that public opinion was continually prejudiced against its principles, the desire of its members to direct a periodical of their own is readily explained. Furthermore, a considerable number of them possessed a literary interest which could not be denied expression. Emerson's letters written to Carlyle during 1835 and 1836 indicate the ardent desire of their author and his associates to own a magazine of their own.[19] As late as 1850 Emerson referred to the journalistic "distemper" in New England and mentioned the fact that both he and Alcott were suffering from a "chronic case."[20]

The periodicals which it has seemed desirable to include in the present study are these:

The Western Messenger (1835-1841)
The Boston Quarterly Review (1838-1842)
The Dial (1840-1844)[21]
The Present (1843-1844)
The Harbinger (1845-1849)
The Spirit of the Age (1849-1850)
Æsthetic Papers (1849)
The Massachusetts Quarterly Review (1847-1850)
The Dial, Cincinnati (1860)
The Radical (1865-1872)
The Index (1870-1886)

Certain other journals are rather closely connected with the transcendental movement, such as *The Christian*

---

[19] During the twenties C. S. Henry and Karl Follen were discussing plans for a journal to set forth the newer philosophy (G. W. Spindler, *Karl Follen, a Biographical Study*, U. of Ill. diss., 1916, p. 126).

[20] Emerson to Samuel Ward, Feb. 24, 1850 (*Letters from R. W. Emerson to a Friend*, ed. C. E. Norton, 1899, p. 79).

[21] The present volume contains very little material relating to the most famous journal of the transcendentalists. Ample reason for this fact will be obtained from a reading of the two-volume introduction written by G. W. Cooke for the Rowfant Club's reprint of *The Dial*, Cleveland, 1902.

Introduction 15

Examiner,[22] the Boston *Commonwealth*, *The Phalanx*, and *The Journal of Speculative Philosophy*; but none of them deserves to be included in the list because of the nature of its contents or because of the fact that it was not controlled by people who were known as transcendentalists. A glance at the dates given in the table above will show that a study of the periodicals of transcendentalism supplies almost a contemporaneous history of the movement from the days when it first attracted attention. However, as will be seen, there is little connection between the various journals represented.

A word should perhaps be said as to the procedure in the discussion of them. Since most of them have little significance to a study of American journalism, the details of publication have been reduced to a minimum. Any notable treatment of transcendentalism itself within their pages has been mentioned. Special attention has been paid to the reaction of the members of the New School to the works and opinions of their fellows—particularly Emerson. Biographical detail has been injected only where circumstances seem to warrant it, as in the case of Orestes Brownson and Elizabeth Peabody, whose importance seems to have been forgotten by later students of the movement. Above all, the attempt has been made by exploring a specialized field to provide material which will supplement the studies of others who have written about the most significant phase of American idealism.

If the study of the periodicals of transcendentalism serves no other purpose, it will convince the reader that the movement had little to do with *belles-lettres*. When one of them was sent to Carlyle, he wrote to Emerson: "*Ach Gott!* These people and their affairs seem all 'melting' rapidly enough, into thaw-slush or one knows not

[22] See Frank L. Mott, "The *Christian Disciple* and the *Christian Examiner*," *The New England Quarterly*, I, 197-207.

what. Considerable madness is visible in them."[23] A similar reaction is still possible, even though one may not be cursed by chronic dyspepsia.

[23] *Carlyle-Emerson Correspondence*, ed. C. E. Norton, 1883, II, 49. The periodical was *The Present*.

CHAPTER II

THE WESTERN MESSENGER AND THE DIAL

The Western Messenger was the product of the literary ambitions of several young Unitarian ministers who desired to arouse in the West an interest in religious philosophy and in literature akin to that which had marked their earlier milieu in New England. Established in Cincinnati in 1835, by James Freeman Clarke, William G. Eliot, and Ephraim Peabody, the periodical announced as its primary object the purpose "to set forth and defend Unitarian views of Christianity,"[1] and bore the legend, "Devoted to Religion and Literature." This combining of a clerical purpose with the desire to provide readers with literary entertainment more or less secular, while no marked innovation in the history of Unitarian journalism,[2] was new to the West.

The attempt was first made to put the *Messenger* in the charge of several editors, but gradually the responsibility for its issue devolved upon Ephraim Peabody. During the first half of the year 1836 the burden fell upon Clarke, under whose supervision the magazine was published at Louisville, Kentucky. An effort has been made to determine the actual circumstances of its editing and publishing, but to little avail.[3] The fact of the matter seems to be that frequently, when the duties of the church called the editors away from the scene of its publication,

---

[1] *The Western Messenger*, I, 1. Hereinafter cited as "*W. M.*"
[2] See, for example, *The Unitarian Advocate*, published in Boston and elsewhere, I, 281 and 304.
[3] The "proposals" for the magazine had announced its name as *The Western Examiner*, doubtless after *The Christian Examiner* of Boston, then the chief Unitarian journal in America. The change was made because a St. Louis periodical had employed the name before the first number was in the press (*W. M.*, I, 1). The best account of its history is to be found in R. L. Rusk, *The Literature of the Middle Western Frontier*, 1925, I, 183.

The Western Messenger was left in the charge of various individuals who had already been regular contributors to its pages. Chief among these were James H. Perkins, Samuel Osgood, and Christopher P. Cranch.[4] Beginning with the number for May, 1839, the first of these three men, together with Clarke and W. H. Channing, assumed responsibility for its editorial policy. The October issue for the same year ended its publication, until May, 1840, when W. H. Channing took charge alone. With the issue for April of the next year it expired, chiefly because Clarke, its prime mover, had returned to New England, and its transcendental nature had caused the loss of subscribers.

Originally engaged most actively in furthering the cause of the Unitarian church in the West, as announced at the beginning of its career, the *Messenger*, under Clarke's influence chiefly, became more and more a literary magazine with a conservative attitude toward abolition and the kindred subjects so vexing to the era of dawning national consciousness. Before it ceased publication, it had become a full-fledged organ of transcendental thought. Under Channing's direction the title-page for the yearly volume had been changed to announce a more catholic devotion, "To Religion, Life, and Literature"; and a preliminary statement of policy declared that *The Western Messenger* "ought never to be the organ of a sect," since "Sectarianism is heresy."[5] The covers for some of the numbers printed in 1840 advertised the fact that the periodical acknowledged no "ecclesiastical author-

---

[4] Perkins had already conducted *The Western Monthly Magazine* with great success (W. H. Channing, *The Memoir and Writings of J. H. Perkins*, Boston and Cincinnati, 1851, I, 89). Cranch states in an account of his activities during his stay in the West, "One number of the 'Messenger' was made up almost entirely of my own writings" (L. C. Scott, *The Life and Letters of Christopher P. Cranch*, 1917, p. 41).

[5] *W. M.*, VIII, 5.

ity"; and this in spite of its having been published at the outset by the Western Unitarian Association.[6]

Aside from its literary merit as one of the most readable of the magazines published in the West of the time, the *Messenger* is eminently noteworthy for the reflection in its pages of the development of American liberalism—from the reaction against the spiritual inhibitions of Calvinism, through the emancipatory stages of interest in the philosophy of Cousin, Goethe, Kant, and Coleridge, to what Emerson termed the "Saturnalia or excess of faith";[7] namely, transcendentalism.

In addition to the products of the *Dial* group of writers, who will be discussed later, *The Western Messenger* printed material from pens so renowned that this fact alone would supply sufficient grounds for its reaching "perhaps the highest point in the literary achievement of early Western magazines."[8] It is now rather well known that Keats's "Ode to Apollo" and two sections of his journal were printed first on its pages.[9]

In the beginning, the editors of the *Messenger* planned to encourage literary activity in the West by conducting a department entitled "Western Poetry," in which were printed and criticized verses by such poets as W. D. Gallagher, C. D. Drake, and M. P. Flint.[10] Before long,

[6] The title-pages of the first three volumes named the Western Unitarian Association as publishers. In 1838 the periodical received financial aid from the American Unitarian Association (*W. M.*, IV, 432).

[7] "The Transcendentalist" (*The Dial*, III, 302). The change in policy of the paper not only lost subscribers, but occasioned some disturbance among the select coterie of contributors. "The tone of the *Western Messenger* at one time caused him [Huidekoper] some disquiet. It was, under W. H. Channing's sanction, giving generous space to a consideration of certain ideas which Mr. Huidekoper looked upon as equally opposed to common sense and safety" (N. M. and F. Tiffany, *H. J. Huidekoper*, 1904, p. 281).

[8] Rusk, *op. cit.*, I, 178.

[9] See *W. M.*, I, 763; I, 772-777; and I, 820-823. For an account of the circumstances of their publication see Rusk, *op. cit.*, I, 180-181; and Amy Lowell, *John Keats*, II, 20-25.

[10] Brief biographies and selections from the poetical effusions of these men may be found in W. T. Coggeshall, *The Poets and Poetry of the West*, Columbus, 1860.

however, the definite interest in the affairs of the West that had marked the first issues subsided in favor of material from Europe and from New England, partly for the reason that underlay one of the editor's complaints: "There is one thing, however, which to us is a matter of regret. Our poetical aspirants are much too numerous."[11]

There is, however, every indication of a keen interest in the more significant literary activities of the country at large. Most of the important works of American litterateurs brought out during the period of its existence prompted critical comment and quotation. For example, Longfellow's *Outre-Mer* was characterized as "somewhat languid";[12] a section of Bancroft's history, "George Fox and the Quakers,"[13] was reprinted; and two of Bryant's poems were reproduced from *The Democratic Review*.[14]

"The Parting Word" of Oliver W. Holmes was first printed in the number for May, 1838.[15] Clarke's early friendship for their author, no doubt, occasioned the appearance of these verses west of the Alleghenies. After Holmes's volume of poems had been brought out in 1836, Clarke remarked in a critique:

> Well do we remember the first appearance of many of them in past college times—"the joy, the triumph, the delight, the madness," with which we heard them read in social circle around a classmate's fire. . . .[16]

In the issue for July, 1838, a sketch by Hawthorne, "Footprints on the Sea Shore," was published.[17] This article, which the editor assured his readers, had "all of Washington Irving's delightful manner, with profounder

---

[11] *W. M.*, I, 272.
[12] *Ibid.*, I, 76.   [13] *Ibid.*, V, 95.
[14] "The Future Life" (*W. M.*, VII, 47); and "The Battle-Field" (*ibid.*, VI, 48).
[15] *W. M.*, V, 78-80. G. B. Ives, compiler of *A Bibliography of Oliver W. Holmes*, fails to note the publication of the poem prior to 1846.
[16] *W. M.*, III, 684. Cf. Holmes's lines, "To James Freeman Clarke," 1880.
[17] *W. M.*, V, 248-257.

meaning and a higher strain of sentiment,"[18] had appeared six months before in *The Democratic Review*.[19] In 1842 Hawthorne included it in the second series of *Twice Told Tales*.

Like all of the professed literary magazines of the day, *The Western Messenger* devoted many of its pages to criticisms and reviews of the works of authors ranging from Wordsworth to Harriet Martineau. But, unlike most of its fellow periodicals, its criticism is marked by a breadth of view and a freedom from national bias that is to be accounted for only when one considers the antecedents of most of its contributors. It is exceedingly doubtful whether any American magazine of the period in question, particularly in the West, could boast a group of writers with better education or a wider acquaintance with continental literature than those who were employed in the service of the *Messenger*. The periodical, in the opinion of an early critic of Western literature, was "essentially an eastern messenger, the organ of New England liberalism in the Valley of the Ohio. Devoted to religion and literature, it was even more literary than religious, and both its theology and its literature were tinctured with transcendentalism."[20]

It has been asserted that the chief claim of *The Western Messenger* to distinction in its service to New England literature was its "defense of Emerson against his critics and its publication of 'almost the first poetical specimens of his writing which have appeared in print'."[21] The purpose of the next few pages of this chapter is to indicate the nature and scope of the relationship established between the Sage of Concord and the Western journal.

---

[18] *Ibid.*, V, 248.
[19] Cf. *The Democratic Review*, I, 190-197.
[20] W. H. Venable, *Beginnings of Literary Culture in the Ohio Valley*, Cincinnati, 1891, p. 72.
[21] Rusk, *op. cit.*, I, 182.

The first article in *The Western Messenger* that evinces any connection with that storm center of Unitarian liberalism is an obituary notice of Charles C. Emerson, who died in New York in May, 1836. The writer of the brief account, Samuel Osgood, spices the usual encomiums with personal incidents which indicate a close intimacy with the family of the deceased, and, fittingly enough, closes with a passage from Goethe's lines on Schiller.[22]

The next contact established seems to be in the issue for January, 1837, which contains a favorable critique of *Nature*, Emerson's rhapsodic utterance of the preceding year. Not only does the writer, Osgood again, launch forth into a typically transcendental elaboration of Nature as the emblem of Divine Wisdom, Beauty, Love, and Power; but contrives by means of numerous quotations to give a succinct paraphrase of the whole work.[23] The chapter on Idealism caused the reviewer to "doubt much the wisdom of the speculation therein contained"; and the Orphic sentences at the end, "which a certain poet sang to the author," appeared "especially dark."[24] Although he appreciated the likelihood that Emerson had not "mingled enough with common humanity" and might possibly have "confounded his idiosyncrasies with universal truth," he termed the work remarkable for those "who consider it to be 'mere moonshine,' as well as those who look upon it with reverence as the effusion of a prophet-like mind."[25] Considering the close relationship, both personal and spiritual, that existed between the guiding lights of the magazine and the New England iconoclast, the review seems remarkably sane and free from prejudice. The chief weaknesses of the Emersonian view of life and living are pointed out in a friendly but unmistakable fashion.

[22] W. M., I, 864. "Notes from the Journal of a Scholar," by Charles Emerson, were printed in *The Dial*, I, 13; and IV, 88.
[23] W. M., II, 385-393.
[24] Ibid., II, 392.   [25] Ibid., II, 387.

The *Messenger* for September, 1837, contained "fillers" from *Nature*. The custom thus initiated was maintained throughout later issues, and here and there, particularly in the numbers for 1840, one finds short passages from the most electric of Emerson's early writings filling out gaps between articles.[26] The importance attached to these by the editors is apparent when one observes that other such quotations were gleaned, for instance, from Sir Thomas Browne, Henry Vaughan, Carlyle, and Madame de Staël.

The Phi Beta Kappa oration of August, 1837,[27] called forth an article by C. P. Cranch, who four months later expressed to the readers of the journal the wish that they might get some idea of "this beautiful and masterly production." "Those who have read 'Nature'," he writes, "will not fail to see traces of the same spirit and style which distinguished that bright little gem in our literature."[28] After an outline of the salient points made in the address, Cranch refers to this product of Emerson's "elevated and fervent spirit" as an indication of the "purer elements struggling to the surface of the stream of society," which he characterizes as "stagnant, unspiritual, and corrupt."[29]

The "elements struggling to the surface" were soon to be given buoyancy of a more efficacious nature by the *Divinity School Address*, of 1838. Like the two preceding documents of the revolt against formalism in metaphysical thought, this also was reviewed in the *Messenger* within a few months after it had set the tongues of theologians wagging.[30] The article, "R. W. Emerson and

---

[26] Cf. *ibid.*, VI, 102, 314, 324, 341, 355; VIII, 404, 424, 467; and elsewhere.
[27] *The Western Messenger* had printed in its first volume a review of the Harvard Phi Beta Kappa address of 1835, delivered by T. Parsons, and had published Ephraim Peabody's poem for the same occasion, "New England Emigration Westward" (*W. M.*, I, 293; and I, 409).
[28] *W. M.*, IV, 184.   [29] *Ibid.*, IV, 188.   [30] *Ibid.*, VI, 37 (Nov., 1838).

the New School," unsigned, but probably the work of Clarke or Cranch, is one of the clearest statements of the circumstances leading to, and connected with, this heretical expression of individualism in religion. "On the whole, we think that the results of this controversy will be excellent," states the critic. "For ourselves, we are convinced that if Mr. Emerson has taught anything very wrong, it will be found out, and then he will quietly drop out of the Unitarian church, or the Unitarian church will quietly fall off from him." "The question is," continues the writer, "has he taught anything wrong? . . . To confess the truth, when we received and read the address, we did not discover anything in it objectionable at all. . . . Parts seemed somewhat obscure."[31] In places the phraseology "hurt"; but, for him, the most charitable and correct view of the matter was to believe that Emerson did not fail to accept the integrity of historical Christianity, but that he was opposing its defects. "The common error is to be satisfied with the historical faith, and it is this error which he thought it necessary to oppose."[32] Some of the best students of the subject agree that such was the purpose of the Poet-Mystic whose speech to the seven graduates, their teachers and friends stirred up the waves of controversy and "frightened Harvard theology back toward at least Unitarian orthodoxy," to quote Barrett Wendell's apt observation.[33]

Immediately following this article appeared another, also unsigned, but probably to be ascribed to Cranch, entitled "The New School in Literature and Religion," which is a reply to a portion of Andrews Norton's attack on Emerson that had been published in *The Boston Daily Advertiser*. The irate professor, whose annoyance at the indirect responsibility for the address urged him to vent

[31] *Ibid.*, VI, 39. [32] *Ibid.*, VI, 41.
[33] See, for example, G. E. Woodberry, *R. W. Emerson*, 1914, pp. 57-59.

his spleen at the expense of all who sought to liberate themselves from the carefully preserved authority inherent in the Harvard orthodoxy of the day, went out of his way to attack his former pupils who had gone "blundering through the crabbed and disgusting obscurity of some of the worst German speculatists." Not content with ascribing the evil to German radicalism, he even censured *The Western Messenger* for having quoted and commended the "Atheist Shelley."[34]

This particularized attack not only prompted a defense of Shelley as an artist, but gave occasion for a statement of the fundamental ideas of the New School.[35] The new group is taken to be the "large and increasing number of the clergy and laity, of thinking men and educated women, especially of the youth in our different colleges, of all sects and all professions, who are dissatisfied with the present state of religion, philosophy, and literature."[36] Cousin, Carlyle, and Schleiermacher are mentioned as the chief foreign sponsors of the movement, while Brownson, Furness, Emerson, and Channing are pointed out as their most eminent American counterparts. After an insistent declaration of the fact that there is no general agreement in thought or purpose to be looked for among the followers of the movement, the writer makes this statement: "If we are asked who is the leader of this New School, we should not name Mr. Emerson so soon as Dr. Channing."[37] Perhaps the theological penchant of the author of the article inclined him to this belief, or perhaps there is some truth in the idea that Emerson's importance in the development of the impulse seeking "the transference of supernatural attributes to the natural constitution of mankind"[38] has

---

[34] *W. M.*, III, 474, an article entitled "Shelley and Pollok," by "D. L." The writer vehemently declared, "We had rather be damned with Percy Bysshe Shelley than go to heaven with John Calvin and Robert Pollok."
[35] *Ibid.*, VI, 42-47.   [36] *Ibid.*, VI, 46.   [37] *Ibid.*, VI, 47.
[38] O. B. Frothingham, *Transcendentalism in New England*, 1876, p. 136.

been grossly exaggerated. At any rate, the writer's location in the West must have given him objective material as the basis of his judgment in the matter.

In *The Western Messenger* for February, 1839, appeared two of Emerson's poems, "Each in All" and "To the Humble-Bee."[39] The following sentences served as an introduction to them:

> Those of our readers who enjoy fine poetry will thank the author of the following verses for communicating them, as well as those on the "Humble Bee," to the reading public. The same antique charm, the same grace and sweetness, which distinguish the prose writings of our author, will be found in his verse. These are almost[40] the first poetical specimens of his writing which have appeared in print. There are others, as we know, behind, not inferior to them in beauty of thought and expression. May we not hope also that these gems may be given to the lovers of the "blameless muse"?[41]

The April number of the same year (1839) contained "Good-Bye, Proud World," and the issue for three months later included "The Rhodora." The changes that the poems underwent at the hands of their author after their initial publication are for the most part minor.[42] The following excerpt from a letter of James Freeman Clarke, dated January 1, 1839, will show how Emerson's verses came to be published in Louisville:

> Had you not given me those poems, I should probably never have asked you for anything; but now I wish you to give me two

---

[39] *W. M.*, VI, 229 and 239.
[40] The "almost" may be due to the occasional rhapsodical passages in Emerson's prose published before this date, or to the fact that the "Concord Hymn" was printed on single sheets in 1837. Cf. W. E. Peck, "A Lost Poem of Emerson?" *The Southwest Review*, XII, 304. Two poems, "Fame" and "William Rufus and the Jew," which appeared in an annual for 1829, have also been assigned to Emerson (*The Offering for 1829*, Cambridge, 1829, pp. 17 and 52).
[41] *W. M.*, VI, 229.
[42] "The Humble-Bee," for example, originally began: "Fine humble-bee! fine humble-bee!"; and after line ten read: "Flowerbells | Honied Cells | These the tents | Which he frequents"; and did not have "Grass with green flag . . ." to "Clover, catchfly . . ." (stanza 5, lines 5-9).

more, namely, "The Rhodora," and the lines beginning,—"Good-Bye, proud world! I'm going home." I have them in my possession, though not by Margaret's [Fuller's] fault; for she gave them to me accidentally among other papers. But, being there, may I print them?[43]

In an essay on "Transcendentalism," by C. P. Cranch, in *The Western Messenger* for December, 1840,[44] there appears the following reference to Carlyle and Emerson: "A certain great writer of England is accused of imitating the Germans; and another writer of our country of imitating him; and these writers in turn, of being imitated by others." The implication is that the charge of such philosophical and literary counterfeiting is false. However true the writer's assertion that the *Zeitgeist* was eminently "the spirit of earnest, free, large enquiry,"[45] rather than that of adjustment to the authority of leadership, no reader of the *Messenger* can fail to see that Emerson's personality and literary products, helped to crystallize the growing reaction against tradition, which played such an important part in the lives of his friends in the West, who, all unconsciously, were making their magazine a vehicle for the expression of the philosophical vagaries inherent in Romantic individualism.[46]

The Dial was founded in 1840 because of the intense passion for self-expression which moved a select group of New England individualists. *The Western Messenger* had been founded a few years earlier for a somewhat similar reason; and, after a few numbers had appeared, had

---

[43] *James Freeman Clarke Autobiography Diary and Correspondence*, ed. E. E. Hale, 1891, pp. 124-125.
[44] *W. M.*, VIII, 407.   [45] *W. M.*, VIII, 408.
[46] In spite of their partisanship the writers for *The Western Messenger* were able to appreciate the humor underlying the tempest in the theological tea-pot. For example, in a notice of the publication of Norton's discourse on "The Latest Form of Infidelity," delivered at Cambridge, July 19, 1839, the following sentence appears: "This discourse we lay aside, with Mr. Emerson's of July, 1838, and *The Boston Quarterly Review* of last April, meaning in our old age to reprint them as curiosities" (*W. M.*, VII, 435).

been conducted on the very same principles as *The Dial.* Indeed, a closer relationship as to origin is established when one remembers that the haphazard assemblage, variously called Hedge's Club, the Symposium, or the Transcendental Club, which fostered *The Dial,* had at its first conference, in 1836, discussed the unhappy plight of the Unitarian church.[47] The purpose of both periodicals, to further the aims of religion, literature, and philosophy, was as identical as their youthful spirit of experiment and naïve disregard for tradition so characteristic of the whole transcendental movement.[48]

The similarity of origin[49] and purpose that one notes in the two magazines is no less striking than the similarity of the lists of their contributors. In 1891 a student of the literature of the Middle West pointed out the fact that at least ten of the writers for the *Messenger* later contributed to *The Dial.*[50] James Freeman Clarke, whose editorial activities in connection with the magazine were the most extensive, furnished at least eight poems and articles to the New England periodical. Moreover, his close association

---

In Louisville Cranch amused his friend Clarke by drawing caricatures of the chief men involved in the controversy, arranging a number of them under the heading, "Illustrations of the New Philosophy." "One of them represents a man lying in bed sipping wine, a copy of *The Dial* having fallen to the floor, while his wife sits at the foot of the bed blacking his boots. This was called 'The Moral Influence of *The Dial*,' and it had this legend from the poem on 'Life':

> Why for work art thou striving,
> Why seekest thou for aught?
> To the soul that is living
> All things shall be brought"

(G. W. Cooke, *The Journal of Speculative Philosophy,* XIX, 236). The drawing described by Cooke is reproduced in *The Life and Letters of C. P. Cranch,* p. 60.

[47] T. W. Higginson, *Margaret Fuller Ossoli,* 1893, p. 142.

[48] For an account of the origin of *The Dial* see G. W. Cooke, Introduction for the Rowfant Club reprint of *The Dial,* 1902, or the same, in *The Journal of Speculative Philosophy,* XIX, 225-265, and 322-323; J. E. Cabot, *A Memoir of R. W. Emerson,* 1887, II, 401-408; and T. W. Higginson, *op. cit.,* cap. IX and X.

[49] It is probably merely adventitious that Emerson planned an organ of the new spirit which Carlyle was to edit, just about the time that *The Messenger* was being established (*Carlyle-Emerson Correspondence,* 1883, I, 58).

[50] W. H. Venable, *op. cit.,* p. 80.

F. H. Hedge, who as early as 1835 was suggested as the editor of the proposed "organ of spiritual philosophy" in Boston,[55] and whose influence upon the spread of German thought among the Unitarians of New England has not been minimized,[56] was also a contributor to both journals. The *Messenger* printed two of his addresses.[57] Another *Dial* writer, Elizabeth Peabody, who has the distinction of having provided for that periodical's publication during its second year, appears also to have been an occasional contributor.

Two others whose literary products were printed in both magazines were C. T. Brooks and Caroline S. Sturgis. The latter, who wrote over the signature "Z," was distinguished by having one of her poems appear in both journals. Under Channing's régime as editor her verses entitled "Pæan" were reprinted in the *Messenger* with the notice, "From *The Dial*."[58]

That strangely sundered soul, Jones Very, not only aided Emerson in his burdensome task of filling the pages of the New England organ of liberalism, but also performed a like service for the editor of *The Western Messenger*. His contribution of twenty-seven "religious sonnets" prompted Channing to devote a few pages to a defense of their author from the charge of being mad, and occasioned the receipt of thirteen more products of his muse.[59]

The more famous mystic, Amos Bronson Alcott, was quoted in the *Messenger*, in reviews of his educational

---

[55] G. W. Cooke, *The Journal of Speculative Philosophy*, XIX, 226.
[56] H. D. Gray, *Emerson, a statement of New England Transcendentalism as expressed in the philosophy of its chief exponent*, 1905, p. 7: "The introduction or rather domesticating of German philosophy, which brought New England Transcendentalism itself into being, was the work, mainly, of F. H. Hedge." This statement appears to be too strong.
[57] *W. M.*, V, 82; and VI, 32 (not complete).
[58] *Ibid.*, VIII, 474. Cf. *The Dial*, I, 217.
[59] *W. M.*, VI, 310-314, 336-373; and VIII, 43, 424, 449, 462, 467, 472, 549-552.

with Emerson, Margaret Fuller, and George Ripley must also have resulted in many suggestions relative to the conduct of *The Dial*, since his own experience as a journalist was of such a nature as to be fruitful of counsel for the untrained editors of the new publication.[51]

Another of the editors of the *Messenger*, W. H. Channing, was responsible for at least three articles in *The Dial*; while C. P. Cranch was the mainstay among its versifiers, as he had been for the Western journal earlier. Samuel Osgood and Ephraim Peabody, who also assisted in directing the affairs of the *Messenger*, did not make any known contributions to the Boston quarterly, but were closely associated with the Transcendental Club.[52]

All of the editors of *The Dial*, in turn, had portions of their work produced upon the pages of the *Messenger*. As has been indicated, Emerson contributed to it four poems, and was frequently used as a source of material for quotation. Margaret Fuller supplied at least four critical essays, ranging from an account of Bulwer's works to an appreciation of Hannah More.[53] George Ripley made no direct contributions, apparently, but was frequently quoted in reviews of his "Foreign Specimens," and, in particular, in a notice of his sermon on "Duties of the Clergy," preached at the ordination of J. S. Dwight, in Northampton, May 20, 1840.[54] After an introductory attack upon the orthodox metaphysicians for driving Kant and Alcott, Coleridge and Emerson, Carlyle and Brownson into a common fold labeled "Transcendentalism," most of the sermon is quoted intact. Dwight himself contributed translations of German poetry to both periodicals.

[51] For Clarke's earlier connection with the "Club," see Cabot, *op. cit.*, I, 245.
[52] Of course, the names of some of the contributors to *The Dial* are not known. All material dealing with the names of its contributors is derived from Cooke.
[53] See *W. M.*, I, 20, 101, 398; and V, 24.
[54] *W. M.*, VIII, 226-236.

treatises,[60] and, later, appears to have sent along the manuscript of his prose-poem, "Psyche, or The Growth of the Soul." But before Channing could print the rhapsody the journal ceased publication. Some of this material, it seems, may have appeared in *The Dial* under the title "Days from a Diary."[61]

Theodore Parker contributed at least one essay to the Western journal, "The Relation of the Bible to the Soul."[62] In general, it may be said that of the "fine constellation of people" who wrote for *The Dial* few of the leading figures had not earlier written for *The Western Messenger*. Thoreau is the most notable exception. However, the absence of his name from the list of contributors to the Western periodical is compensated for by the presence of the names of W. H. Furness, Convers Francis, and Dr. W. E. Channing,[63] men who meant more to their day than a thousand writers like Thoreau.

From the similarities that have been observed in their origin, purpose, and lists of contributors, it is but natural that there should be a marked likeness in the contents of *The Western Messenger* and *The Dial*. H. C. Goddard, speaking of the latter, observes:

> The journal discussed questions of theology and philosophy; it contained, besides many other things, papers on art, music, and literature, especially German literature; translations from ancient "Oriental Scriptures," original modern "scriptures" in the form of Alcott's *Orphic Sayings*; and, finally, a good deal of verse.[64]

This description of the contents of the periodical would fit *The Western Messenger* very aptly.

In the field of art, for example, the Eastern mag-

---

[60] Cf., for example, *ibid.*, III, 540 and 678.
[61] *The Dial*, II, 409.
[62] *W. M.*, VIII, 337 and 388. For Parker's authorship of this essay see John Weiss, *Life and Correspondence of Theodore Parker*, 1864, I, 123.
[63] Cf., for example, *W. M.*, I, 383; II, 340; and IV, 343.
[64] *Studies in New England Transcendentalism*, 1908, p. 37.

azine's interest in Allston, exemplified by Margaret Fuller's article on her impressions of the artist's exhibition in 1839,[65] finds a very close parallel in an account of the "Allston Exhibition," written by W. H. Channing for *The Western Messenger*.[66] Not content with a criticism of the canvases under consideration, the Western journal reproduced at the same time two of the painter's poems: "Rosalie," and "The Spanish Maid."[67] A few months later another of his poems, "Ursulina," was printed, along with a portion of one of his essays, originally published in the first volume of *The American New Monthly Magazine*.[68]

In its religious tone *The Dial* presents another similarity to *The Western Messenger*. One has only to note such articles as Parker's "Thoughts on Theology,"[69] or Elizabeth Peabody's "A Glimpse of Christ's Idea of Society"[70] to realize that the New England periodical was scarcely more secular than its Western counterpart. Margaret Fuller as editor did not feel that her journal was unsuitable for such an essay as W. D. Wilson's "The Unitarian Movement in New England."[71] Indeed, it has been affirmed with eminent justice that "philosophical and religious elements constantly tended to overbalance the literary" quality of *The Dial*.[72] No one appreciated this fact more than Emerson himself, who observed in his journal, "*The Dial* is poor and low, and all unequal to its promise."[73]

Alcott's "Orphic Sayings," which were "an amazement to the uninitiated and an amusement to the profane"[74] readers of the Boston magazine, find a counterpart in Clarke's translations from Goethe, also entitled "Orphic

---

[65] *The Dial*, I, 73.
[66] *W. M.*, VII, 200.
[67] *Ibid.*, VII, 204.
[68] *W. M.*, VII, 327.
[69] *The Dial*, II, 485.
[70] *Ibid.*, II, 214.
[71] *Ibid.*, I, 409.
[72] H. C. Goddard, *op. cit.*, p. 196.
[73] *Journals*, V, 471.
[74] Frothingham, *op. cit.*, p. 133.

Sayings."[75] In view of the poems of Very to be found in both periodicals, and the numerous essays inspired by the most unmitigated type of transcendentalism, a relationship in regard to the mystical character of the two magazines was inevitable.[76]

The Dial has long been regarded as a pioneer journal in presenting the ancient Oriental literatures to American readers. But even in this respect *The Western Messenger* was earlier in the field. Thoreau's "Ethnical Scriptures"[77] and "Sayings of Confucius"[78] find earlier counterparts in the selections from Saadi, published in 1837,[79] and "Chinese Rules of Conduct," printed two years later.[80]

In the era of Romantic expansiveness, with its turmoil of socialism, abolition, and religious controversy, no figure stood out more prominently before the eyes of the educated public in New England than the singular Orestes A. Brownson, whose *Boston Quarterly Review* aroused discussion, and opposition, in the pages of many of its fellow journals. Although a member of the group who founded *The Dial*, his combativeness of disposition had made him *de trop* with Hedge's Club, so that his proposals that his own magazine be made the organ of the new movement were rejected.[81] Nevertheless, *The Dial* and *The Western Messenger* rallied to his defense when his economic views and theological vagaries induced attack. For the first volume of *The Dial* George Ripley wrote an essay on "Brownson's Writings," in which he referred to the man as "a writer whose native force of mind, combined with rare philosophical attainments, has elevated him to a prominent rank among the living authors of this country."[82]

---

[75] Cf. *The Dial*, I, 85; and *W. M.*, II, 59.
[76] See, for example, *The Dial*, II, 382; and III, 406.
[77] *The Dial*, IV, 205; and elsewhere.
[78] *Ibid.*, III, 493.
[79] *W. M.*, III, 806, 814, and 826.
[80] *Ibid.*, VI, 389-390.
[81] T. W. Higginson, *op. cit.*, p. 148.
[82] *The Dial*, I, 22.

The *Western Messenger* not only espoused his cause to such an extent that subscribers were thereby lost, but printed several of his articles and letters. Indeed, it may well be said that not even Emerson or Dr. Channing occupied the attention of the writers of the magazine more than he.[83] The reader of its later numbers does not have far to seek to find an essay reprinted from his *Review*, or a discussion of his position in regard to the various problems of the day. The opinion that he entertained of the *Messenger* is indicated by the following excerpt from a letter to Clarke, dated January 18, 1837:

> I place it [*The Western Messenger*] among the best, ablest conducted and most useful of our American periodicals, and bespeak for it the support of every one who loves God and Humanity, or religion and his country. It must be a blessing to the West and to the East.[84]

No more outstanding similarity in the contents of the two magazines is to be observed than in their criticism and translation of German literature. The importance of *The Dial* in this regard is too well known to require comment; and, as for the *Messenger*, the fact that it devoted many of its pages to the works of German writers at so early a date gives it a place unique among the periodicals of the West. In 1836 Clarke began to print his translation of De Wette,[85] which later was included in George Ripley's "Specimens of Foreign Standard Literature." From time to time throughout subsequent issues, portions of the works of Goethe, Schiller, Richter, Herder, Uhland, and others were brought out. A student of the relationship

---

[83] For Brownson's connections with *The Western Messenger*, see III, 529-539, 601, 618; V, 104; VII, 67; VIII, 316-330, 420, 433-449.
[84] Quoted in *W. M.*, III, 602.
[85] G. W. Cooke, *op. cit.*, p. 244: "In 1841 he [Clarke] translated De Wette's 'Theodore' for Ripley's 'Specimens'." This, of course, was the date of its publication by Ripley. For the significance of the "Specimens" see Frothingham, *op. cit.*, p. 116.

between American periodicals and the literature of Germany makes the following comment upon the magazine:

The Western Messenger contains a large number of favorable criticisms and original translations, many from the pen of Mr. Clarke himself, and is particularly worthy of notice, in that it is one of the first western journals to take active part in the discussion of a question which at that time was attracting so much attention in New England.[86]

The similarities in the contents of the two publications could be carried out into further detail. The department of the *Messenger* entitled "Monthly Record," for example, became the "Record of the Months" in *The Dial*. Thoreau's articles on Natural History find parallels in such essays as W. B. Powell's "Geology of the Mississippi," and the sketches of Mann Butler.[87] *The Dial* even obtained Keats's "Remarks on John Milton . . . Written in the Fly-Leaf of 'Paradise Lost,'" through the interest of James Freeman Clarke, who had previously been permitted by the poet's brother to copy them from the volume in question.[88]

Suffice it to say, in conclusion, that, in view of their kindred origin and purpose, and the identity of so many contributors, it is but natural to find such a striking sameness in the contents of the two magazines. The reader of *The Dial* and *The Western Messenger* finds scarcely any type of material which is not common to both journals. The chief exception is made by Thoreau's translations from Pindar, "Anacreon," and Aeschylus, which have no counterpart in the Middle Western publication.

The material presented in this chapter seems to indicate that *The Western Messenger* had an influence on *The Dial* that is altogether noteworthy and important. It

---

[86] S. H. Goodnight, "German Literature in American Magazines Prior to 1846," *Bulletin of U. of Wisconsin*, Madison, 1907, p. 51.
[87] *W. M.*, III, 552. Cf. also *ibid.*, V, 384.
[88] *The Dial*, III, 500-504.

appears that the Boston periodical has often been regarded as *the* organ of transcendentalism rather than *an* organ of the movement. Nothing is further removed from fact than such a categorical statement as that of G. W. Curtis, who, speaking of *The Dial,* affirmed: "There had been nothing like it in this country."[89] Of course, the student of the journalistic expression of American Romanticism must view that magazine in its proper perspective, along with similar publications, particularly *The Western Messenger* and *The Boston Quarterly Review.*

Moreover, it is apparent that the literary apprenticeship of some of the less known writers of the period has not received the attention which this study seems to justify. The poetical activity of C. P. Cranch, or the earlier critiques written by Margaret Fuller, for example, might well be viewed in connection with the rise of Unitarian journalism in the West.

Then, too, it may be maintained that there was such a thing as transcendentalism outside of New England. In a sense, it is perfectly just to consider *The Western Messenger* as a graft on Eastern stock; but the fact that its editors sought to develop the latent literary possibilities of the Ohio Valley implies an interest in American letters beyond mere sectionalism.

The Western Messenger is eminently worthy of the attention of one who wishes to learn just what was the best contemporary opinion of the New School and its leaders. Its editors and chief contributors had not only the inestimable advantage of an intimate acquaintance with the men most active in the East, but also the opportunity of gaining an objective view of their accomplishments by a remoteness from the scene of affairs. No better illustration of the soundness of judgment manifested by the

---

[89] "Ralph Waldo Emerson and *The Dial,*" *The Journal of Speculative Philosophy,* XVI, 330.

writers for the *Messenger* could be had than the following excerpt from a criticism of *The Dial* for October, 1840:

> Thus far, to speak frankly, we do not think that they [the contributors to *The Dial*] have shown the power they possess. The articles in the number before us, if we except two or three, will, we think, do little good. However, we know that among the writers for this work are some dozen of the purest, clearest, and truest minds in the land, and such as will be felt and felt deeply. We wish them all success.[90]

Finally, if it is true that "the transcendental movement yet remains the most important influence that has affected American literature,"[91] a study of its early development in the West is of unusual interest, particularly in view of its great influence upon the East. As early as 1836 *The Western Messenger* had close to one hundred subscribers in New England alone,[92] while the subscription list of *The Dial* at no time reached three hundred names all told.[93]

[90] *W. M.*, VIII, 303.
[91] G. W. Cooke, *The Poets of Transcendentalism*, 1903, Introduction, p. 3.
[92] *W. M.*, II, 352.
[93] G. W. Cooke, *The Journal of Speculative Philosophy*, XIX, 229.

CHAPTER III

ORESTES A. BROWNSON AND *THE BOSTON QUARTERLY REVIEW*

Like most of the transcendentalists, Orestes A. Brownson was a man of strong emotions. In his spiritual autobiography, *The Convert*, written after he became a Catholic, he gives an account of his early communings with Christ, and even with the Virgin Mary.[1] As a result, his interest in religion was something more than the usual dutiful acquiescence to family tradition. Of the earlier phases of his philosophical and religious evolution he writes as follows:

> Like most English and Americans of my generation, I had been educated in the school of Locke. From Locke I had passed to the Scottish school of Reid and Stewart, and had adhered to it without well knowing what it was, till it was overthrown by Dr. Thomas Brown, who . . . revived the scepticism of Hume, and drove me into speculative atheism, by resolving cause and effect into invariable antecedence and consequence, thus excluding all idea of creative power or productive force. Still young, I rushed into pure sensism and materialism, and was prepared intellectually to join with Frances Wright and her followers, when they appeared. Gradually I had elaborated a sort of philosophical sentimentalism, depending on the heart rather than the head. . . . In this half-dreaming state, with vague feelings, and vaguer notions, I encountered the philosophical writings of Cousin, first, I think, in 1833, and yielded almost entirely to the witchery of his style . . . although I made from first to last certain reserves.[2]

The chief circumstances of his "outer" life during the period covered by the above remarks are of equal importance. Born in Stockbridge, Vermont, in 1803, almost completely self-educated, Brownson in 1822 became a

---
[1] *The Convert, or Leaves from My Experience, The Works of Orestes A. Brownson*, Detroit, 1884, V, 5. Cf. the dream of Margaret in S. Judd's *Margaret*, 1851, cap. XIV.
[2] *Ibid.*, 124-125.

member of the Presbyterian church. Two years later he "avowed himself a Universalist," and after a short visit to Detroit, preached Universalism in his native state. This stage of his career lasted three years, during which he contributed to, and later edited, *The Gospel Advocate*, an organ of the Universalists of New York. Soon he was aroused by the socialistic theories of Frances Wright, and became the corresponding editor of her paper, *The Free Enquirer*. At the same time he was actively engaged in spreading the views of Robert Owen and his Workingmen's Party. In February, 1831, he began to preach in Ithaca, New York, as an independent minister, and there published a weekly periodical called *The Philanthropist*.

Moved by the sermons of Dr. W. E. Channing, which he first read in 1829, he gave up his journal and his charge in 1832, to become the pastor of the Unitarian society in Walpole, New Hampshire. There he first studied French, choosing as his reading five volumes of Benjamin Constant. From Walpole he made frequent trips to Boston, where he became acquainted with the leaders of the denomination with which he was associated. His unusual ability as a writer was soon employed in the service of *The Unitarian*, edited by Bernard Whitman, *The Christian Register*, which George Ripley conducted for a time, and, more notably, *The Christian Examiner*, for which his first contribution, dealing with the philosophical notions of Constant, was made in 1834.

In that year he accepted a charge at Canton, Massachusetts. During the winter of 1834-1835 he had as a boarder and fellow student of German, Henry Thoreau, who was teaching school in the village.[3] It is interesting to note that Thoreau later referred to his six weeks' stay with Brownson as "an era in my life—the morning of a

[3] W. E. Channing, *Thoreau the Poet-Naturalist*, 1902, p. 32.

new *Lebenstag*."⁴ In 1836 Brownson moved to Chelsea and began to establish his Society for Christian Union and Progress in Boston, a project which attracted the interest of the Unitarian reformers who were bent upon converting "agrarian infidels." As an aid in his work he edited *The Boston Reformer*. In the following year he received the appointment from George Bancroft as steward of the Marine Hospital in Chelsea, a position which he held four years.⁵

In addition to his activities as a social reformer and journalist, Brownson came to the fore as a protagonist of the New School by publishing in 1836 *New Views of Christianity, Society, and the Church*, a transcendental treatise based in part upon Constant and Schleiermacher.⁶ Four years later Ripley, in his essay on "Brownson's Writings," published in the first number of *The Dial*, said of the work, "It has already formed a conspicuous era in the mental history of more than one who is seeking for the truth of things, in the midst of painted, conventional forms."⁷ Convers Francis, the oldest member of the Transcendental Club, noted in his journal for 1836:

> I find that George Ripley is publishing *Discourses on the Philosophy of Religion;* besides, Brownson is out with his *New Views*, and Alcott with *Questions* [sic] *on the Gospels*, for Children. Then there is Furness' book, *Remarks on the Gospels*, so that it seems the spiritualists are taking the field in force. I have long seen that the Unitarians must break into two schools—the old one, or English School, belonging to the sensual and empiric philosophy, and the new one, or the German School (perhaps it may be called), belonging to the spiritual philosophy.⁸

---

⁴ Thoreau to Brownson, in H. F. Brownson, *Orestes A. Brownson's Early Life*, Detroit, 1898, p. 204. Sanborn, accounting for a paradoxical argument in one of Thoreau's early essays, ascribes it in part to the "strong impression" made by Brownson (*The Life of Thoreau*, 1917, p. 141).
⁵ For all the preceding biographical information see H. F. Brownson, *op. cit.*, pp. 1-213. This work will hereinafter be cited as *E. Life*.
⁷ *The Dial*, I, 30.   ⁶ Cf. *Works*, IV (1883), 2.
⁸ John Weiss, *Discourse Occasioned by the Death of Convers Francis*, Cambridge, 1863, p. 28.

Naturally enough, Brownson soon came to be closely associated with the chief leaders of the "party of Progress," and was one of the earliest members of the Transcendental Club. Dr. Channing recognized in his Society of Union and Progress "a promise of true social regeneration."[9] Emerson, in 1836, was discussing a "question out of Brownson's book."[10] Alcott visited him, and noted in his diary: "Emerson and Hedge promise more than others amongst us; with Furness, Brownson, and Ripley, they furnish the best talent in the liberal church."[11] Of the group who later met in the rooms of Elizabeth Peabody to discuss the vexing subject of socialism, a group interested in the establishment of Brook Farm, Brownson was one of the most influential.[12] Moreover, he was responsible for the enlisting of several recruits for the enterprise, most notably Isaac Hecker.[13] His earlier experience with Fanny Wright and Owen must have been of particular value to the prime mover of the Roxbury community, George Ripley, who was, without question, his closest friend among the Unitarian clergy. In a letter relating to Brownson's son, who was a pupil in the school at Brook Farm, Ripley expressed his obligations in these words:

We have truly sympathized as few men have done; you have always quickened my love for humanity; and for no small share of what mental clearness I may have am I indebted to the hours of genial, pleasant intercourse I have enjoyed with you. If I had never known you, I should never have been engaged in this enterprise. I consider it as the incarnation of those transcendental truths which we have held in common, and which you have done much to make me love.[14]

[9] W. H. Channing, *The Life of William Ellery Channing, D.D.*, Boston, 1882, p. 482.
[10] *Journals*, IV, 166.
[11] Sanborn and Harris, *A. Bronson Alcott*, 1893, I, 269.
[12] G. B. Kirby, *Years of Experience*, New York, 1887, p. 91.
[13] I. Hecker, "Dr. Brownson in Boston," *The Catholic World*, XLV, 466-472.
[14] *E. Life*, p. 313.

Indeed, so eminent was Brownson in the New England renaissance that he was, in his day, usually considered to be one of its chief leaders. In 1841, for example, a writer for *The New York Review* announced the fact that Brownson, Parker, and Emerson were to be held as "the new world apostles" of the "new Christianity."[15] One needs not marvel, then, that Lowell, in *A Fable for Critics*, described him immediately after Emerson and Alcott. Despite the obvious caricaturing, upon which the *Fable* rests for no small portion of its interest, the following extract is essentially illuminating:

> Close behind him [Alcott] is Brownson, his mouth very full
> With attempting to gulp a Gregorian bull;
> Who contrives, spite of that, to pour out as he goes
> A stream of transparent and forcible prose.
> He shifts quite about, then proceeds to expound
> That 'tis merely the Earth, not himself, that turns round.
> . . . .
> That of two sides he commonly chooses the wrong;
> If there is only one, why he'll split it in two,
> And first pummel this half, then that, black and blue.

As indicated by the above lines, Brownson was noted for "a gladiatorial vigor," as Higginson has aptly expressed the idea.[16] He, like Emerson, believed that the great soul has little to do with consistency. With the tremendous energy of which he was possessed he attempted to make his opinions pass current as truth. As he later confessed, he at one time regarded himself as "the precursor to the new Messias" that the New School was to produce.[17] The natural effect of this emotional extravagance upon his contemporaries is revealed by this passage from Emerson's *Journals:*

[15] *The New York Review*, X, 220.
[16] *Margaret Fuller Ossoli*, 1884, 144.
[17] *The Convert, Works*, V, 81.

But Charles Lane gives a very good account of his conversation with Brownson, who would drive him to an argument. He took his paper and pencil out of his pocket, and asked Brownson to give him the names of the profoundest men in America. Brownson stopped, and gave him one, and then another, and then his own for a third. Brownson never will stop and listen, neither in conversation, but what is more, not in solitude.[18]

The guiding geniuses of the New Spirit were ready to hail with delight his declarations of the necessity of "a new dispensation in perfect harmony with the new order of things,"[19] but excess was excess—even to the transcendentalists.

But the factor that is perhaps most largely responsible for the failure of scholars to recognize the importance of Brownson's efforts to extend the scope of transcendentalism in America is not his emotional exuberance or his inordinate lack of intellectual restraint, but the fact that in 1844 he joined the Catholic church, and immediately began to subject his erstwhile associates, along with himself, to criticism of the most acrid character. Parke Godwin, in *The Harbinger* for January 15, 1848, summed up the situation in these words:

> The great difficulty, now as ever, with Mr. Brownson is that he sees only one truth at a time, or rather one side or aspect of truth, which he is driven to assert as the whole and only truth in the Universe. . . . The absolute is his forte. His God is absolute, his church is absolute, his metaphysics are absolute, and all his reasonings and statements are absolute. By this unhappy want of integrity of mind, he was whirled about in former times by every wind of doctrine, and he has now become, for the same reason, a Catholic who out-herods Herod.[20]

---

[18] *Journals*, VI, 297. Emerson's reaction indicates only too well why Brownson soon found himself *de trop* with the Transcendental Club.
[19] *A Discourse on the Wants of the Times*, Boston, 1836. Harriet Martineau appended a great part of this work to her *Society in America*, London, 1837 (III, 342).
[20] *The Harbinger*, VI, 84.

With the foregoing facts and opinions in mind, one may more readily undertake a consideration of the rôle played by *The Boston Quarterly Review* in spreading the propaganda of transcendentalism. In 1836 Brownson had written, "The time is not far distant when our whole population will be philosophers, and all our philosophers will be practical men."[21] And his magazine, which he conducted from January, 1838, to October, 1842, undertook to eliminate as much of the distance as it could.

The chief circumstances connected with the publishing of *The Boston Quarterly Review* are given by Brownson in *The Convert* (1857), as well as in the various notices to the readers which appeared from time to time within the pages of the periodical. The introductory article announced that its owner and editor had no definite object to accomplish, but that he would "probably be very heretical, and show a fellow feeling for heretics of every name and nature."[22] "I undertake this Review," he wrote, "for myself; not because I am certain that the public wants it, but because I want it."[23]

As he explained, he was not at a loss for a means of bringing his views before the public. *The Christian Examiner*, for example, had willingly received his contributions, which aimed at combining the new spiritual philosophy with the notion of social progress. Indeed, according to Ripley, his articles in the *Examiner* had formed "a new era in the history of that able journal."[24] Ripley himself, it should be said, along with F. H. Hedge and others, had done all that was possible to make the organ

---

[21] *New Views, Works*, IV, 49.
[22] *The Boston Quarterly Review*, I, 5 and 6. Hereinafter cited as "*B. Q. R.*"
[23] *Ibid.*, I, 4.
[24] *The Dial*, I, 25. Brownson's contributions to the *Examiner* were these: "Benjamin Constant on Religion" (XVII, 63); "Principles of Morality" (XVII, 283); "Progress of Society" (XVIII, 345); "Education of the People" (XX, 153); "Cousin's Philosophy" (XXI, 33); and "Recent Contributions to Philosophy" (XXII, 181).

of the Unitarians a vehicle for the newer philosophy. But tradition was against them. And when Francis Bowen, reviewing Emerson's *Nature* for the *Examiner*, launched forth into a bitter assault upon transcendentalism,[25] all the progressives realized that the time had come for a periodical of their own.

In *The Boston Quarterly Review* for October, 1839, Brownson announced that its publication would be suspended.[26] However, the magazine reappeared at its regular time, with the notice that the public was not concerned with the reason for the resumption of his editorial duties, and that "several distinguished literary friends" had promised their help.[27] The same notice reasserted the magazine's devotion to "Religion, Philosophy, Politics, and General Literature," and added that "the great idea" in their treatment was "freedom." In politics the journal was to support "democratic principles and measures." But the editor might well have spelled "democratic" with a capital letter. Of his own opinions he wrote:

> I am myself an eclectic, and I seek to carry the spirit of eclecticism into all departments of life and thought; but the Transcendentalists, the Mystics, the Theosophists, the Idealists, may make this journal at all times, if they choose, their medium of communication with the public....[28]

At the end of the third volume Brownson stated that the aid promised by his friends had been little and that the entire number for October, 1840, had been written by himself. He had decided to discontinue the magazine at that time, but the attacks prompted by his articles on the laboring classes had aroused such discussion that he was unwilling to desert the field. He denied definite allegiance to the Democratic Party, but promised in the future

---

[25] *The Christian Examiner*, XXI, 371 (Jan., 1837).
[26] *B. Q. R.*, II, 517.
[27] *Ibid.*, III, 1. [28] *Ibid.*, III, 19.

to have "less to do" with politics. Finally, he appealed to all readers who dared "to look the boldest heresy in the face."[29]

At the end of the fourth volume he stated that the subscription list of his journal had increased during the year, and that the reception of his views in and around Boston had been particularly gratifying.[30] The increased popularity of the work, it should be said, was not due to any sudden growth in the vogue of Romantic philosophy in America, but to Brownson's articles dealing with the laboring classes, which were republished by the politicians as campaign material.

In the final number of the magazine its editor stated that the *Boston Quarterly* should be taken "very much in the light of a private journal," and announced that it was to be merged with *The Democratic Review*, for which he had promised to write.[31]

In January, 1844, after Brownson had withdrawn his support from *The Democratic Review*, and was converted to Catholicism, he started a new periodical, called *Brownson's Quarterly Review*. In the first issue of it he referred to his former quarterly as the product of his mind "in process of formation," not aimed at positive instruction, but at exciting inquiry. Its subscribers were "few, but serious, honest, earnest, and affectionate."[32] How many they were cannot be stated with any degree of definiteness.

Fifteen years after the last number of *The Boston Quarterly Review* appeared, Brownson wrote of it as follows:

I established, in January, 1838, a Quarterly Review, which I conducted almost single-handed for five years . . . devoted to religion, philosophy, politics and general literature. It had no

---

[29] *Ibid.*, III, 518-520.
[30] *Ibid.*, IV, 524.
[31] *Ibid.*, V, 513 and 515.
[32] *Brownson's Quarterly Review*, I, 2 and 5.

creed, no distinct doctrines to support on any subject whatever, and was intended for free and independent discussion of all questions which I might regard as worth discussing.... My aim was not dogmatism, but inquiry.... I aimed to startle, and made it a point to be as paradoxical and extravagant as I could, without doing violence to my own reason or conscience.[33]

As Frothingham has pointed out,[34] *The Boston Quarterly Review* dealt with a very wide range of subjects, and handled them all by the transcendental method, so to speak. The periodical would serve as an unusually effective means of determining what problems were discussed by the intellectual element of the population of New England during the period. At least one Boston newspaper occasionally used the magazine as a means of rehearsing topics of current interest.[35] From a consideration of the President's messages to Congress, a discussion of the soundness of an opinion expressed by Longinus, and a glowing exposition of "The Rights of Woman,"[36] the articles ranged to the more esoteric problems of philosophy. Each number usually contained about six essays, almost always prompted by a newly published work, and a series of brief "Literary Notices." Except for the quotations in the critiques there was no poetry.

The problem of determining who the various contributors were is, for the most part, an insoluble one, because of the then current practice of allowing the identity of magazine writers to remain unknown. Occasionally, however, initials are to be found. Brownson's own work can often be determined because he usually appended a footnote here and there to indicate that his own views were at variance with those of the contributor. Moreover,

---

[33] *The Convert*, p. 89.
[34] *Transcendentalism in New England*, 1876, pp. 128 and 131.
[35] Cf., for example, *The Boston Morning Post* for Jan. 4, April 3, July 8, and Oct. 21, 1839.
[36] *B. Q. R.*, IV, 371; II, 385; and II, 350.

the discussion aroused by his own opinions soon led him to mark his essays "By the Editor." Among the writers for the periodical, according to Henry F. Brownson, were George Bancroft, George Ripley, Bronson Alcott, Margaret Fuller, Anne C. Lynch (Botta), Sarah H. Whitman, Miss R. A. Tyler, Elizabeth Peabody, B. H. Brewster, H. S. Patterson, A. H. Everett, and Theodore Parker.[37] Albert Brisbane contributed an article on "Association and Reform," and John F. Tuckerman one on Beethoven.[38] Tuckerman, it may be said here, wrote at least one article for *The Dial*.[39] The writers for the first volume of the *Boston Quarterly*, according to the marginal notes written in his own copy by Theodore Parker,[40] were, besides Brownson, J. S. Dwight, W. H. Channing, S. D. Robbins, Bancroft, and Parker himself.

The work of the transcendentalists that can be identified will be considered later. The articles that can be ascribed to the other contributors are as follows: Bancroft, "On the Progress of Civilization, or Reasons Why the Natural Association of Men of Letters Is with the Democracy";[41] B. H. Brewster, "Charles Lamb," and "Milton's Select Prose Works";[42] A. H. Everett, two essays on "The Currency";[43] Miss R. A. Tyler, "The Rights of Woman";[44] and Henry S. Patterson, "Shelley's Poetical Works."[45] There is good reason for believing that Bancroft and Everett made other contributions, but no external evidence can be presented to determine what they were.

For the purposes of this study it will be necessary to give little or no consideration to the problems of economics

---

[37] *E. Life*, 214, 215, 220, 227, 230, 231, 233, and 237.
[38] *B. Q. R.*, V, 183; and III, 332.
[39] *The Dial*, I, 539.
[40] In the Boston Public Library.
[41] *B. Q. R.*, I, 389.
[42] *Ibid.*, IV, 214; and V, 322.
[43] *Ibid.*, II, 298; and III, 80.
[44] *Ibid.*, II, 350.
[45] *Ibid.*, IV, 393.

and politics discussed in *The Boston Quarterly Review*. The essential quality of the magazine is the strange mixture of literature, religion, and philosophy so characteristic of all the products of the transcendental movement. It must be admitted, however, that the heresies on property and industry thrown out by Brownson were in themselves part and parcel of the New Spirit. After all, there is an undeniable connection between the attempt to uphold the idea of the divinity in man and the effort to better the conditions of the working classes and to abolish slavery. The Romantic movement can not be said to have confined its scope to philosophy and literature. In undertaking a sketch of the transcendental aspects of the periodical, however, the economic phases of the problem will be passed by. Emerson's connection with the review will be considered by itself.

When Brownson projected his *Boston Quarterly* he depended upon his intimate friends to aid him in the work, and at first he seems not to have been disappointed. According to Parker's marginal notes, J. S. Dwight contributed to the first volume a review of the poems of W. T. Bacon (Boston, 1837); W. H. Channing wrote critiques of Emerson's Phi Beta Kappa oration, and of Carlyle's *French Revolution;* Parker himself provided a fifty-page essay dealing with J. G. Palfrey's work on the Pentateuch (Boston, 1838); and S. D. Robbins furnished "Thoughts on Unity, Progress, and Government."[46] The rest of the first four issues of the periodical seems to have been written by Brownson, unless, as is quite possible, George Ripley aided in the preparation of the literary notices.

Of the transcendental utterances in the first volume

[46] *Ibid.*, I, 74, 106, 407, 261, and 192.

none seems more striking than Robbins's "Thoughts." The essay begins with these words:

> All truth, whether in science, philosophy, religion, or politics, is one. The one truth is God's idea, the Right, the Expedient, the Indispensable.
>
> The soul is also a unity. It has no dualism, either in its powers or its requisites. Humanity has but one law, as the Deity has but one mind.[47]

The idea of unity expressed in the above is applied to education and to government, and the note of philosophical evolution is struck by an ardent prophecy of true progress based upon "the inward worship of the Divinity" within man. The application of this idea to religion is contained in these words:

> The present age is prophetic. The seers are on the watch towers, gazing with serene eye upon the moral firmament, reading the aspect of the lights and shadows which alternate in the moral heavens, solving the problems, interpreting the prophecies, and opening the parables which are written in the history of man, which are uttered by the experience of society.
>
> The inspiration of nature is the music in all our hearts. Brotherhood, the warm tide that, flowing through the arteries of the universal frame, connects the unit to the whole, and the whole to the parts by a life-current of quick loves. Individual minds are the best interpreters of the Divinity. The original thinkers, the single-eyed, the holy-hearted, are the purest conductors of infinite truth, the Christs of God. The word is incarnate in every Godchild. The oracles of the Father-mind issue warm from the bosoms of his Well-beloved, in all generations. Revelation is confined to no age. No man can invent truth; all men may discover it. God reveals himself to all orders of spirits equally, as the sun illumines all alike, even the blind. . . .
>
> Forms may grow old, altars decay, and prophets die, creeds change, and dynasties crumble in the dust, but man shall always be priest and king, so long as he shall be true to the Urim and Thummin stamped on his heart, so long as he shall obey the oracle

[47] *Ibid.*, I, 192.

of his own spirit, and fulfil the inwritten commandment of his Godlike nature.[48]

It will readily be seen that Robbins set forth the central theme of Emerson's *Divinity School Address* some months before it was delivered. Accordingly, that famous protest against what was esteemed the dominion of delusion needs to be considered rather as a concrete manifestation of a general movement than as the expression of a critical stage in the evolution of an individual.

Brownson himself elaborated a point of view somewhat similar in two articles maintaining that "Christianity was not an original revelation with Jesus."[49] However, he first showed the vigor of his style in an article entitled "Philosophy and Common Sense," which took issue with the unfortunate Francis Bowen, who had written on "Locke and the Transcendentalists" in *The Christian Examiner* for November, 1837. After a brief reference to the recent dawning of American interest in speculative philosophy, Brownson wrote:

Apparently the article was intended to vindicate the character of Locke as a metaphysician, and to put the community on its guard against certain individuals whom its author denominates Transcendentalists. Who these Transcendentalists are, what is their number, and what are their principal tenets, the writer does not inform us. Nor does he tell us precisely the dangers we have to apprehend from their labors; but so far as we can collect his meaning, it would seem that these dangers consist in the fact that the Transcendentalists encourage the study of German literature and philosophy, and are introducing the habit of writing bad English. . . . So far, however, as our knowledge extends, there is no overweening fondness for German literature and philosophy. We know not of a single man in this country who avows himself a disciple of what is properly called the Transcendental Philosophy. The genius of our countrymen is for Eclecticism.[50]

---
[48] *Ibid.*, I, 193 and 199 (April, 1838). In connection with this article, see "Some Remarks on Emerson's *Divinity School Address*," by the present writer (*American Literature*, I, 27-31).
[49] *B. Q. R.*, I, 8 and 129.   [50] *Ibid.*, I, 86.

The passage above reveals Brownson's early effort to evade the term "transcendentalism."

Already in his articles in the *Examiner* he had made the attempt to create a vogue for Cousin's term, "Eclecticism,"[51] and he was possibly one of the first to express in print the impropriety of applying the name "Transcendentalists" to a varied group of men who had little in common save an interest in religious philosophy and literature. The attempt to avoid the use of the word was exceedingly wise, since it already had a connotation of foreign skepticism, obscurity in terminology, and rabid speculation. As a matter of policy, Brownson's attempt to win favor for his chosen name of eclecticism was well justified.

The editor of the *Boston Quarterly*, however, was not an advocate of the quixotic notions of some few of the "Newnessites." William A. Alcott, a now forgotten cousin of Amos Bronson Alcott, published at Boston, in 1838, *The Mother in the Family, or Sayings and Doings at Rose Hill Cottage*, in which he set forth his ideas about a reformation in diet. Brownson was so inspired that he delivered himself of an essay on "Ultraism,"[52] in which he pointed out the folly of advocating the unnatural, and showed himself a master of ridicule. A large portion of this essay was republished in *The Western Messenger*.[53]

Amos Bronson Alcott's *Conversations with Children on the Gospels* also aroused the editor of the *Boston Quarterly*—but in another fashion. "The author," Brownson wrote, "as a man, is singularly evangelical, pure minded, in love with all that is beautiful and good, and devoted soul and body to what he deems truth, and the regenera-

---

[51] See, for example, *The Christian Examiner*, XXII, 181.
[52] *B. Q. R.*, I, 377.
[53] *W. M.*, V, 313. *The Western Messenger* frequently reprinted pages from the *Boston Quarterly* (cf. *W. M.*, V, 104 and 173; and VIII, 316 and 433).

tion of man." But, he continued, "Mr. Alcott appears to us not to discriminate with sufficient accuracy between the Creator and the Creation." The critic summarized in excellent fashion the educational theories of Alcott, and explained their source in a philosophy of intuition, which he deemed necessary to counteract the prevalent materialism. Yet, he cautioned: "The instincts, as Mr. Alcott calls them, are no doubt from God; they deserve to be studied and reverenced. We must, however, be on our guard that we do not become exclusively devoted to them, for if we do we shall become mystics."[54] Although Brownson had an eye for fundamental weaknesses, and was unwilling to sanction unmitigated mysticism, his genuine appreciation of Alcott's merits made this review unquestionably one of the most discerning that appeared during the life of the philosopher of the Concord porch.

The particular variety of transcendentalism that Brownson favored, that of Victor Cousin, was first presented in quantity to the readers of the *Quarterly* in the number for October, 1838, the occasion being a review of the first work brought out by Ripley in his series of "Specimens of Foreign Standard Literature," *Philosophical Miscellanies of Cousin, Jouffroy and Constant* (Boston, 1838). Brownson began by expressing his faith in American letters and thought, maintained that the use of foreign ideas was, under the circumstances, altogether fitting, and expressed his belief that the genius of France and Germany would be effective in overcoming the tyrannical sway of English writings over the American mind. Cousin he considered to be "if not the first, one of the first philosophers of the age."[55] The reason for this statement has already been indicated in the passage from *The Convert* in which he acknowledged his indebtedness to Cousin. The *New Views*, the articles in the *Examiner*, and the fre-

[54] B. Q. R., I, 417-432.   [55] Ibid., I, 443.

quent references to the Frenchman's opinions in earlier numbers of the *Boston Quarterly* all prove that he was an avowed disciple of the foreign master.

Cousin early began to correspond with Brownson,[56] and in the third edition of his *Fragments Philosophiques* (1838) made this reference:

> En 1836 et 1837, M. Brownson a publié une apologie de mes principes où brille un talent de pensée et de style qui, régulièrement développé, promet à l'Amérique un écrivain philosophique du premier ordre.[57]

The influence of French eclecticism upon the development of American transcendentalism deserves a special study.[58] However, it may be said here that it appears to be quite possible to trace the history of the movement along a line of thought derived from Cousin and his like, as well as along the line of influences exerted by Coleridge, Carlyle, or Goethe. Some significance may be attached to the fact that Ripley chose as the first of his "Specimens" not German idealism, but the spiritual philosophy of France. But Ripley and Brownson were not the only ones interested. In *The North American Review* for July, 1829, A. H. Everett had written an essay upholding Cousin's ideas against those of Locke.[59] In 1832 H. G. Linberg had brought out in Boston, Cousin's *Introduction to the History of Philosophy*. Caleb S. Henry published his *Elements of Psychology*, with an introductory essay and notes, at Hartford, in 1834, a work which after 1838 went through several editions. In 1840 W. H. Channing furthered the cause by translating Jouffroy's *Introduction*

---

[56] See E. *Life*, 394.   [57] Introduction, p. vi.
[58] Cf. in this connection Howard M. Jones, *America and French Culture*, Chapel Hill, 1927, pp. 461 ff. Walter L. Leighton found "the slenderness of French influence somewhat disappointing" (*French Philosophers and New England Transcendentalism*, U. of Virginia diss., Charlottesville, 1908, p. 94). Mr. Leighton, however, cannot be said to have studied the matter thoroughly.
[59] *The North American Review*, XXIX, 67.

to *Ethics* as the fifth and sixth volumes of the "Specimens of Foreign Standard Literature."

There is no need for wonder, then, that *The Princeton Review* in its attack on Emerson included Cousin's treatises as a chief source of the New England heresy.[60] Francis Bowen, in *The North American Review* for July, 1841, began his assault by asserting, "The writings of Cousin form the popular philosophy of the day."[61]

Since Brownson regarded himself as the chief disciple of Cousin in America, *The Boston Quarterly Review* naturally took a leading part in spreading French idealism. The second volume, for example, contained three essays dealing with the subject: "The Eclectic Philosophy," a discussion of Cousin's *Cours de Philosophie* (Paris, 1836); "Eclecticism—Ontology," a continuation of the above; and a critique of his *Fragments Philosophiques* (Paris, 1838).[62] The first two of these articles were written by Brownson, and constitute a very readable exposition of his opinions concerning the principles set forth by his master.

"There is manifested," wrote Brownson, "a singular pertinacity in confounding M. Cousin with certain persons among ourselves, who, for some reason not known to us, have received the appellation of Transcendentalists." Continuing, he asserted:

> We say again that M. Cousin is not a Transcendentalist, as the term appears to be understood in this community. It is not easy to determine what people mean by the term Transcendentalist; but we suppose they mean to designate by it, when they use it as a term of reproach, a man who, in philosophizing, disregards experience and builds on principles obtained not by experience, but by reasoning *a priori*. In this sense Cousin is no Transcendentalist. Nor, indeed, was Kant.[63]

---

[60] *The Princeton Review*, XI, 37.
[61] *The North American Review*, LIII, 1.
[62] *B. Q. R.*, II, 27, 169, and 435.
[63] *Ibid.*, II, 27 and 29.

Then follows an explanation of the chief differences between the ideas of Kant and Locke, with an elaboration of the elements of Cousin's philosophy, which is considered to be, like that of Bacon and Descartes, experimental. According to the reviewer, the student of the system must begin by ascertaining what the facts of consciousness are. Then, "if we find among our ideas, ideas which are unquestionably facts of consciousness, certain ideas which could not have been generated by the senses, we have a right to infer that we have another source of ideas than the senses."[64] After this comes an ingenious illustration:

> There are in the case of voluntary causation, the *me*, or personality willing or making a voluntary effort, and the motion of a part of the body in obedience to the will. I will to raise my arm. Here we must note: 1st, the volition; 2nd, the muscular contraction; 3rd, the rising of the arm. Now the senses take cognizance of the rising of the arm, and, if you please, of the muscular contraction, but not of the volition, much less of the fact that the volition is the cause of the phenomena succeeding it. The sensation I am conscious of in this case is the result of the muscular effort, not of the voluntary effort. How then by sensation alone am I to connect my volition, or, more properly, myself, with the muscular contraction and the rising of my arm, as their cause? I am conscious of the fact. I want no reasoning to prove to me that the connexion implied does really exist. I cannot for one moment doubt that I am the cause of the phenomena in question. Whence comes this feeling of certainty, this conviction, this conception of myself as cause? It cannot come from sensation.[65]

The elaboration of the postulate explained by the above quotation leads to the assertion: "Inferences from Sensibility cannot go beyond the experience of Sensibility."[66] The argument up to this point is summed up as follows:

> We have the idea of cause; that we conceive of cause always as something which creates, or produces effects; and that this idea,

---

[64] *Ibid.*, II, 38.   [65] *Ibid.*, II, 43.   [66] *Ibid.*, II, 47.

whether it be true or false, cannot be derived from the experience of the senses, nor from the experience of the Activity; but must be derived from the Intelligence, the Reason, or whatever that is in us by virtue of which we are knowing, as well as feeling and acting beings. It must therefore be an intuition of the reason. It is the reason that sees the relation of cause and effect in the phenomena presented by experience, and the reason that furnishes us the principle, that nothing can begin to exist but by virtue of a cause. If we are correct in this, it must be admitted, that there are facts in the consciousness which have not an empirical origin, but a rational origin.[67]

It will be noted that Brownson's use of the word "reason" is a typically transcendental one. The demonstration of the basis for intuition as a psychological necessity is carried on in a briefer analysis of facts of consciousness other than that of cause; namely, the notion of space, and the idea of the infinite. With the same deft logic he points out the shortcomings of the school of Locke.

In the second essay, "Eclecticism—Ontology," he expounds his belief that "ontology must have its root in psychology" by quoting copious extracts from Cousin dealing with the fundamental points of variance between the school of Locke and that of Kant.[68] He amends Cousin's statement that reason is objective by a suggestion of his own:

Perhaps it would not be amiss to divide the Reason into objective reason and subjective reason. By the objective reason we may understand the eternal Reason, the immaterial world, the world of necessary Truth which overshadows us, underlies us, and constitutes the ground of our intelligence, identical with the Logos of the Apostle and the Greek Fathers, the "inner light" of the Quakers. . . . In this sense Reason is not mine, nor any man's. It is impersonal and absolute. . . .

By the subjective reason we may understand . . . our general faculty of knowing, that by virtue of which we are intelligent beings, capable of intelligence. . . . But we apprehend that a

[67] *Ibid.*, II, 49.   [68] *Ibid.*, II, 169-176.

careful analysis of the facts of consciousness would go far to identify this subjective reason with the objective reason, so far at least as to prove that our reason must be in immediate relation with the impersonal Reason—that it is, in fact, as it has been called, "a fragment of the Universal Reason."[69]

Evidently, not all of the transcendentalists were dispensers of mere moonshine, unable to balance philosophic accounts, and for that reason counting upon an Orphic aspect to mask their essential inability to think in a consecutive fashion.

Brownson promised a further treatment of the same subject for the next number of his magazine, but failed to keep his promise. In the issue for October, 1839, however, a contributor, possibly Ripley, briefly summarized Cousin's newly published *Fragments Philosophiques*. Another contributor, writing on "The Development of Humanity," undertook to prove that Pure Reason existed from eternity, and took issue with Cousin upon certain aspects of his philosophy.[70] Brownson smoothed matters over by means of a footnote about four pages in length, but allowed the same writer, "T, of Wheeling, Virginia," to develop his opinions further in *The Boston Quarterly Review* for April, 1840.[71] His chief addition to the central belief in intuition which characterized the views of both the editor and himself was this: "Personality is the active principle in man; it is all that portion of our minds not included in the Pure Reason."[72]

In addition to the pages devoted to Cousin, the second volume of the periodical had other transcendental features. There was, for example, a very flattering review of the third volume of Ripley's "Specimens," *Select Minor Poems from Goethe and Schiller*, translated by J. S.

---

[69] *Ibid.*, II, 178-179.
[70] *Ibid.*, II, 449-477.
[71] *Ibid.*, III, 193.
[72] *Ibid.*, III, 201.

Dwight and others of the New School.[73] An essay on "The Poetical Works of Wordsworth" contained these words:

> Spontaneity is the divine in man. It is the voice of the universal reason, or Word of God, uttering itself in us. It is in immediate relation with God, and consequently with the primal source of truth, beauty, and goodness. It reveals to us truth, beauty, goodness, which are but different phases of absolute being—God.[74]

Yet the critique strikes one as singularly sound.

On the polemic side, the second volume of *The Boston Quarterly Review* is of interest in that it contains Brownson's inimitable handling of Andrews Norton, the archenemy of all that savored of the New Spirit, the denouncer of Emerson, and the antagonist of Ripley. The occasion was a review of Norton's *Evidences of the Genuineness of the Four Gospels* (Boston, 1837). Brownson wrote: "When we heard that this work was announced as actually published, we trusted it would wipe out that suspicion of infidelity which had long been attached to the author . . . but we are sorry to say that, to a certain extent at least, we have been disappointed."[75] When it is remembered that Norton had actually been suspected of holding heterodox views in his earlier career, but had not, on that account, hesitated to attack transcendentalism as "The Latest Form of Infidelity,"[76] the point of Brownson's words is readily seen.

---

[73] *Ibid.*, II, 187. Cf. Emma G. Jaeck, *Madame de Staël and The Spread of German Literature*, New York, 1915, pp. 303-307.

[74] *Ibid.*, II, 141.   [75] *Ibid.*, II, 87.

[76] The Ripley-Norton controversy really began in 1836. Ripley published an article on Martineau's *Rationale of Religious Inquiry* in *The Christian Examiner* (Nov., 1836) and Norton, in *The Boston Daily Advertiser*, condemned it as a presumptuous indication of infidelity. Ripley printed a rejoinder in the same paper the next day (O. B. Frothingham, *George Ripley*, 1882, pp. 95 and 96).

In addition to newspaper letters and the like, the chief documents in the controversy are these: *A Discourse on the Latest Form of Infidelity*, A. Norton, Cambridge, 1839; *The Latest Form of Infidelity Examined*, a letter to Mr. Andrews Norton occasioned by his discourse before the Association of the Alumni

How little the transcendentalists needed the *Evidences* is indicated in the following:

> There are persons who believe that the truths of Christianity bear on their face a certain stamp of divinity, which the soul is capable of recognising; that "the inspiration of the Almighty, which giveth men understanding" enables us to see, and know, and be well assured of the great truths of the Gospel. To these persons the question of the genuineness of the Four Gospels is a matter of comparative indifference.[77]

Brownson continued by discounting the idea that miracles can prove divinity, and argued that even the philosophy of Locke, whose chief disciple in America Norton was considered to be, would not admit of resting the basis of Christianity upon the miraculous.[78] After summoning Jonathan Edwards as a witness of the untenableness of Norton's position, he continued:

> Edwards, it may be urged, did not regard this power of seeing, apprehending the truth and reality of the Gospel revelation, as one of the original powers of the soul, but as superinduced upon the soul in the fact of regeneration. But this makes no practical difference.[79]

The essay concludes with a brief reference to Norton's opposition to the New School, in part as follows:

of the Cambridge Theological School, on the 19th of July, 1839, by an alumnus of that school [Ripley], Boston, 1839; *Remarks on a Pamphlet Entitled "The Latest Form of Infidelity Examined,"* by Andrews Norton, Cambridge, 1839; *Defence of "The Latest Form of Infidelity Examined"* [Spinoza], by George Ripley, Boston, 1840; *A Third Letter to Mr. Andrews Norton* [Schleiermacher and De Wette], by George Ripley, Boston, 1840; *A Letter to Andrews Norton on Miracles as the Foundation of Religious Faith* [Richard Hildreth], Boston, 1840; *Two Articles from the Princeton Review, Concerning the Transcendental Philosophy of the Germans and of Cousin, and Its Influence on Opinion in This Country*, Cambridge, 1840 [Published by Norton] (The two articles from *The Princeton Review* were: "Transcendentalism," by J. W. Alexander and A. B. Dod, *The Princeton Review*, XI, 37 (Jan., 1839); and "The School of Hegel," by Charles Hodge, *The Princeton Review*, XII, 31 (Jan., 1840); and *The Previous Question Between Mr. Andrews Norton and His Alumni Moved and Handled in a Letter to All Those Gentlemen*, by Levi Blodgett [Theodore Parker], Boston, 1840.

[77] *B. Q. R.*, II, 87.   [78] *Ibid.*, II, 106-110.   [79] *Ibid.*, II, 104.

We have grieved to witness, of late, certain demonstrations of uncharitableness on his part towards some of our friends, and of a determination to check, by the use of hard names, and by severe denunciations, the free action of thought, and the bold utterance of honest opinion. In this he is inexcusable; for it is well known that the brand of heresy is and long has been as deep on him as it can be on any one else.... He would do well, then, not to fill the newspapers of this city with too many denunciations of a young man who chances to say a good word for the poet Shelley.[80]

The final remark dealing with Shelley appears to have been a keen thrust at Brownson's opponent, who, it must be remembered, strove to be a literary critic as well as a theologian. In his unsigned article "The New School in Literature and Religion," published in *The Boston Daily Advertiser* for August 27, 1838, Norton not only attacked Emerson for his heretical utterance before the graduating class of the Divinity School, but, as has been seen, made a great ado about an article praising Shelley which had appeared in *The Western Messenger*. But his exposition of Shelley's "atheism" was based upon an inadequate knowledge of the poet's works; and when his charges were shown to have been in a great many points groundless, he replied with a half-hearted reiteration of his opinion that Shelley had been after all "improperly commended."[81] James Freeman Clarke had prompted the partial retraction by a letter to the *Advertiser*, in which he pointed out the fact that the original article on Shelley had carefully given attention to those views of the poet which were open to censure, and suggested, "Perhaps your correspondent was scandalized at anything good being said of an atheist."[82] The Shelley affair was practically the only part of the controversy in which Norton was made to feel ridiculous, and Brownson, accordingly, showed keen judgment

---

[80] *Ibid.*, II, 112-113.
[81] *The Boston Daily Advertiser*, Oct. 5, 1838.
[82] *Ibid.*, Sept. 28, 1838.

in using it, along with the former charge of infidelity, as an effective means of nettling the champion of the opposition party.

However, the article in the *Boston Quarterly* was more than a clever means of taunting the supposed liberal Unitarian with mistaken judgment and intolerance. Its chief value lay in the fact that Brownson used the method of Locke against the school of Locke. As a consequence, the essay deserves a high place among the numerous tracts that sought to lay the Harvard Goliath low.

In the preliminary statement to the third volume of the periodical Brownson referred to the spiritual situation of New England in these words:

> The dominion of Locke is broken up, and he now has only a few adherents, and they are men of yesterday,[83] who can exert no influence on tomorrow. The tendency is just now to an opposite extreme, to what among us is called Transcendentalism, a system of philosophy—if that may be called a system which disclaims all system—which builds upon an order of facts proceeding from an origin which *transcends* the senses and the operations of the understanding. The source of this order of facts is called by some Instinct, by others Spontaneity, and by others still Inspiration. They are intuitive and immediate. All among us, who are denominated sometimes the New School, contend for the reality of this order of facts, and so far all who have broken with the past are agreed.[84]

But, he continued, there were some in the group who held reason and logic in slight esteem, and despised a demand for proof of their statements. "With these individuals," he wrote, "I do not entirely agree. If I started with them, I could not stop short of exclusive mysticism."[85]

The first contribution to the third volume is a thirty-seven-page critique of Margaret Fuller's translation of

---

[83] In 1835, Emerson, when urging Carlyle to come to America to edit the proposed organ of the spiritual philosophy, spoke of the opposition in these words: "If we get a good tide with us, we shall sweep away the whole inertia, which is the whole force of these gentlemen, except Norton" (*Carlyle-Emerson Correspondence*, 1883, I, 61). [84] B. Q. R., III, 11. [85] *Loc. cit.*

Eckermann's *Conversations with Goethe* (Boston, 1839). Its author, Sarah H. Whitman, Poe's friend, proves by her review to have been strongly inclined toward transcendentalism. Margaret Fuller herself supplied for this volume two dialogues entitled "Chat in Boston Bookstores."[86] These two "conversations" are interesting to the student of the transcendental movement in that they give the views of both the conservatives and radicals of the day in regard to contemporary literature, and the theological quarrel raging in Boston. For example, the information is afforded that most of the people who were reading about the Ripley-Norton controversy took sides with Norton. Spinoza, we are told, had suddenly become more than a mere name. Jones Very's *Poems and Essays* are described sympathetically.[87]

During this year, 1840, it will be remembered, the discussion of a new magazine of the idealistic type reached a head, and *The Dial* was started. Probably in April, 1839, Brownson made a final proposal that the new periodical should be combined with his own. Alcott was made the advocate for the project, but Margaret Fuller and Emerson rejected the offer.[88] As has been said, Brownson announced that the *Boston Quarterly* would not appear after the final number for 1839, possibly because he still entertained the hope of uniting his literary labors with those of his friends. Little effort, however, is necessary to discover a reason for the failure to join the two publications, a step which would seem to have been a very logical one, since many of the transcendentalists had written for the earlier magazine. A suggestion is contained in Alcott's diary for March 27, 1839:

[86] *Ibid.*, III, 127 and 323.
[87] *Ibid.*, III, 328 ff. and 132.
[88] T. W. Higginson, *Margaret Fuller Ossoli*, p. 148.

Brought home with me Brownson's *Boston Quarterly Review* for April. This is the best journal now current on this side of the Atlantic, but falls far below the idea of the best minds among us.[89]

In that last clause one may find the reason. Emerson and his associates aimed at the stars even in the publishing business, a fact brought out by their keen disappointment at the ineptitude of their own *Dial*. Moreover, Brownson's periodical was esteemed to be an organ of the Democratic Party, and he was one of the "reform men."

The Boston Quarterly Review for July, 1840, the month in which *The Dial* first appeared, contained as its feature article an essay, by Brownson, elicited by Norton's reprint of the two contributions to *The Princeton Review*. The essay is a very sound survey of the controversy with Norton, and, as might be expected, a clever defense of Cousin from the charges brought by the Princeton opponents. In it Brownson shows that he had given up the attempt to force the public to recognize the distinction between transcendentalism and eclecticism. Of the New School, he wrote:

They differ widely in their opinions, and agree in little except in their common opposition to the old school. . . . Some of them embrace the Transcendental philosophy, some of them reject it, some of them *ignore* all philosophy, plant themselves upon their own instincts, and wait for the huge world to come round to them. Some of them read Cousin, some Goethe and Carlyle, others none at all. Some of them reason, others merely dream. . . . The movement is really of American origin, and the prominent actors in it were carried away by it before ever they formed any acquaintance with French or German metaphysics; and their attachment to the literatures of France and Germany is the effect of their connexion with the movement, not the cause.

Moreover, there are no members of the movement party who would adopt entirely the views of any of the distinguished foreigners named. We are inquiring for ourselves, and following

[89] *Ibid.*, p. 143.

out the direction of our own minds, but willing to receive aid, let it come from what quarter it may. . . . We have nothing to do with Hegel, or Schelling, or Kant, or Cousin, any further than our own inquiries lead us to approve their speculations.[90]

The transition from the third to the first person in the above is significant. At the end of the essay, after an elaboration of "Cousin's Transcendentalism," Brownson carefully stated that he was one of the party that recognized the "capacity of knowing truth intuitively," but maintained that he could not place "dreaming above reflection."[91]

In the same number of the *Boston Quarterly*, the editor brought out his first article on the laboring classes, using Carlyle's *Chartism* (Boston, 1840) as a point of departure. Of Carlyle and his American imitators he spoke slightingly, and insisted that the genius of the Englishman was essentially destructive. "Priests," he wrote, "are in their capacity of priests, necessarily enemies to freedom and equality."[92] In a similarly bold fashion he set forth various heresies about property and the condition of laborers. This essay, with its sequel in the next issue, marked a crisis in Brownson's career, and caused his name, with that of his review, to be spread throughout the country. Ripley and Alcott sought to relieve their feelings about social injustice by forming communities in which the evils of the existing order were to be excluded by the mere operation of the will. Brownson, in his more active, even vehement, fashion, strove to shock the world into sensibility, hoping that logic, plus rhetoric, would win the day. The reaction to the essay is indicated in a passage from

[90] *B. Q. R.*, III, 270-271. The reference to those who "plant themselves upon their instincts" is, of course, to Emerson.
[91] *Ibid.*, III, 322-323. Brownson was perhaps irritated by the idea set forth in *The Princeton Review*: "The principles upon which Mr. Emerson proceeds, so far as he states them, are the same as those of M. Cousin" (Norton's reprint, p. 66).
[92] *B. Q. R.*, III, 386.

the journal of Theodore Parker, who also had interesting views on the subject of labor:[93]

> Brownson has recently written an article on the laboring-classes calculated to call the philosophic to reflection. He thinks inherited property should be given up; that the relation of master and servant, employer and employed, should cease; that the priest is the chief curse to society. This makes a great noise. The Whigs, finding their sacramental idea—money—in danger, have come to the rescue with fire-brands and the like weapons. . . . I like much of his article, though his property notions agree not with my view.[94]

As a consequence of the interest aroused by the essay, *The Boston Quarterly Review* was occupied for several numbers with slightly more than the usual amount of economic discussion. The general spirit of the times is reflected in "Conversations with a Radical, by a Conservative,"[95] a document of some value to one who is bent upon tracing the ramifications of the Romantic rebellion in various phases of American life of the period. More pertinent to this study is a brief review of *The Dial*, which appeared among the literary notices. The substance of it is contained in these excerpts:

> The Dialists belong to the genus *cullotic*, and have no fellowship with your vulgar *sans-cullottes*. . . . Some of its prose pieces are more poetical than most of its pieces in verse. . . . "The Problem," however, in the first number, is not merely verse; it is poetry, and unsurpassed, if equalled, by any production of the American muse with which we are acquainted. . . . To our taste, they [the contributors] want robustness, manliness, and practical aims. They are too vague, evanescent, aerial; but, nevertheless, there is a "sad sincerity" about many of them; and one cannot help feeling that these after all are the men and women who are to shape our future.[96]

---

[93] See, for example, his *Collected Works*, London, 1864, VIII, 31.
[94] O. B. Frothingham, *Theodore Parker*, 1874, pp. 134-135.
[95] *B. Q. R.*, IV, 1 and 137.
[96] *Ibid.*, IV, 132.

The fourth volume contained other matter of interest to the student of transcendentalism: Brownson's essay, "Truth Is Not a Lie," his criticism of Parker's *The Transient and Permanent in Christianity*, a letter from Albert Brisbane, and Alcott's contribution of a few of his "Orphic Sayings." "Truth Is Not a Lie" was prompted by the editor's perusal of William Wollaston's *Religion of Nature Delineated* (London, 1731). It is important not only because it indicates Brownson's wide range of reading, which, oddly enough, included contemporary fiction, but because it exhibits the growing meaning of the word "transcendentalism." Since Wollaston had studied Plato, the critic wrote, he had "a tendency to a spiritual philosophy, or, as we say in these times, to Transcendentalism."[97]

In his review of Parker's famous discourse he expressed his hearty appreciation of the idea of progress in religion which lay back of the work, and of its denial of the plenary inspiration theory of the Bible; but, as usual, he noted a few weaknesses in logic.[98] In general, the reader receives the impression that substantially the same point of view was taken by the two men.

Albert Brisbane's letter was written to the *Quarterly*[99] to develop "a very contracted idea" of Fourier's notions, which Brownson had described, in a favorable manner, in an essay entitled "Social Evils and Their Remedy."[100]

Just why Alcott, "in place of a contribution requested from himself," sent the editors of *The Dial* a poem by Henry More, but furnished a dozen of his Orphics for the issue of the *Boston Quarterly* which appeared in the very same month (October, 1841), is an insoluble problem.[101] Two of the number are especially striking:

[97] *Ibid.*, IV, 341.
[98] *Ibid.*, IV, 436-474.
[99] *Ibid.*, IV, 494.
[100] *Ibid.*, IV, 265.
[101] *The Dial*, II, 137.

Beauty
Beauty is the health of goodness,
Beneficence
God hath, and is all things; yet gives all things, himself, away. Go, churl, and do thou likewise.[102]

Immediately after the receipt of the number containing Alcott's contribution, A. H. Everett, from his college in Louisiana, wrote to Brownson as follows:

> I see that you have become the organ of Orpheus Alcott. What is the meaning of this? Is *The Dial* defunct? Does that mysterious Horologue no longer "repeat the progress of the hour and the day"? I have some doubts, however, whether the presence of Orpheus in the quarterly will do it much good. Eurydice-Fuller, whom you appear to have lost from your pages, was to my taste the better contributor. How fares it, in general, with Transcendentalism about these times? How are Norton and Ripley carrying on the war? What is the prevalent opinion on the doctrine of Spinoza?[103]

The final volume of *The Boston Quarterly Review* is of interest largely because it reveals the beginning of another change in Brownson's philosophy and religion—a change that was marked by a growing belief in the efficacy of external authority. He was not wholly satisfied with the attitude he had assumed in his *New Views*, of 1836, and his *Charles Elwood*, written earlier, for the most part, but published in 1840. Accordingly, he ventured to review both of these works in his magazine.

He still considered his *New Views* to be the "most genuine statement" of his whole thought, and accordingly, set about supplying an exposition of the fundamental ideas of the work, ideas which, when stripped of supplementary social and religious opinions, reduce themselves to an insistence upon the necessity of adjusting inherited theology, philosophy and sociology to the exigencies of the *Zeit-*

---

[102] *B. Q. R.*, IV, 492.   [103] *E. Life*, p. 234.

geist.[104] Its general tone is one of prophecy. The addition made by him in the review of the work is contained, for the most part, in the following:

> The time has come to affirm, and to affirm with emphasis. The race is tired of mere analysis, criticism, dissecting, which gives not life but takes it away. It demands a broad and generous synthesis, positive convictions, positive institutions, and a positive mission. It would act.[105]

Like most of the progressives of the Unitarian church, Brownson was looking for an Everlasting Yea, instead of "pale negations." In the end he found it, not in a glorification of the divinity of self, but in the authority of the Catholic church.

Of *Charles Elwood, or the Infidel Converted* he had more to say. After pointing out that the fiction contained in his book was little, and that the experiences of the hero were largely his own, he expressed the desire to refurbish some of the philosophy it contained.[106] What he had in mind, as he later explained, was this. After several ministers have tried in vain to satisfy the intellectual demands made by the Infidel, Charles Elwood, a certain Mr. Morton, a thorough-going transcendentalist,[107] converts the hero to a philosophy based largely upon the ideas of Cousin and Constant. Although Morton avoided most of the errors into which he might have fallen, he is esteemed to have been in error in regard to three points: the origin of religion in human nature, the impersonality of reason, and the division of reason into spontaneous reason and reflective reason.[108] The first of these shows the influence

---

[104] *B. Q. R.*, V, 1, 16 and 17.
[105] *Ibid.*, V, 26.　　　　　　[106] *Ibid.*, V, 146.
[107] Morton begins his work of conversion by explaining: "Man, I take it, in his forms of religious faith and worship, seeks successfully or unsuccessfully, to realize his conceptions of the true, the beautiful, and the good. These conceptions are the fundamental elements of religion; and they are also under one aspect the fundamental elements of reason, without which reason would not be reason" (*Works*, IV, 265).　　　[108] *B. Q. R.*, V, 149.

of Constant, and the other two, of Cousin, according to Brownson. One who has read his exposition of his chosen type of transcendentalism readily sees in these three topics the framework of his psychological demonstration of the philosophy of intuition.

It would be perhaps futile to attempt to summarize the nice discriminations and the adroit manipulation of philosophical commonplaces which Brownson employs in stating the "progress" of his thoughts. Suffice it to say here that he definitely restricts the utter license which, in spite of his assertions, had marked his exploitation of intuition as the panacea for all ailments in logic. These words are perhaps illuminating:

By *intuition* we understand merely the power of the soul to perceive ideas, and by ideas we mean objects or realities of that world which transcends time and space. All ideas—and we use the term in the original Platonic sense—are transcendental. In asserting man's power to perceive them we coincide with the transcendentalists; but in asserting, as we also do, that it is out of the soul, out of the *me* and not in it, that they exist, and that we perceive them, we depart from what we suppose is a characteristic feature of American transcendentalism.[109]

One may question whether many of the transcendentalists could have realized that Brownson was no longer to be called a brother. But the use of the word "transcendental" in the quotation is again of interest. In his attempt to make the movement square with philosophy Brownson had gone all the way from insisting upon the use of the term as a distinct element in a very special jargon, to an acceptance of the word as a synonym for idealism. Accordingly, one may appreciate the distress of parents whose sons at Harvard tried to explain the nature of the much-discussed heresy.[110]

[109] *Ibid.*, V, 152-153.
[110] See, for example, a letter of F. D. Huntington to his mother, May 16, 1840, in A. S. Huntington, *Memoir and Letters of Frederick D. Huntington*, Boston, 1906, pp. 53-54.

The last volume of *The Boston Quarterly Review* also contained an essay on "Association and Reform,"[111] the first of a proposed series of articles by Albert Brisbane, which were calculated to explain the doctrines of Fourier. However, with the suspension of publication after the number for October, 1842, Brisbane was forced to continue his series in another magazine. It is significant that the rest of his essays in the group were not published in *The Dial*, but in *The Democratic Review*.[112]

The April number of the *Boston Quarterly* included a defense of Theodore Parker, written by Elizabeth Peabody.[113] That she, too, did not use *The Dial* as the means of getting her article before the public is worthy of attention. Perhaps the reason lies back of this postscript in a letter of Margaret Fuller's to Emerson, dated April, 1842, the same month in which the article appeared:

> Let me before I forget it guard you, if need be, against trusting E. P. P. to write the slightest notice or advertisement. I never saw anything like her for impossibility of being clear and accurate in a brief space.[114]

In the final volume Brownson took occasion to vent his displeasure at the passive attitude of some of his friends.

> The great end of life is not to be, but to do; and, in doing, being is developed and enlarged. This cant of the followers of our transcendentalists about being, and cultivating one's being, is quite nauseating.... There is for us no sadder image than that of a man who sets out "with malice aforethought" to cultivate himself.[115]

---

[111] B. Q. R., V, 183.
[112] See *The United States Magazine and Democratic Review*, new series, X (1842), 30, 167, 321, and 560. [113] B. Q. R., V, 201.
[114] MSS. dealing with M. F. Ossoli, in the Boston Public Library.
[115] B. Q. R., V, 82. Hawthorne, of Margaret Fuller: "It was such an awful joke, that she should have resolved—in all sincerity, no doubt—to make herself the greatest, wisest, best woman of the age" (Julian Hawthorne, *Nathaniel Hawthorne and His Wife*, 1885, I, 261).

These remarks form part of an excursus in his essay on "Reform and Conservatism," which he had been moved to write by one of the published sermons of James Freeman Clarke, *The Well-Instructed Scribe* (Boston, 1841). Like Clarke, he said, "We have been for years blowing hot and cold with the same breath, though unwittingly and unintentionally; and, like him, have mistaken an imbecile eclecticism for a powerful and living synthesis."[116]

Further evidence of the change which he was undergoing at this time is supplied by his article of sixty-five pages dealing with Saint-Simonism,[117] and his review of Parker's *Discourse on Matters Pertaining to Religion* (Boston, 1842). The latter, which occupied the entire final number of *The Boston Quarterly Review*, is an exposition of Parker's ideas of the religious sentiment, inspiration, Christ, the Bible, and the Church. The critic expressed his own opinions when they were at variance with those of the author. Perhaps the most significant ideas in Brownson's discussion are his continual assertions that intuition is to be regarded as a fact of experience, and his belief that "the perfection of nature" is "the greatest of all absurdities."[118] Unlike Emerson and Parker, he was determined to find a supernatural origin for the Bible.[119] But, as he later said in *The Convert*, his views were, in general, much like those of Parker.[120]

Nevertheless, there can be no question about the shift in philosophical outlook manifested by Brownson's "ripest views," as he called them, and his consequent withdrawal from the New School. The mental and religious evolution of any man alive to the stirring spirit of the New England renaissance is apt to be a baffling study. Just why Brownson was moved to decide that Cousin's ideas, if in-

---
[116] *Ibid.*, V, 61.
[117] *Ibid.*, V, 257.
[118] *B. Q. R.*, V, 397, 408 and 439.
[119] *Ibid.*, V, 481-485.
[120] *The Convert*, 152.

terpreted from an objective point of view, became "a system of absolute pantheism," and that "there is no purely subjective, or purely objective knowledge,"[121] within such a short time after he had taken pains to prove the contrary —who can tell?

His sincerity, in spite of his many spiritual "somersets," can scarcely be questioned. After his attack upon his former opinions made in the review of *Charles Elwood*, he wrote:

> The criticisms on ourselves will be taken, we presume, in good part; but those on Cousin, considering the relation we have been supposed to hold to his philosophy, will most likely excite some surprise, and call forth a new edition of the old stereotyped charge that we have changed our opinions again. . . . Yet, we resolve never to be the slave of our own past—the slave of our own shadow.[122]

That *The Boston Quarterly Review* should be of unusual interest in its attitude toward Emerson goes without saying. When Brownson was preparing material for the first number of his review, he asked Emerson for a contribution dealing with Carlyle. The letter which he received in answer to his request, dated November 15, 1837, expressed pleasure at the prospect of the "literary-philosophic" enterprise, but stated that a promise made to James Walker, editor of *The Christian Examiner*, of a critique of Carlyle, and the press of work in preparation for a course of lectures forbade compliance.[123] The vague suggestion that Emerson held out of a future contribution seems never to have passed beyond the realm of hope. There appears to be no evidence to confirm the statement that Emerson had been writing for Brownson's periodical before *The Dial* was begun.[124] On the other hand, there

---
[121] *B. Q. R.*, V, 165 and 176.
[122] *Ibid.*, V, 178-179.   [123] *E. Life*, pp. 214-215.
[124] A. Tassin, *The Magazine in America*, 1916, p. 263.

are no corroborative facts for Edward Emerson's note that Brownson contributed to *The Dial*;[125] although, as has been said, Ripley wrote for it a very enthusiastic essay on "Brownson's Writings," and Emerson supplied a noncommittal review of his *Letter to Rev. W. E. Channing* (Boston, 1842).[126] But the *Boston Quarterly* was more generous of its space, seventy-three of its pages, in addition to scattered references, being devoted to the discussion of Emerson's works.

The first number of the quarterly contained a review of the Phi Beta Kappa discourse, written, according to Parker's marginal note, by W. H. Channing. The critic liked the style of the work much better than that of *Nature*, announced a preference for the expression "American Author" instead of "Scholar," and proceeded to give his own notions as to the proper training and task of the national writer. "We shall never have a healthy American literature unless we have an American spirit, an American manner of life," he concluded. Channing's attitude toward Emerson himself is revealed in these words:

He seems to us true, reverent, free and loving. We cheerfully tolerate, therefore, any quaint trappings in which a peculiar taste may lead him to deck his thoughts.[127]

After having used his pen in Emerson's defense in *The Boston Morning Post*, Brownson employed the issue of his own periodical for October, 1838, to set forth at length what he thought of the *Divinity School Address*. Much of the work he admired greatly. But its tone seemed "somewhat arrogant," its philosophy "undigested," and its reasoning "inconclusive."[128] He observed that there was in Emerson's work, as well as that of "his masters, Carlyle and Goethe," a "transcendental selfish-

---
[125] Emerson's *Journals*, VI, 297.   [126] *The Dial*, I, 22; and III, 276.
[127] *B. Q. R.*, I, 107, 108, 113, and 120.
[128] *Ibid.*, I, 501.

ness" or "pure egotism."[129] He expressed the usual objections to a passive yielding to "instincts," and demanded "reflection as well as spontaneity." If by his attack on historical Christianity Emerson meant only to arouse interest in the spirit rather than the letter, Brownson was ready to approve heartily, but he insisted upon the necessity of a continuity with past tradition.[130] So much for Brownson the philosopher. Brownson the transcendentalist went on to say:

> Nevertheless, let not the tenor of our remarks be mistaken. Mr. Emerson is the last man in the world we should suspect of conscious hostility to religion and morality. No one can know him or read his productions without feeling a profound respect for the singular purity and uprightness of his character and motives. The great object he is laboring to accomplish is one in which he should receive the hearty coöperation of every American scholar, of every friend of truth, freedom, piety, and virtue. Whatever may be the . . . moral, philosophical, or theological system which forms the basis of his speculations, his real object is not the inculcation of any new theory on man, nature, or God; but to induce men to think for themselves on all subjects, and to speak from their own full hearts and earnest convictions. His object is to make men scorn to be slaves to routine, to custom, to established creeds, to public opinion, to the great names of this age, of this country or of any other. He cannot bear the idea that a man comes into the world today with the field of truth monopolized and foreclosed. To every man lies open the whole field of truth, in morals, in politics, in science, in theology, in philosophy. The labors of past ages, the revelations of prophets and bards, the discoveries of the scientific and the philosophic, are not to be regarded as superseding our own exertions and inquiries, as impediments to the free action of our own minds, but merely as helps, as provocations to the freest and fullest spiritual action of which God has made us capable.
> This is the real end he has in view, and it is a good end. To call forth the free spirit, to produce the conviction here implied, to provoke men to be men, self-moving, self-subsisting men, not

[129] *Ibid.*, I, 504.   [130] *Ibid.*, I, 510.

mere puppets, moving but as moved by the reigning mode, the reigning dogma, the reigning school, is a grand and praiseworthy work, and we should reverence and aid, not abuse and hinder him who gives himself up soul and body to its accomplishment.[181]

The second volume of the *Boston Quarterly* started out with the editor's review of Emerson's oration delivered to the literary societies of Dartmouth, published at Boston, in 1838. After an excellent summary of its contents, the critic said of the author:

He is a poet rather than a philosopher—and not always true even to the laws of poetry. He must be read not for a work of art, which shall be perfect as a whole, but for the exquisite beauty of its details, not for any new or striking philosophical views, but for incidental remarks, frequent aphorisms, valuable hints, rich and original imagery and illustration.[182]

He agreed with Emerson's belief in the necessity of "spiritual independence," but, like Whitman, proclaimed:

Genius has come out of the cloister and the university, and creates in the ship-yard and the smithy, reasons on change, and sings in the music of the axe, the hammer, and the loom, giving dignity to labor and the empire of the world to the laborer.[183]

Brownson's belief that nature ordained provision for the body before the soul led him to write:

It is said that the whole nation has been absorbed in the pursuit of wealth. We admit it, and rejoice that it has been so. It is a proof of the unity of our national life.... It proves that the pursuit of wealth can be only a temporary pursuit, that we must soon satisfy our material wants, and be ready to engage with similar intenseness in providing for the wants of the soul.[184]

Other ideas, not without interest to the student of American critical theory, are expressed in the following excerpts:

[181] *Ibid.*, I, 513-514.
[182] *Ibid.*, II, 4.
[183] *Ibid.*, II, 8.
[184] *Ibid.*, II, 11.

The business world is in no sense inferior in active intellect to the world of letters; all the difference is in the application.

The great merit and wide circulation of our newspapers and periodicals are doubtless the cause of the meagreness of our "book" literature.

Few things are less independent of mere will or arbitrariness than literature. It is the expression and embodiment of the national life.

Great men do not make their age; they are its effect.

Literature cannot come before its time. We cannot obtain the oracle before the Pythoness feels the God.[135]

The characteristic quality of Brownson's theory of American literature, along with the milieu doctrine, is an ardent love for the democratic—the over-earnest type of the social reformer, not that of the Emersonian "solitary soul." An apt illustration is supplied in the following words:

It will be because a man has felt with the American people, espoused their cause, bound himself to it for life or for death, time or eternity, that he becomes able to adorn American literature; not because he has lived apart, refused "to serve society," held lone reveries, and looked on sunsets, and sunrises.[136]

When a study is made of the numerous essays on American literature which helped to fill the pages of the magazines of the period, this review of Brownson's will, in all probability, deserve particular attention.[137]

When the first series of Emerson's *Essays* appeared the editor of the *Boston Quarterly* soon printed a review, written by himself, in the number for July, 1841. He said, in part:

To most persons who read these Essays, they will seem to be wanting in unity and coherence. They will always strike as

---

[135] *Ibid.*, II, 17, 18, 19, 20 and 23.   [136] *Ibid.*, II, 26.
[137] V. G. Michel's *The Critical Principles of O. A. Brownson*, Catholic U. diss., Washington, D. C., 1918, fails to give consideration to the matter.

beautiful, often as just, and sometimes as profound; but the reader will be puzzled to round their teachings into a whole, or to discover their practical bearing on life or thought. Yet they have unity and coherence, but of the transcendental sort. The author seems to us to have taken, as far as possible, his stand in the Eternal, above time and space, and tried to present things as they appear from that point of vision—not in their relation to each other as seen in the world of the senses, but in their relation to the spectator who views them from above the world of senses. . . . He is to be regarded as a Seer, who rises into the regions of the Transcendental, and reports what he sees, and in the order in which he sees it. His worth can be determined, that is, the accuracy of his reports can be properly judged of by none except those who rise to the same regions and behold the universe from the same point of view.[138]

Not only does Brownson anticipate Arnold in his belief that Emerson's value is to be ascertained only by "those who would live in the spirit," but he also explains the essays as a product of the New School. Of the new spirit itself he has much to say. After a brief, and neat, tracing of the movement from Puritan days, he continues, "All our ideas of truth, justice, love, beauty, goodness, are transcendental."[139] Fox, Penn, Edwards,[140] Price, "nearly all the Germans," and the French eclectics he calls transcendentalists. He notes that the essays frequently remind him of Montaigne, and explains their pantheistic tendency as the natural product of an effort to bring up "a pole of truth" that has been too long depressed.[141] Perhaps these words should also be quoted:

There is a sacredness about them, a mystic divinity, a voice issuing from them, saying to critics, "Procul, O Procul, este, pro-

---

[138] *B. Q. R.*, IV, 292.   [139] *Ibid.*, IV, 300.
[140] In a copy of the first volume of Edwards's works, New York, 1844, given by him to the Harvard library, Convers Francis wrote: "In an article in the *British Critic*, Vol. XV (1834), p. 333, metion is made of 'Edwards and other *transcendental* divines. . . .' There is more good reason for applying this epithet to Edwards than most readers of his works are aware of."
[141] *B. Q. R.*, IV, 304.

fani!" To do them justice, they should be read with reverence, with a yielding spirit, an open heart, ready to receive with thankfulness whatever meets its wants or can be appropriated to its use. The rest, what is not congenial, should be left with pious respect.[142]

Enough has been given here, perhaps, to show that Brownson had an eye for more than the philosophical shortcomings of the Sage of Concord.

In his criticism of Parker's discourse, which, it will be remembered, occupied the entire final number of *The Boston Quarterly Review*, Brownson quoted from "The Problem," a favorite with him, and maintained that the lines,

> Out from the heart of nature rolled
> The burden of the Bible old,

seemed to take a higher view of the scriptures than Parker had attained.[143] Continuing, he wrote:

> According to Mr. Emerson, it is not man that speaks out from himself, but the mighty Over-Soul—answering nearly to what we term the Ideal; that hovers over man, underlies him, thinks in his thought, loves in his love, and lives in his life. This is the mighty, the one, universal, living Spirit, Nature, what you will, the Power from which all forms proceed, the form in which the infinite I Am is revealed. This is the Creator. It is one, whether it create in what men call nature, or in what they call art; whether it bloom in a violet or in a Madonna, rear an Andes, or with human hands, a St. Peter's. All genuine, all authentic productions are its creations. . . .
> We are every day led to suspect that his [Emerson's] thought lies deeper, and is altogether broader, than we have usually given him credit for; and in doubting his religious faith or religious feeling we have done him great wrong. The more progress we seem to ourselves to make in true philosophical science, the more do we discover in his writing, and the profounder is our reverence for his genius. . . . We apprehend that it will ultimately be found that his seeming denial of God comes from his deep sense of a uni-

---

[142] *Ibid.*, IV, 298.   [143] *Ibid.*, V, 479.

versal Presence which he stands in awe of, before which he shudders with fear, love, and delight, but which he does not name.... Mr. Emerson, may we not say, appears to be often irreligious in consequence of the very excess of his devoutness?[144]

It is apparent from the foregoing discussion that Orestes Brownson played no small part in spreading the ideas of transcendentalism in the United States. Early a member of Hedge's Club, he devoted his pen to the service of the cause, chiefly in his *New Veiws*, his *Charles Elwood*, his contributions to *The Christian Examiner*, and the powerful *Boston Quarterly Review*, the most philosophical of all the periodicals connected with the movement. As a disciple of Cousin, his exposition of the Eclectic School's method of demonstrating the psychological necessity for a belief in intuitions was an important contribution to the overthrow of the dominion of Locke and the Scotch theologians in America. It may well have been as influential as James Marsh's prefatory essay to his edition of Coleridge's *Aids to Reflection* (1829) and Hedge's article on Coleridge in *The Christian Examiner* for 1833. That it appeared when the controversy over transcendentalism was at its height must have given it additional weight. Of all the economic theorists numbered with the New School, without question, Brownson commanded the widest interest during his day. His influence upon George Ripley, in this connection, deserves special attention.[145]

The Boston Quarterly Review is also to be considered as an important forerunner of *The Dial*, in view of its contents and contributors. That it presents material for a study in the growth of the transcendental movement, as

[144] *Ibid.*, V, 479-480.
[145] C. A. Dana(?) wrote, in *The New York Sun*, July, 1880, about Ripley during the Brook Farm period: "He had very few intimate friends then or at any time, yet three men were especially near to him, influencing his mind by their conversation and writings. These men were George Bancroft, Orestes A. Brownson and Theodore Parker" (J. H. Wilson, *The Life of C. A. Dana*, New York, 1907, p. 453).

well as perhaps the most convincing criticism of Emerson brought out during the period, is obvious. The attitude of one of the most outstanding leaders of the party of progress toward the periodical is indicated in these words of W. H. Channing:

In an age like this, superficial and perplexed, and yet learning, as it is, its own ignorance at least . . . a man must be akin to a seraph or a stock not to change. The only consistency one would now desire to keep is the *consistency of progress,* and this Mr. Mr. Brownson may proudly claim. . . . It is heard with uncommon pleasure that there is a prospect of renewing the *Boston Quarterly*. Take it all in all, it was the best journal this country has ever produced, at once the most American, practical and awakening; the more so because its editor was a learner and shared his studies with his readers.[146]

Theodore Parker, whose contributions to *The Dial* promoted the sale of that magazine more than those of any other writer,[147] remarked in a letter to Convers Francis, dated December 18, 1840:

Apropos of *The Dial,* to my mind it bears about the same relation to the *Boston Quarterly* that Antimachus does to Hercules, Alcott to Brownson, or a band of men and maidens daintily arrayed in finery, "walking in a vain show," with kid mitts on their "dannies," to a body of stout men in blue frocks, with great arms and hard hands, and legs like the Pillars of Hercules. If I were going to do the thing in paint, it should be thus: I would represent a body of minute philosophers, men and maidens, elegantly dressed, bearing a banner inscribed "The Dial." A baby and a pap-spoon and a cradle should be the accompaniment thereof. The whole body should have "rings on their fingers and bells on their toes" and go "mincing as they walk," led by a body of fiddlers, with Scott's Claude Halcro "playing the first violin and repeating new poetry." This body of the excellent should come out of a canvas city of Jerusalem set upon a hill. On the other hand

---

[146] *The Present* (1843), p. 72.
[147] Parker's article on the "Hollis Street Council" (*The Dial*, III, 201) sold out the entire issue in which it appeared (Cabot, *A Memoir of R. W. Emerson*, II, 407).

should come up a small body of warriors looking like the seven chiefs before Thebes, and swearing as they did, with just about as modest devices on their shields. They should be men who looked battles, with organs of combativeness big as your fist. They should be covered with sweat and blood and dust, with an earnest look and confident tread. . . . At their head should stand Orestes Augustus Brownson, dressed like Daniel, with Goliath's sword in one hand, and that giant's head in the other.[148]

[148] O. B. Frothingham, *Theodore Parker*, p. 139.

CHAPTER IV

THE PRESENT

In the second series of his *Imaginary Conversations*, published in 1826, Walter Savage Landor put into the mouths of Franklin and Washington a woefully dull discussion of much pompous inanity. During the course of the conversation Franklin, who is made out to be little more than a subservient flatterer, expresses himself as follows:

> I do not believe that the remainder of the world contains so many men who reason rightly as New England. Serious, religious, peaceable, inflexibly just and courageous, their stores of intellect are not squandered in the regions of fancy, nor in the desperate ventures of new-found and foggy metaphysics, but warehoused and kept sound at home. . . .

Whether these remarks adequately characterize the New England of Revolutionary times may be doubted. But if one were to search for a description of the intellectual state of New England during the period of its renaissance, no words could be found so far removed from the truth as those of Landor. One needs only to read Emerson's vivid account of the Chardon Street Convention, held in 1840,[1] to realize how completely the intellect of the northeastern states was being "squandered in the regions of fancy."

Old John Quincy Adams, vainly endeavoring to understand the changes of the new era, wrote in his diary for August 2, 1840:

> A young man, named Ralph Waldo Emerson, a son of my once-loved friend William Emerson, and a classmate of my lamented son George, after failing in the every-day avocations of a

---

[1] *The Dial*, III, 100, reprinted in *Lectures and Biographical Sketches*. In connection with the Chardon Street Convention see also *William Lloyd Garrison, the story of his life, told by his children*, New York, 1885, II, 422 ff.

CHAPTER IV

THE PRESENT

In the second series of his *Imaginary Conversations*, published in 1826, Walter Savage Landor put into the mouths of Franklin and Washington a woefully dull discussion of much pompous inanity. During the course of the conversation Franklin, who is made out to be little more than a subservient flatterer, expresses himself as follows:

I do not believe that the remainder of the world contains so many men who reason rightly as New England. Serious, religious, peaceable, inflexibly just and courageous, their stores of intellect are not squandered in the regions of fancy, nor in the desperate ventures of new-found and foggy metaphysics, but warehoused and kept sound at home. . . .

Whether these remarks adequately characterize the New England of Revolutionary times may be doubted. But if one were to search for a description of the intellectual state of New England during the period of its renaissance, no words could be found so far removed from the truth as those of Landor. One needs only to read Emerson's vivid account of the Chardon Street Convention, held in 1840,[1] to realize how completely the intellect of the northeastern states was being "squandered in the regions of fancy."

Old John Quincy Adams, vainly endeavoring to understand the changes of the new era, wrote in his diary for August 2, 1840:

A young man, named Ralph Waldo Emerson, a son of my once-loved friend William Emerson, and a classmate of my lamented son George, after failing in the every-day avocations of a

---

[1] *The Dial*, III, 100, reprinted in *Lectures and Biographical Sketches*. In connection with the Chardon Street Convention see also *William Lloyd Garrison, the story of his life, told by his children*, New York, 1885, II, 422 ff.

Unitarian preacher and schoolmaster, starts a new doctrine of transcendentalism, declares all the old revelations superannuated and worn-out, and announces the approach of new revelations and prophecies. Garrison and the non-resistant abolitionists, Brownson and the Marat Democrats, phrenology and animal magnetism, all come in, furnishing each some plausible rascality as an ingredient for the bubbling cauldron of religion and politics.[2]

Obviously, the old gentleman's acceptance of Emerson's responsibility for the despised transcendentalism of the day is much too simple; but, at any rate, he was able to point out some of the causes for the intellectual ferment that makes the period of the forties so "fabulous" to us.

A competent observer of the times, blessed with a proper perspective, would have mentioned also the name of William Henry Channing, who was by all odds the most active of the New School in his interest in reform—no matter how it manifested itself. Endowed with a warmth of nature so noticeably lacking in his uncle, the Apostle of Unitarianism, Channing had passed through a period of doubt consequent upon his ministry in the Middle West, and in the early years of the forties began to preach a kind of "socialism" that embraced all the favorite reforms of the age—from abolition to temperance.[3] When one remembers that the fundamental principle of Dr. William Ellery Channing's teaching was "the dignity of human nature," it is easy to see a close connection with the ideas that prompted his nephew to turn his back upon the formal activities of a Unitarian clergyman, and embark upon a career that was to take him among the ranks of the propagandists and reformers.

As a preliminary step in the direction of overcoming the "insufficiency of individual exertion" in spreading his

---

[2] *Memoirs of John Quincy Adams*, ed. C. F. Adams, Philadelphia, 1876, X, 345.
[3] O. B. Frothingham, *Memoir of William Henry Channing*, 1886, pp. 7, 94 *et passim*.

views, he established in New York and Brooklyn a society for "Christian Union." In a statement of the principles upon which this organization was effected he observed:

> We begin to perceive that through all varieties or creeds, through the thousand-fold forms of mythology and theology, through the systems of philosophers and the visions of poets, has spoken more or less audibly one Eternal Word. Sublime analogies present themselves between the spiritual and natural worlds.[4]

Back of these words, of course, one can see again the catholicity of spiritual interest so characteristic of American transcendentalism, and in the "sublime analogies," the potential symbols of mysticism.

As another means of bringing his ideas before the public, in 1843 Channing established a monthly magazine in New York. As has been seen, he was at that time a welcome contributor to *The Dial*, and it might have been expected that he should have employed that journal as a medium. But Emerson's attitude toward his activities as a reformer, so plainly brought out later in the ode inscribed to him, might have occasioned trouble with "the evil time's sole patriot." Moreover, the existence of the Boston quarterly was too precarious to justify an attempt to extend its scope. However, that *The Dial* recognized the merits of *The Present*, as the new periodical was called, is to be seen in one of its critical notices for January, 1844:

> Mr. Channing's *Present* is a valiant and vivacious journal, and has no superior in the purity and elevation of its tone, and in

---

[4] *A Statement of the Principles of the Christian Union*, New York, 1843, p. 5. It should be remembered that Dr. Channing himself had never regarded himself as a subscriber to any creed of Unitarianism, so to speak. On August 8, 1841, he wrote to Professor George Bush: "I do not speak as a Unitarian but an independent Christian. I have little or no interest in Unitarianism as a sect. I have hardly anything to do with them. I can endure no sectarian bonds. With Dr. Priestley, a good and great man, who had most to do in producing the late Unitarian movement, I have less sympathy than with many of the 'Orthodox'" (W. H. Channing, *The Life of William Ellery Channing*, 1880, p. 427).

the courage of its criticism. It has not yet expressed itself with much distinctness as to the methods by which socialism is to heal the old wounds of the public and private heart; but it breathes the air of heaven, and we wish it a million readers.[5]

On the cover of the first number of his periodical, that for September, 1843, the editor published a prospectus, which stated:

The Present, as its name indicates, is designed to reflect the Signs of the Times. Its aim will be to aid all movements which seem fitted to produce union and growth in Religion, Science, and Society. It will seek to reconcile faith and free inquiry, law and liberty, order and progress; to harmonize sectarian and party differences by statements of universal principles; and to animate hopeful efforts on all sides to advance the Reign of Heaven on earth. It will endeavor to discuss the various questions of Reform which are now interesting our communities with sincerity and candor; to encourage and note the progress of spiritual and humane enterprises to remove ignorance, vice, and suffering; to record discoveries and inventions which promise to elevate man's condition; and by notices of native and foreign books, with extracts and translations, by descriptions and criticisms of artistic creations, as well as by tales and poems from our own authors, to unite beauty with truth and love. Its pages are open to all who can express their convictions with good sense and feeling; and the aid of friendly contributors is requested.

In a very diffuse introductory article he further announced that the special aim of his journal would be "to show the grounds of reconciliation between the sects and parties, native and foreign, the controversies, theological and political, the social reformers and prudent conserv-

[5] *The Dial*, IV, 407. The spirit of this notice is similar to that of Channing's recommendation of *The Dial*, in the last number of *The Western Messenger* (VIII, 571): "We have not said a word of *The Dial*, for we are slow to praise our own family, and the writers in this Periodical are our own dear friends. Therefore, one word only, Readers! Believe not the geese, who have hissed their loudest at this new comer. Such foolish creatures cannot save the Capitol. *The Dial* marks an era in American literature; it is the wind-flower of a new spring in the Western world. For profound thought, a pure tone of personal and social morality, wise criticism, and fresh beauty, *The Dial* has never been equalled in America. Subscribe for it as you love yourselves."

atives, the philosophers and poets, prophets and doubters, which divide these United States."[6] The first number of *The Present* also contained a "Salutation to Contemporaries and Subscribers," in which Channing offered a greeting to the journalistic world, and outlined to his "brother reformers" some matters of special consequence, such as capital punishment, labor, and slavery. "Let puritan rigidity," he wrote, "unbend before the courteous manliness of a freer age."[7]

At the outset he acquired the subscription lists of several reform journals,[8] and later received at least the moral support of a certain element among the socialists, for the Social Reform Convention held at Boston in December, 1843, "earnestly recommended to the friends of Human Progress" *The Present*, along with the organ of the Fourierists called *The Phalanx*.[9] It was the enthusiasm engendered at this assembly that induced Channing to print in his January number a prospectus for a second volume, to begin in May, in which he announced as the central doctrine of the journal the idea that "modern civilized society is tending to the organization of associations of families and individuals, united in all the interests of life."[10] At the same time, he stated that assistance had been promised from a number of "able writers of quite opposite modes of thinking." But circumstances did not permit him to realize his expectations, for no number of the journal appeared during February, 1844, and the issue for the following April brought the magazine to a close.

Already in the March number the editor had acknowledged that he had issued the prospectus for a second volume "under the hopes excited by the New England Convention," and that sober thought had "hinted" that

[6] *The Present*, on cover.
[7] *Ibid.*, p. 35.
[8] *Ibid.*, p. 36.
[9] *Ibid.*, p. 287.
[10] *Ibid.*, p. 288.

a material enlargement of the number of subscribers was an absolute necessity.[11] However, in the final notice to the readers of the periodical he did not mention the financial situation as a reason for suspending publication, but stated that the "near and sacred duty" of preparing a memoir of his uncle, Dr. W. E. Channing, forbade further journalistic activity on his part. In the same announcement he attempted to explain the reason for "the abstract and 'transcendental' cast" of the speculations contained in his own articles, and expressed his obligations to the doctrines of Charles Fourier.[12]

Perhaps the chief reason for the early failure of *The Present*, however, was Channing's inability to adjust himself to the exigencies of an editor's duties. His journal, like *The Dial*, which terminated during the same month, offered no distinctive product to its readers. As its prospectus indicated, its aims were entirely too broad. Moreover, its editor, to quote Lindsay Swift, "had an overenthusiasm and lack of definiteness well calculated to wreck any project dependent on him alone to shape its course."[13] The final notice to the readers of the periodical suggested the possibility of renewing publication as soon as circumstances would permit, but by the time that Channing had finished his biographical work the Brook Farm organ, *The Harbinger*, was ready to give its space to anything he might write. In the interim that elapsed between the publication of the last number of *The Present* and the first issue of *The Harbinger* the friends of reform concentrated their interests upon *The Phalanx*, which Albert Brisbane had founded after he had ceased to edit a column in Greeley's *Tribune*.[14]

[11] *Ibid.*, p. 360.
[12] *Ibid.*, p. 432. J. H. Noyes, in his *History of American Socialisms*, Philadelphia, 1870, p. 516, claims that it was W. H. Channing who "converted" Brook Farm to Fourierism. [13] *Brook Farm*, 1900, p. 217.
[14] For a sketch of "the literature of Fourierism" see J. H. Noyes, *op. cit.*, cap. XVIII.

In its general quality—its interest in religion, philosophy, and literature—*The Present* was at first similar to its contemporary, *The Dial*. But as succeeding issues tended to exhaust the supply of better material the magazine devoted more space to problems of reform, particularly Fourierism. Yet its editor was able to avoid the appearance of narrow-minded sectarianism in spite of the intensity of his convictions, and at no time did the journal manifest an uncompromising attitude. In a note appended to a contribution Channing wrote: "I hold myself responsible for nothing which is not professedly from my pen; and *The Present* is conducted upon the *only catholic* principle, as it seems to me, of giving free room to writers whom I respect, even when I differ from them, to express their own views in their own words."[15]

With the second number, that for October, 1843, a department was started headed by the caption "Signs of the Times." This contained announcements and short discussions, largely from the editor's pen, which had a special interest for the reformers alone. The initial notice in this department was a brief welcome to *The Phalanx*, the first number of which had just come from press.[16] The "Signs of the Times" not only announced conventions and discussed works of interest to the Associationists, but ventured into politics in expressing a hearty disapproval of "the plot to annex Texas."[17] The most interesting of its items, however, are not those dealing with pauperism, capital punishment, and similar subjects, but those announcing progress at Fruitlands and Brook Farm.

The October number mentioned a visit in New York from "the Essenes of New England," Charles Lane and

---

[15] *The Present*, p. 337.
[16] *Ibid.*, p. 70. *The Phalanx*, which shared with *The Present* the subscription list of *The Independent Magazine*, frequently printed notices of Channing's journal, and at times took issue with certain of its assertions relative to Fourier (cf. *The Phalanx*, p. 42, for example). [17] *The Present*, pp. 137 and 428.

Amos Bronson Alcott, "the gardeners of Fruitlands." While admitting a profound respect for these "Therapeuts," Channing wrote:

> But I am willing to own for one, that I have little confidence in a mysticism, which does not steadfastly exercise the function of conscious rational volition, as the appointed means of receiving divine communications in the soul; and neither have I a wish to imitate any who would undervalue the body and sensible enjoyments as a condition of health of the spirit. The experiment has too often failed.[18]

Yet, in a few remarks introductory to Ripley's announcement that Brook Farm was about to begin a partial experiment with Fourierism, he became very enthusiastic in urging contributions to the cause of "unity, freedom and order, progress and peace," and serenely continued: "If they fail, no harm is done. If they prosper, they will be the embodiment of our professed principles of Christian love, and of Liberty."[19]

But Lane and Alcott were evidently not offended by Channing's frank disapproval of their beliefs, since the former contributed several well written articles to *The Present*,[20] and the latter, twenty-five of his "Orphic Sayings."[21] Among these Delphic utterances was one of an unusually mundane nature, which exhibited Alcott as the *pater familias* of Fruitlands rather than as an American Plotinus:

Eden

Eden is a garden, not a farm; and Adam, not an husbandman, but gardener. Tillage, pasturage, involve trade, slaughter, servitude, and lucre. The divine man dwells amidst gardens and orchards, a grower of plants and fruits; a handler of spades and

---
[18] *Ibid.*, p. 71.
[19] *The Present*, p. 350.
[20] "The Third Dispensation" and "The True Life" (*ibid.*, pp. 110 and 312). Lane was also a contributor to *The Dial* (cf. *The Dial*, III, 417; IV, 65 and 188; and IV, 351).
[21] *The Present*, p. 170 (Dec., 1843); and p. 261 (Jan., 1844).

pruning knives; not a goader nor throttler of oxen, nor stripper of udders, nor scavenger of cattle, nor feeder of swine. He neither breeds herbs, nor cherishes muckpiles; nor is a marketer of fatlings in shambles, nor debauches his acres, nor imbrutes his households, by debasing toils, diets, bargains, and gains. Husbandry, pasturage, trade and wages, are lapses from primeval innocency; the doom of expulsion from Paradise. 'Tis of toils and competitions that guile and extortion are born, and lust of gain is the progenitor of guilt. Not in the stir of towns, of bales and banks, chapmen and publicans, breathes Honesty, but harvests indigenous bread from virgin soils, amidst hills and waters.[22]

Of an oracular nature somewhat similar to Alcott's Orphics was a group of short "Affirmations," which Channing used as "fillers" for his magazine.[23] These were written by James P. Greaves, who had named his Pestalozzian school at Ham, near London, after Alcott, and who had died in 1842, after an "abstention for thirty-six years from fermented drinks and animal food." The appearance of his "Affirmations" in *The Present* was probably due to Lane, who was his literary executor.[24]

The magazine contained a considerable amount of material written by Englishmen other than Greaves and Lane. Philip Harwood, a rationalist lecturer in Finsbury, London, sent articles on "Unitarianism" and "The Hebrew Prophets and the Christian Gospel."[25] A few of the productions of John C. Prince, a poet whose bitter experiences as a victim of British capitalism made him interesting to the reformers, were published, as well as a critique and biographical account of the author, by Parke Godwin.[26] An essay on Victor Cousin, calculated to show the lack of originality in the philosophy of eclecticism, was

---

[22] *The Present*, p. 171.
[23] See, for example, *ibid.*, pp. 155, 164, 196, 229, 265, and 268.
[24] For Greaves see Emerson's sketch in *The Dial*, III, 228; and Sanborn and Harris, *A. Bronson Alcott*, 1893, I, 310 ff.
[25] *The Present*, pp. 122 and 156.
[26] *The Present*, pp. 94, 227 and 235; and 45 and 98.

reprinted from *The British and Foreign Review*.[27] More significant, perhaps, was a lengthy discussion of Swedenborg's life and works,[28] reproduced from the London *Monthly Magazine*, a journal which excited no little attention among the transcendentalists.[29]

Channing, whose interest in the similarities of the doctrines of Swedenborg and Fourier led him to venerate the founder of the New Church, intimated in a note that this article failed to do justice to the great mystic, and took issue with one of its statements about Emerson. John Heraud, the author of the essay, in quoting from the Phi Beta Kappa oration, had referred to Emerson as one of "Carlyle's own disciples in America." The editor of *The Present* added these words:

> This error has also been committed here. Mr. Emerson is a brother of Mr. Carlyle, not his son. And the points of contrast between them outnumber those of similitude. The former is a Painter dashing off frescoes, the latter a Sculptor working in basreliefs, or even in medals, though both take for subjects the gods of Olympus. What is common to these two writers belongs to the Spirituality of the Age. The merits of each are peculiar.[30]

Channing's efforts to minimize the influence of Carlyle were no doubt aimed to counteract a general impression, for, as has been seen, Andrews Norton, in his first assault on transcendentalism, had mentioned the "Germanized Englishman" as one of those whom he esteemed respon-

---

[27] *Ibid.*, p. 80.
[28] *Ibid.*, pp. 252, 329, and 386. A good account of Swedenborgianism in America is to be found in an essay by Wm. L. Worcester in *The Religious History of New England*, Harvard U. Press, 1917, cap. VIII. The student of transcendentalism will find some interesting material in B. F. Barrett, *Swedenborg and Channing, showing the many and remarkable agreements in the beliefs and teachings of these writers*, Philadelphia, 1879.
[29] T. W. Higginson, *Margaret Fuller Ossoli*, 1884, pp. 145 ff.
[30] *The Present*, p. 253. Various writers for *The Present* occasionally referred to Carlyle (see, for example, *ibid.*, pp. 126, 186, and 349). For Carlyle's influence upon Emerson see Frank T. Thompson, "Emerson and Carlyle," *Studies in Philology*, XXIV, 438-453.

sible for much heresy. Moreover, on July 18, 1840, Dr. Channing himself had written to a friend:

> Will you tell me what place Carlyle holds among you, whether he influences opinion? We have some signs among us of a "transcendental" school, as it is called, i.e., we have some noble-minded men, chiefly young, who are dissatisfied with the present, have thrown off all tradition, and talk of deriving all truth from their own souls.[81]

In February, 1840, a reviewer for *Blackwood's* feared that the genius of Carlyle was responsible for having familiarized the minds of the American public "with a phraseology belonging to systems which the more flippant and shallow among them were certain to misunderstand and misuse."[82] Channing's opinion relative to the intellectual relationship of Carlyle and Emerson is of great value, since he himself was thoroughly familiar with the ideas of both men. Already in 1837 he had talked about the author of *Heroes and Hero Worship* with the enthusiastic W. H. Furness, and in the same year had discussed the English writer with Emerson himself.[83]

In the first number of *The Present*, immediately after the introductory article, there appeared Goethe's "Road-Song" ["Mason's Song"], translated by Carlyle:

> The future hides in it
> Good hap and sorrow;
> We press still thorow,
> Naught that abides in it
> Daunting us,—onward.
>
> And solemn before us
> Veiled, the dark portal,
> Goal of all mortal;

---

[81] *Correspondence of W. E. Channing, D.D., and Lucy Aiken*, ed. A. L. Le Breton, Boston, 1874, p. 367.

[82] *Blackwood's Edinburgh Magazine*, XLVII, 179. The writer continued by pointing out "Orlando E. Brownson" as the "Coryphaeus" of the Americans.

[83] O. B. Frothingham, *op. cit.*, p. 142.

> Stars silent rest o'er us,
> Graves under us silent.
>
> But heard are the voices,
> Voices of the sages,
> The worlds and the ages;
> Choose well, your choice is
> Brief and yet endless;
>
> Here eyes do regard you,
> In eternity's stillness;
> Here is all fulness,
> Ye brave, to reward you;
> Work and despair not.[34]

Much more voluminous than the material from England, however, were the effusions of French socialists which helped to fill the pages of *The Present*. A short "Social Confession" was translated from the Paris newspaper *La Démocratie Pacifique*, and a section from a work by Abel Transon was reproduced, in the version of a writer for *The London Phalanx*.[35] Portions of the manifesto of the so-called Humanitarian School, Pierre Leroux's *De l'Humanité*, appeared in translation,[36] as well as extracts from the writings of Victor Considerant, one of the most ardent of Fourier's adherents.[37] Parke Godwin supplied the journal with an exhaustive treatise on "Constructive and Pacific Democracy," which followed closely the "profound and eloquent *Manifeste*" of Considerant.[38]

The scheme for the reorganization of society which Parke Godwin proposed is fairly typical of the various socialistic panaceas with which *The Present* and its fellow journals abounded. The evils of the existing order are pointed out in a neat fashion, and the general nature of the remedy desired is set forth in a good journalistic style, but there is little or no attempt to present in detail the

---

[34] *The Present*, p. 5.
[35] *The Present*, pp. 317 and 361.
[36] *Ibid.*, pp. 65, 105, 203, and 237.
[37] *Ibid.*, pp. 19, 52, and 129.
[38] *Ibid.*, pp. 181 and 338.

means whereby the economic conventions of workaday life are to be superseded by something better. Godwin, at least, realized the situation, and apologized for his abstractions by asserting that his object had been to give "only the most elementary view," and that he could "prove scientifically" that the plan he sketched was "designed by God."[39] Unfortunately, the scientific proof was never forthcoming!

Although the chief foreign influence acting upon the journal was French, a slight interest in German letters was also exhibited.[40] Goethe was represented not only by Carlyle's translation but by a brief "Legend."[41] There were also a "Song of Consolation," marked "from the German," a tale by Ludwig Tieck, and an allegory from Novalis, the last translated by F. S. Stahlknecht.[42]

The poetry that the magazine contained was of an order rather better than that of the average journal of the day. As has been stated, there were verses by J. C. Prince. For the first issue C. P. Cranch supplied two poems,[43] and, subsequently, two of Lowell's were reprinted.[44] Among the first verses of T. W. Higginson to be printed was a poem entitled "La Madonna Di San Sisto," which appeared in *The Present* for December, 1843.[45] The same writer, it may be said here, also furnished a review of Lydia M. Child's *Letters from New York*. Mrs. Fanny Kemble Butler contributed at least one poem, as did also C. A. Dana.[46]

But the chief supply of poetical effusions for the journal came from William Ellery Channing, of Concord.[47]

---

[39] *The Present*, p. 343.
[40] V. L. Parrington, in *The Romantic Revolution in America, 1800-1860*, 1927, p. 379, has rightly mentioned French Utopianism as one of the chief creative influences acting upon the New England renaissance.
[41] *The Present*, p. 205.   [43] *Ibid.*, pp. 10 and 19.
[42] *Ibid.*, pp. 196, 197, and 56.   [44] *Ibid.*, pp. 300 and 425.
[45] *Ibid.*, p. 165. See his *Cheerful Yesterdays*, 1900, pp. 101-102.
[46] *The Present*, pp. 93 and 80.   [47] *Ibid.*, pp. 44, 65, 136, and 266.

Numerous quotations from Emerson's "philosopher," as Longfellow called him, were also printed in a critique of his verse written by the editor. "Your daily thoughts," he wrote, "are better poems than you can write. . . . Why always of Nature, dear cousin; why not sometimes of Humanity, which is greater than Nature?"[48] Very probably the critic appreciated the limitations of his relative's muse. Emerson, too, despite his enthusiasm for his Concord neighbor, seems to have been aware of the poet's shortcomings, for he wrote in the back of his own copy of Channing's volume published at Boston in 1843:

"'Tis a wail in the air, but a wail in the air
The song that thou singest, O child so new—"

In accordance with its multifarious aims outlined in the prospectus, *The Present* sought to display an interest in arts other than literature. An essay on "Crawford's Orpheus" contained some remarks on sculpture, and an article dealing with the violinist Ole Bull provided a bit of musical criticism.[49] The author of the latter was George W. Curtis, the future occupant of *Harper's* "Easy Chair."

Two other contributors who achieved a national reputation as writers were Lydia M. Child and Margaret Fuller. The former lady supplied the journal with a short story entitled "The Remembered Home," a humanitarian essay on "Progress and Hope," and an account of the activities of Dorothea L. Dix, the "missionary of prisons."[50] Margaret Fuller's contribution was her "conversation" entitled "The Two Herberts," "intended chiefly as a setting for the Latin poems of Lord Herbert,"[51] and later reprinted in her *Papers on Literature and Art.*

[48] *Ibid.*, p. 30.
[49] *Ibid.*, pp. 32 and 404.
[50] *The Present*, pp. 11, 230 and 210.
[51] *Ibid.*, p. 301.

As was frequently the case with periodicals like *The Present*, the editor himself wrote a considerable amount of what he published. Channing's articles were all compounded of religion and social philosophy, and were meant to supply an exposition of the necessity for a "Christian Union"; but back of them all the reader can see the shaping influence of Fourier's doctrines of association. As has already been pointed out, Channing's final notice to his readers expressed his obligations to the ideas of the French reformer. At the same time he might very well have mentioned his indebtedness to Swedenborg.

Perhaps the best written of the editor's literary products is a series of three essays entitled "The Call of the Present."[52] The first of these is a treatment of "Social Reorganization," a denunciation of the "error of the modern doctrine of liberty," selfish individualism. The second is headed "Science of Unity," and attempts to show a way out of the chaos of social and intellectual disorder. As an example of American distaste for intelligent reading Channing mentioned the unpopularity of Brownson's "instructive papers on synthetic philosophy," and then continued:

Again, consider that *The Dial*, opening unexplored mines of purest thought, brilliant with wit, rich with beauty, and pervaded by a tone of serene, cheerful, manly piety and wisdom as it is, has only a circulation of a few hundred—while week by week, novels by tens of thousands are sent like hampers and boxes of French wines, to make giddy our boys and girls, all over the land. . . .[53]

The third essay in the series is a metaphysical discussion of the "Oneness of God and Man." In the course of the remarks made about the manifestation of the Creator in the Created these words occur:

The same tendency which . . . led the Rationalist and Eclectic to an oftentimes indiscriminate approval of all phases of human

[52] *Ibid.*, pp. 37, 73, and 145.   [53] *The Present*, p. 76.

opinion, has led the Transcendentalist to a liberal estimate of virtue, which repeats the words of Peter's vision, "Why callest thou any thing that God has made common or unclean." Every instinct of man, says the Transcendentalist, is holy. Evil is only in disproportion. Give full and harmonious development to every power. Accept the life which from the unseen and eternal flows by with its river of joy. Dream not of the past, fear not for the future. Live now with all thy energies.[54]

This optimistic philosophy Channing proclaimed also in his most profound article, "Heaven Upon Earth," in which he carefully considered the problem of evil, and then elaborated an ideal which gave point to the title chosen for his essay.[55] Although he did not attempt to dodge the issue after the fashion of Jonathan Edwards, he contented himself with sketching the various theories of the origin of evil, and then proceeded to a demonstration of the triumphant power of good. In the last analysis, his conclusions appear to have been based upon intuition and upon a sincere belief in the possibility of conscious spiritual evolution. Channing's optimism, however, was not of the fatalistic variety which Charles Eliot Norton found so exasperating in Emerson,[56] but was permeated by a faith in the efficacy of "Christian Socialism." Mankind was to him a host of individuals in need of a gospel—not a collection of self-sufficient entities.

More revelatory of Channing's philosophy than any other of his articles in *The Present* is his "Confession of Faith," which appeared in the first number. According to his own admission, he purposed only to sketch his "present faith," without completeness or "scientific accuracy," and was unconcerned as to the originality or novelty of any of his ideas. His articles of belief are divided into five sections: 1. The Divine Being, Nature, Spirits, 2. The Hu-

[54] *Ibid.*, p. 153 (Dec., 1843).   [55] *Ibid.*, pp. 289 and 411.
[56] *Letters of Charles Eliot Norton*, 1913, I, 504 ff.

man Race, 3. The Jewish Tribes and Jesus Christ, 4. The Kingdom of Heaven, and 5. The United States a Member of Christendom.

In view of his connections with Unitarianism his idea of Jesus is of particular interest. Channing believed:

That in the fullness of time, when the civilizations of East and West had borne their fruits and were falling into decay, when floods of untamed, vigorous tribes were gathering to oversweep and cover with fresh soil the exhausted nations, when universal man stood watching in mournfulness and longing, was born Jesus; conceived in holiness by a devout mother, cradled in her solemn aspirations, nurtured on the prophetic hopes of his nation and age, filled, in his human nature, with the fullness of a super-human life, a son of man transfigured by goodness, and made a Son of God—a divine man.

That he was commissioned and anointed to be the image of the Father, the Adam of a spiritualized and reunited race, the prophecy of redeemed humanity, the desire of all nations, the way, the truth, the life; and that, by his life and death of perfect self-sacrifice, by his words of inspired wisdom, by his purely disinterested deeds, in the joy of oneness with God and man and nature, he had the glory of founding upon the new commandment, love, the kingdom of Heaven on earth.[57]

The longest section of Channing's "Credo" gave consideration to the United States as a "member of Christendom." That he devoted so much space to such a topic in outlining his religious convictions is an indication of the tremendous power exerted by the nationalistic spirit of the day, a power that was to manifest itself most notably in Whitman. Like the author of *Leaves of Grass*, Channing believed that the United States were "manifestly summoned to prove the reality of human brotherhood," and that our "robberies of the Indians, our cruel and wanton oppressions of the Africans," and our national greed had thwarted the accomplishment of "our providential mission to fulfil the law of love."[58]

[57] *The Present*, pp. 7 and 8. [58] *Ibid.*, p. 9.

At the end of his confession of faith he stated that he had "studied in many schools, ancient and modern," and that he had sat at the feet of many teachers, among whom he mentioned "with particular gratitude" Coleridge, Fénelon, Herder, Lessing, Carlyle, Cousin, Leroux, Swedenborg, and Fourier.[59] The presence of Coleridge's name at the head of the list is perhaps significant, as is also the predominance of French writers. It is unfortunate that he did not give the names of "the writers of our own land, more than one," whom he considered "too near to name with praise."

The seven numbers of *The Present* offer more to the student of American thought and letters than the example of another unsuccessful journalistic experiment. The magazine not only throws much light upon the earlier development of Fourierism in this country, but contains in its pages a well written elaboration of many aspects of the general philosophy of the times, particularly as applied to the problems of a centrifugal society. The writers for the periodical were firm believers in perfectionism and the power of mere ideas to work wonders in the realm of facts. Finally, the journal supplies perhaps the most lucid account of the peculiar philosophical, religious, and social beliefs held at the time by William Henry Channing, one of the most active of the transcendentalists.

[59] *Ibid.*, p. 10.

Chapter V
THE HARBINGER

With the adoption of a new constitution on May 1, 1845, the Brook Farm Institute of Agriculture and Education became a Phalanx, fashioned in many ways after the system of Charles Fourier, which Albert Brisbane had modified to meet the needs of America. The consequences of the change were numerous. The community lost its unique character, and became one of a surprisingly large number of experiments conducted in various parts of the country by the Associationists. Persons of very doubtful qualifications sought to become members. Fanatics and freakists with all sorts of grievances against society tried to make West Roxbury their rendezvous. The more or less naïve disregard for regulations and systematic organization that had prevailed during earlier days gave way to an elaborate scheme of Groups and Series, which was intended by Fourier to provide a scientific solution for the manifold problems presented by the necessity of a division of labor at once equitable, efficient—and pleasant. The situation that had existed in earlier days is to be seen in this excerpt from the Brook Farm records for February, 1843:

A special meeting called to consider the importance of more deliberation and accurate examination of facts before acting upon propositions, and after a discussion of internal economic changes, adjourned.

J. Burrill Curtis, Secretary.[1]

[1] MS. records of Brook Farm in the library of the Mass. Hist. Soc. It should be stated that Fourierism had influenced the activities of the community before 1845. In *The Dial* for April, 1844 (IV, 473), Elizabeth Peabody wrote: "We understand that Brook Farm has become a Fourieristic establishment." At that time Ripley and his associates began experimenting with the system, but it was not until the next year that the community was made a Phalanx.

But after the new system went into effect the state of affairs changed. Money was still the chief need of the community, but every possible means was employed to regulate expenditures. Whenever a member needed tobacco or a pair of socks he was referred to the special group in charge of purchases, and a record was kept of the transaction. If bookkeeping alone could have served to insure success, the scheme of the French socialist would have vindicated itself.

The meticulous provision made for every type of labor which the members of the Phalanx were capable of performing included the establishment of groups of carpenters, masons, tailors, shoemakers, waiters, and so on. And since several printers were living in the community,[2] a press was bought so that they should be provided with the means of employing their special qualifications. Because Brook Farm had also among its number a few men who were unusually gifted along literary lines, the Associationists naturally availed themselves of the opportunity presented to transfer their official organ to its care. Accordingly, on June 14, 1845, *The Harbinger,* "devoted to social and political progress," made its appearance as the successor to *The Phalanx,* which Albert Brisbane and Osborne Macdaniel had edited with indifferent success from October 5, 1843, to May 28, 1845. Their efforts had been aided by numerous articles written by Hugh Doherty, an English apostle of Fourierism, and by Parke Godwin. Occasionally, Horace Greeley, Lydia M. Child, W. H. Channing, and others had supplied material. But the difficulties connected with the publication of the paper

[2] Among the signers of the constitution of 1844 were the following printers: Minot Pratt, Jonathan Butterfield, George W. Houghton, and Thomas H. Blake. The day book of the Printers' Group for 1846 indicates that the following were engaged in printing *The Harbinger*: Blake, Butterfield, C. H. Codman, E. Palisse, W. Saxton, T. Treadwell, and, at times, W. Lanton, L. Kleinstrup, and J. Palisse (MS. in the library of the Mass. Hist. Soc.).

were so many that its appearance was very irregular, and the plan to make it a weekly journal was never fulfilled. Two other periodicals may be said to have been the predecessors of *The Harbinger: The Present,* which has already been discussed, and *The Social Reformer*,[3] which was fused with *The Phalanx* when the Brook Farmers projected their paper.

The editor of *The Harbinger* was at first George Ripley, who was assisted chiefly by his associates, C. A. Dana and J. S. Dwight. The prospectus, written by the editor, stated, in part:

> It is proposed to publish a weekly newspaper, for the examination and discussion of the great questions in social science, politics, literature, and the arts, which command the attention of all believers in the progress and elevation of humanity.... *The Harbinger* will be devoted to the cause of a radical, organic social reform as essential to the highest development of man's nature, to the production of those elevated and beautiful forms of character of which he is capable, and to the diffusion of happiness, excellence, and universal harmony upon the earth. The principles of universal unity as taught by Charles Fourier, in their application to society, we believe, are at the foundation of all genuine social progress; and it will ever be our aim to discuss and defend these principles, without any sectarian bigotry, and in the catholic and comprehensive spirit of their great discoverer.[4]

Ripley further asserted that the periodical would not be limited to criticism, but that it would accept "all that in any way indicates the unity of Man with Man, with Nature and with God." The determination to make the paper's broad interest manifest from the outset prompted him further to indicate its purpose in an introductory notice which reaffirmed the intentions expressed in the prospectus. In this an appeal was made to "the aspiring

---

[3] *The Social Reformer* was owned by John Allen, who joined the Brook Farmers in March, 1845 (*Letters from Brook Farm 1844-1847* by Marianne Dwight, ed. Amy L. Reed, Poughkeepsie, 1928, p. 71).

[4] *The Harbinger,* I, 16.

and free-minded youth of the country," and promises were made that there should be no polemics. In politics, the notice added, *The Harbinger* was to be "entirely democratic."

In spite of such a broad purpose, there is no evidence for believing that the paper circulated among many readers other than the friends of social reform. Scattered references and correspondence show that most of its subscribers were living in New York, Massachusetts, and Ohio, where Fourierism was particularly rife. In 1846 *The Harbinger* had "a good list of subscribers" in and around New Orleans, one of whom supplied funds so that the periodical was sent to the senior class of "every college in the United States, with few exceptions."[5]

In the number for July 12, 1845, a notice stated, "We have now a circulation of over one thousand."[6] Later, the desire was expressed to have three thousand subscribers by the beginning of the third volume, but whether that number was the product of an extravagant hope or an attainable ideal, it is impossible to say. However, in the first number of the third volume, that for June 13, 1846, the editor wrote that although the reception of the paper had "far surpassed" his warmest hopes, there had never been sufficient patronage to justify expenses except in an Association, where the economies of combined activity made possible the expenditure of much time and labor.[7] Soon afterward, Ripley announced that the editors had not been paid for their services, and that, unless additional support was forthcoming, the final number of the third volume would be the last to appear.[8] But friends came to the rescue, and the journal managed to continue its work.

---

[5] *The Harbinger*, II, 271 and 300. [6] *Ibid.*, I, 79.
[7] *Ibid.*, III, 12. In a letter of July 28, 1846, Marianne Dwight referred to *The Harbinger* as one of the sources of revenue for Brook Farm (*Letters from Brook Farm*, p. 169).
[8] *Ibid.*, III, 272.

With the transfer of *The Harbinger* from the Brook Farm Phalanx to the American Union of Associationists, in the spring of 1847, the financial situation seems to have been temporarily relieved, for in July of that year it was announced that subscriptions were coming in as well as could be expected.[9] At the same time the statement was made of the paper:

> Like all advocates of truths that are in advance of the public sentiment, it must depend for its existence on the exertions and sacrifices of its friends, rather than upon popular support.

Similar confessions of the failure of the journal to command attention beyond the narrow limits imposed by its reformatory nature were all too frequent. But *The Harbinger* unquestionably made a greater appeal to the average reader after the transfer mentioned above took place, for with the gradual decline of Brook Farm the paper had suffered in direct proportion. When the West Roxbury community was abandoned, and the journal was moved to New York, Parke Godwin became its editor. He was assisted by Dana and Ripley, in New York, and by W. H. Channing and Dwight, who continued to reside in Boston. Very naturally, the change in location and editors served to revive interest.

More effective, however, was the change in the character of the journal which was brought about in November, 1847, when Godwin assumed charge. A new prospectus announced:

> In conducting *The Harbinger* for the future the editors intend to relieve it of the abstract character which, to a certain degree, it has hitherto borne, and to give much larger space to General Topics, to the News of the Day, and to comments on Passing Events.[10]

[9] *The Harbinger*, V, 80.
[10] *The Harbinger*, VI, 16.

At the same time that the paper was made a liberal newssheet, with the wide range of interest demanded by an effort to attract the general public, the size of its sixteen pages was increased so that about one half more of printed matter was contained. However, the neat appearance which the printers at Brook Farm had given the publication was lost.

The transfer to New York also resulted in an increase of the number of advertisements that *The Harbinger* carried. Previously, the Brook Farm school had received space, and, for a time, a New York hotel, which prided itself upon special accommodations for vegetarians. A few numbers also had carried advertisements of books and lectures. But under Godwin's editorship the paper became a more desirable means of advertising.

After the new policy had been in vogue for a short time, *The Harbinger* became so desired as an exchange that only the best of its fellows were chosen as a favored few. The number of subscribers again "surpassed expectations." However, in a letter to Dwight, urging him to come to New York to assume charge of "the artistic department," Godwin expressed his belief that his journal was the best in the country, and went on to say, "I see no reason why we cannot make the paper pay for itself."[11] Accordingly, the "expectations" could not have been very great. The same letter includes this revelatory query: "By the way, what has become of the Boston editor [Channing]? Or does he mean to write only once in six weeks?" But, in spite of the comparatively modest hopes of its editor, *The Harbinger* had increased its subscription list by fifty per cent within a half year after its removal to New York.[12]

As a consequence, one is at a loss to account for the

[11] G. W. Cooke, *John S. Dwight*, 1898, p. 111.
[12] *The Harbinger*, VII, 13.

sudden decision to suspend the publication of the paper after the issue for February 10, 1849. There may have been a decline in the number of contributors during the last months of *The Harbinger's* existence, so that the periodical could not be continued, but a more probable reason is that the men who did most of the writing for the journal could not continue their support when the greater part of their time was occupied by other literary activities. It will be remembered that Dana and Ripley, for example, were working for Horace Greeley's *Tribune*.

In the number immediately preceding the final issue of *The Harbinger*, Godwin announced that the Associationists would transfer their interests to another weekly paper or to a monthly magazine. He himself seemed inclined to believe that a monthly periodical would be decided upon, and, accordingly, outlined the type of material that would be offered in it.[13] However, the meeting of the executive committee of the Associationists called by Greeley to decide the matter seems to have availed little, and no new organ was immediately forthcoming. W. H. Channing, with his customary devotion to the cause, carried on the work in his *Spirit of the Age*, and Dwight assumed charge of three columns of *The Daily Chronotype*, published in Boston, which he undertook to fill, with the assistance of Albert Brisbane and others. These two periodicals may be said to have been the successors of *The Harbinger*.

The contributors to the paper were, for the most part, of two groups: the Brook Farmers and their close friends, and the Fourierists who had little connection with the transcendental movement in the narrower sense. The names of the writers for the first volume, as given in the index, are these:

Albert Brisbane, New York   Otis Clapp, Boston
W. H. Channing, New York   C. P. Cranch, New York

[13] *Ibid.*, VIII, 116.

G. W. Curtis, New York
C. A. Dana, Brook Farm
A. J. H. Duganne, Philadelphia
J. S. Dwight, Brook Farm
G. G. Foster, New York
Parke Godwin, New York
E. P. Grant, Canton, Ohio
Horace Greeley, New York
T. W. Higginson, Cambridge
J. R. Lowell, Cambridge
Osborne Macdaniel, New York
D. S. Oliphant, Batavia, N. Y.
G. Ripley, Brook Farm
L. W. Ryckman, Brook Farm
J. A. Saxton, Deerfield, Mass.
Francis G. Shaw, West Roxbury, Mass.
W. W. Story, Boston
J. G. Whittier, Amesbury, Mass.

The index to the second volume included these names:[14]

Albert Brisbane
W. H. Channing, Brook Farm
Wm. F. Channing, Boston
Walter Channing, Boston
J. F. Clarke, Boston
C. P. Cranch
G. W. Curtis
C. A. Dana
J. S. Dwight
G. G. Foster
Parke Godwin
E. P. Grant
T. W. Higginson
Osborne Macdaniel
John Orvis, Brook Farm
G. Ripley
Francis G. Shaw
W. W. Story.

The third volume contained original contributions from the following:

S. P. Andrews, Boston
Albert Brisbane
W. H. Channing
Wm. Ellery Channing, Concord
C. P. Cranch
G. W. Curtis
C. A. Dana
J. S. Dwight
E. P. Grant
F. H. Hedge, Bangor, Me.
T. W. Higginson
Marx E. Lazarus, Wilmington, N. C.
J. H. Pulte, Cincinnati
G. Ripley
Samuel D. Robbins, Chelsea, Mass.
Francis G. Shaw
W. W. Story.

[14] After the first appearance of a contributor's name, the place of his residence has been supplied only when changed.

The fourth volume included contributions by:

Albert Brisbane
W. H. Channing
G. W. Curtis
C. A. Dana
J. S. Dwight
Parke Godwin
T. W. Higginson

Marx E. Lazarus
J. R. Lowell
Osborne Macdaniel
John Orvis
G. Ripley
Francis G. Shaw
W. W. Story.

The fifth volume was written by:

John Allen, Boston
W. H. Channing
Joseph J. Cooke, Providence
G. W. Curtis
J. S. Dwight
T. W. Higginson,
   Newburyport, Mass.
Marx E. Lazarus

Osborne Macdaniel
N. Neidhart, Philadelphia
John Orvis
Jean M. Palisse, Brook Farm.
E. W. Parkman, Boston
G. Ripley
Miss E. A. Starr,
   Deerfield, Mass.

The sixth volume, which, it will be remembered, appeared in New York under the editorship of Parke Godwin, came from the pens of the following:

George H. Calvert,
   Newport, R. I.
W. H. Channing
Joseph J. Cooke
C. A. Dana
J. S. Dwight, Boston
Parke Godwin
E. Ives, Jr., New York
Henry James, New York
W. H. Kimball,
   Concord, N. H.

Marx E. Lazarus
Osborne Macdaniel
Jean M. Palisse, New York
Mary S. Pease, Philadelphia
G. Ripley, New York
James Sellers, Philadelphia
Francis G. Shaw, New York
James J. G. Wilkinson,
   London.

The seventh volume was written by:

C. A. Dana
J. S. Dwight
Edward Giles, New York
Parke Godwin

Henry James, New York
Marx E. Lazarus
W. H. Muller,
   Zelionople, Pa.

G. Ripley
James Sellers
Eliza A. Starr

Edmund Tweedy, New York
James J. G. Wilkinson.

For the final incomplete volume there is no index. It should be stated here also that several contributors are not listed in the indexes, perhaps because they desired to remain unknown. For example, there are in the fourth volume several poems signed 'X', and 'E. Y. T.' A review of G. H. Calvert's poetry which appeared later, however, mentions the fact that he had employed the initials 'E. Y. T.' in signing his verses.[15] The index to the sixth volume fails to include the name of Poe's friend, Frances Osgood, who contributed a poem entitled "Stanzas for Music."[16] The material reprinted from other periodicals was almost invariably credited to its source.

A glance at the list of writers for *The Harbinger* is sufficient to indicate the genuine literary quality which the paper sought to develop. It is to be observed that at least eleven of the contributors to the periodical had earlier written for *The Dial*: Ripley, Dwight, Dana, Saxton, Hedge, Clarke, Lowell, Cranch, W. H. Channing, William Ellery Channing, and Curtis.

From the outset the problem that confronted Ripley and his associates was that of producing a more or less literary paper which might advance the cause of Fourierism. Of the various activities at Brook Farm *The Harbinger* purposely steered clear. In an early number the editor wrote: "We trust that our brothers of the different Associations in the United States will not regard *The Harbinger* as the exclusive organ of the Brook Farm Phalanx."[17] When a subscriber ventured to ask for an account of the life led by the residents in the West Roxbury community, he was told that the purpose of the periodical was

---
[15] *The Harbinger*, V, 25.
[16] *Ibid.*, VI, 194.
[17] *The Harbinger*, I, 47.

not to present what had already been accomplished, but to make clear the aims and ideals of the Associationists.[18] The only notable exception to this policy was made in the number for March 14, 1846, which contained an account of the burning of the partially completed Phalanstery.[19] But to supply a sauce for the weighty editorials dealing with various aspects of socialism, the translations from Fourier and other French believers in "Unity," and the essays by American advocates of the cause, the guiding spirits of the journal decided to include regularly several poems, book reviews, musical criticism, and, at first, fiction.

Of the Fourieristic propaganda and the translations from the works of French socialists little need be said here, except that the bulk of the material was written by Ripley, Dwight, Shaw, Godwin, and Brisbane. The sincerity with which these men, and their fellows, elaborated Utopian notions about reforming society seems incredible, unless one gives due consideration to the tenor of the age, and to the fact that the underlying idealistic philosophy made a definite appeal. An important London socialist, Hugh Doherty, resolved the essence of Fourier's beliefs into the following:

> Unity of man with God.
> Unity of man with Man.
> Unity of man with the Universe.[20]

The Romantic idealism, the devout belief in the sovereignty of the ineffable One, which was at the heart of Fourierism, came as a confirmation of the inarticulate longings of the mystic, and, at the same time, offered to

---
[18] *Ibid.*, I, 192.
[19] *Ibid.*, II, 221. Ripley, with his customary idealism, found some alleviation for the loss in the fact that the building had not endeared itself by "the tender and hallowed associations of home." Marianne Dwight's impassioned description of the fire is of interest (*Letters from Brook Farm*, p. 145).
[20] Parke Godwin, *A Popular View of the Doctrines of Charles Fourier*, New York, 1844, p. 119. It may be remembered that Ripley had embodied Doherty's analysis in the prospectus of *The Harbinger*.

the more active reformer an apparently simple and logical solution for the problems presented by the perplexing chaos into which a selfish economic system was esteemed to have plunged humanity. When one understands the broad nature of the type of socialism under consideration, it is easy to see its connection with the problems of education, women's rights, capital punishment, slavery, and even vegetarianism,[21] all of which were discussed in *The Harbinger*.

The fiction which appeared in the journal was one of its particular attractions during the earlier days of its existence. Francis G. Shaw, a neighbor of the Brook Farmers, provided copyrighted translations of George Sand's *Consuelo*, and her *Countess of Rudolstadt*, which enlivened the paper, and aided in giving it a reputation for unusual literary merit. At the same time, the translations relieved the Brook Farmers of some of the work, which, after the supply of fiction was exhausted, was so heavy that *The Harbinger* rapidly assumed the "abstract" character that Godwin later commented upon. Then, too, the serials must have been calculated to aid in the acquisition of an increased number of regular subscribers. After the two novels had run their course there was no more fiction in the paper. Instead, a constantly increasing number of cullings from other periodicals and "fillers" appeared. After the transfer to New York a regular department of such material was established under the caption "Weekly Gossip."

[21] A long treatise on vegetarianism, entitled "Cannibalism," written by Marx E. Lazarus, who believed in "the application of Natural History to Psychology," ran through numerous issues. Its conclusion is as follows: "The vegetable eater must be first a poet (in the higher sense, not necessarily a writer), secondly, a lover, thirdly, a religious enthusiast. If he cannot attain those natural, social, and psychical conditions which develop in him one of these three sides of an integral character, he must perforce remain a cannibal, or in the attempt to resign the life of the brute, without gaining that of the true man, will sink into comparative impotence" (*The Harbinger*, V, 132-133).

The padding which Ripley was forced to employ during the time of his editorship is illustrated by the two following excerpts:

The Bavarian Government, by a rescript of the Minister of the Interior, has forbidden the use of steel pens in the public records.

We believe that Evil has no absolute cause in the Nature of Man, who is the Son of God, and whose native faculties and tendencies, in their essential character, are fixed and immutable; on the contrary, we believe that the Cause of Evil resides in the imperfection of Social Institutions, which are essentially variable, and hence, capable of being meliorated, perfected, or totally changed by Human Intelligence and Will.[22]

The first is a fair sample of *The Harbinger* at its worst; the second, of *The Harbinger* in one of its most typical aspects.

The musical criticism that appeared in the paper, written by Dwight, with occasional assistance from G. W. Curtis, Dana, and others, is unquestionably one of the chief merits of the journal, because of the discerning discussion of the chief musical events of Boston and New York that took place during the period. Indeed, it may be claimed with some justice that *The Harbinger* contained the first noteworthy criticism of the ethereal art in the history of American journalism. From the outset the periodical included also an occasional critique of plastic art, such as W. W. Story's essay on "Allston's Belshazzar";[23] and when Godwin became its editor, the "artistic department" devoted several pages to the discussion of Powers's Greek Slave and kindred subjects.

The poetical department of the organ of the Fourierists was apparently one of the most difficult to provide for, since even the first volume contained many verses that were reprints. The following extracts from a letter of

---

[22] *The Harbinger*, V, 46.   [23] *Ibid.*, I, 55.

C. A. Dana, dated July 3, 1845, are illuminating in this connection:

> Friend Whittier:
> I received your letter today, but the book has not reached me.... I am glad that you like *The Harbinger*. The testimony of a person like yourself not pledged to its special doctrines, is an evidence that we are not wrong in the manner of setting forth our views.... Will it be too much to ask of you an occasional contribution to our pages whether of prose or verse? You will see in this week's paper a little piece of yours which, I fear, by the way, the paper from which we copied it, did not print correctly.
> Our poetical department is not an easy one to fill. The *New Spirit* has hardly yet made its way among the gentler Muses, though when the *Poet* has once comprehended the Destiny of Man, such strains will burst from his lips as the world has never yet echoed with.[24]

In response to the above request Whittier sent the verses entitled "To My Friend on the Death of His Sister."[25] Lowell, perhaps because of Dwight's contribution to his own magazine, *The Pioneer*, sent *The Harbinger* two poems, "To a Pine Tree," and "Si Descendero in Infernum, Ades."[26] Thomas Wentworth Higginson, then setting out to win his literary spurs, supplied ten poetical effusions.[27] Dana and Dwight, with their manifold labors, managed to turn out verses for the paper, while Cranch and Curtis lent their aid before they left for Europe, in 1846. Story included several poems among his contributions, and William Ellery Channing sent along

---

[24] *Whittier Correspondence*, ed. John Albree, Salem, 1911, p. 94. The "piece" referred to was "The Moral Warfare," which, however, was correctly printed.

[25] *The Harbinger*, I, 108.

[26] *Ibid.*, I, 122; and IV, 94. See *The Pioneer*, I, 26 and 56.

[27] Since the bibliography appended to Mary T. Higginson's *Thomas Wentworth Higginson*, 1914, mentions only five of the number, a complete list is here given: "Tyrtaeus" (I, 332); "The Railroad" (II, 269); "Holiness Unto the Lord" (III, 28); "Hymn of Humanity" (III, 44); "Hebe" (III, 59); "Cradle Song from Rückert" (III, 59); "Dawn and Day" (IV, 94); "De Profundis Clamavi" (IV, 125); a sonnet beginning "There are great souls among us" (IV, 125); and "Earth Waits for Her Queen" (V, 58).

various products of his muse. Hedge and Robbins wrote one poem each for the journal. As has already been mentioned, George H. Calvert and Frances Osgood also contributed verse.

After Dana and Dwight had exhausted their supply of poetry, and Cranch and Curtis, followed a year later by Story, departed for Europe, *The Harbinger's* verse consisted largely of reprints. Among the favorites chosen were Whittier, Lowell, Longfellow, Bryant, Bayard Taylor, Anne Lynch (Botta), and William Davis Gallagher. One of Jones Very's poems, "How Long," was reprinted from *The Christian Register*.[28] The English poets whose work appeared most frequently were Hood, Mrs. Southey, and Blake. James Freeman Clarke's sole contribution to the paper, a review of an edition of Keats,[29] included a reprint of the "Ode to Apollo," which had appeared first in *The Western Messenger*.

The reviews that the periodical contained were also a means whereby the editors relieved their journal of its abstract character. Until late in the year 1846, when he became city editor of Greeley's *Tribune*, C. A. Dana was the chief literary critic. Indeed, for the earlier numbers he was the most voluminous contributor. The first volume, for example, included sixty separate items from his pen. Even after his entrance upon his new duties in New York, he continued to write for the paper, and when he sailed for Europe, in June, 1848, he contracted to supply *The Harbinger* weekly letters, for each of which he received five dollars.[30]

Dana's reviews appear to be marked by no extraordinary penetration, and at times reflect the contentious spirit which was accepted as a regular feature of the jour-

---

[28] *The Harbinger*, II, 404.   [29] *Ibid.*, II, 234.
[30] J. H. Wilson, *The Life of Charles A. Dana*, 1907, p. 62. Cf. *The Harbinger*, VII, 52.

nalistic practice of the period. The reader receives the impression that he was particularly anxious to combat the views of Emerson and his disciples, but that he was restrained by the policy of the paper.[31] It is a notable fact in this connection that the works written by friends of the New School were soon reviewed by Dwight, or Ripley himself. Of the numerous books that were noticed, none, excepting a few with a socialistic or Swedenborgian interest, commanded Dana's unreserved commendation. William Gilmore Simms was given credit for "talent, but not genius";[32] and Cooper was characterized as rather dull.[33] A striking feature of many of the critiques is the frequency with which Fourierism was injected. A good example is afforded by Dana's review of Melville's *Typee*.[34] He was frank in expressing his interest in the work, and believed it to be the first book to appear that was worthy of being compared with *Two Years Before the Mast*, with its "fresh and natural interest." He admitted being perplexed as to whether Melville's depiction of the life led by the savages was authentic or not; but, assuming that little fiction was involved, he burst forth into an ardent glorification of "associated, coöperative labor" as an effective means of civilizing mankind. At times, however, Dana approximated what may be considered to be the "modern" point of view. For example, he believed that Longfellow's poetry was "like sugar candy—pleasant in small quantities." Of the poet himself he wrote:

> He is undoubtedly the most elegant sentimentalist that the literature of New England has produced, or is likely to produce.... As a thinker and creative artist his rank cannot be marked by any high figure.[35]

---

[31] See, for example, *ibid.*, II, 157 and 268.
[32] *Ibid.*, I, 316.
[33] *The Harbinger*, I, 122.   [34] *Ibid.*, II, 263.
[35] *Ibid.*, II, 173. A more favorable review of *Evangeline*, by Dwight, elicited a letter from the poet (Samuel Longfellow, *Life of Henry Wadsworth Longfellow*, 1899, II, 102).

The reaction of *The Harbinger's* reviewers to Poe is perhaps more interesting. Dana undertook to criticize the 1845 volume of tales, and found little to comment upon except "the power of disease."[36] Dwight gave thoughtful consideration to the *Raven* volume, granted that its author had deservedly acquired "some fame" by his literary powers, but insisted, "Edgar Poe does not write for Humanity."[37] Aroused by the obvious truth of Dwight's assertion, Poe dubbed the Brook Farm paper "the most reputable organ of the Crazyites," and reprinted the whole critique in *The Broadway Journal* for December 13, 1845, adding his customary severe comments.[38]

In the selection of books to be reviewed Ripley and his henchmen at first showed a decided penchant toward the ideas of the New School. The very first critique to appear in *The Harbinger* was an enthusiastic discussion of a translation by Taylor Lewis, *Plato Against the Atheists* (1845).[39] The criticism of works written by the transcendentalists was, with the exception of that by Dana, predominatingly favorable. Dwight early expressed his pleasure at the opportunity presented in the new journal to give his opinions as to the merits of several "books by our friends," among them being Cranch, Lowell, C. T. Brooks, Story, and Lydia M. Child.[40]

Hawthorne's *Mosses from an Old Manse* was heartily recommended to the readers of *The Harbinger* by W. H. Channing.[41] William Ellery Channing's *Conversations in Rome* (1847) was less cordially received by Dwight.[42] The memoir of the great apostle of Unitarianism, the writing of which had occasioned the lapse of *The Present*, was, of course, highly praised. Parke Godwin, who re-

---

[36] *The Harbinger*, I, 73.
[37] *Ibid.*, I, 410-411.
[38] *The Complete Works of Edgar Allan Poe*, ed. J. A. Harrison, n.d. (1902), XIII, 27-32.
[39] *The Harbinger*, I, 7.
[40] *Ibid.*, I, 41.
[41] *Ibid.*, III, 43.
[42] *Ibid.*, V, 69.

viewed the work, dwelt particularly upon the fact that Dr. Channing had been quick to embrace "new views of truth" in regard to social reform. His remarks included these words:

> It is well known that the experiment at Brook Farm, so beautiful while it lasted, was undertaken chiefly by men who had derived their impulses from Dr. Channing's ardent convictions on this head.[43]

A better proof of the high regard in which the Associationists held the famous clergyman is afforded by the fact that the editorial motto of their periodical was taken from his works. It reads as follows:

> Of modern civilization the natural fruits are contempt for others' rights, fraud, oppression, a gambling spirit in trade, reckless adventure, and commercial convulsions, all tending to impoverish the laborer and to render every condition insecure. Relief is to come, and can come only from the new application of Christian principles, of Universal justice and Universal love, to social institutions, to commerce, to business, to active life.

There is one exception, however, to the general high regard in which the writers for *The Harbinger* held Dr. Channing. Henry James, Sr., with his usual cantankerous disposition, wrote for the paper a letter on "Dr. Channing and the Moral Life," in which he took issue with the notion that "disinterested benevolence" was "the Deity" worshiped by the clergyman.[44]

Frequently the periodical gave some of its space to a consideration of the sermons of Theodore Parker,[45] whose

---

[43] *Ibid.*, VII, 23. Emerson also was impressed by Channing's influence upon Brook Farm. See "Historic Notes of Life and Letters in New England," in *Lectures and Biographical Sketches*. W. H. Channing, however, insisted upon giving all the credit to Ripley (O. B. Frothingham, *Memoir of William Henry Channing*, 1886, p. 209).

[44] *The Harbinger*, VII, 29.

[45] See, for example, *ibid.*, II, 157; III, 75 and 361; and IV, 137 and 376. In his notebook for 1844 Parker listed several subjects *"for the Harbinger,"* but if he made any contributions to the paper his name was not signed (MS. in the library of the Mass. Hist. Soc.).

views on social problems made his statements particularly interesting to his many friends among the reformers. George Ripley usually reviewed his discourses.

In regard to a volume of verse which Christopher Cranch published in 1844, Dwight wrote:

> Mr. Cranch's Transcendentalism, or whatever you may choose to call it, has given us some of the most perfect little gems of poetry which have yet been mined in America.[46]

The critic was particularly impressed by the poem "Enosis,"[47] which had earlier appeared in *The Dial* as "Stanzas." The new title, Dwight explained, meant "the making into one." The works of other kindred spirits, such as John Weiss and W. H. Furness, also came in for favorable notice in the paper.[48]

Ripley praised Hedge's *Prose Writers of Germany* (1848), but went on to question the value of German thought:

> We have here the ultimate results of what philosophical speculation and literary culture have been able to accomplish among the best minds of the nineteenth century, and to what does it amount?[49]

A further indication of Ripley's doubt as to the merits of German idealism is given in his review of J. B. Stallo's *General Principles of the Philosophy of Nature: with an outline of some of its recent developments among the Germans* (Boston, 1848). After an assertion that the

---

[46] *The Harbinger*, I, 107. Poe even granted Cranch, "the least intolerable of the school of Boston Transcendentalism," remarkable vigor and "vivacity of fancy" ("Christopher Pearse Cranch," *The Complete Works of Edgar Allan Poe*, XV, 69).

[47] The peculiar type used in Cranch's volume probably accounts for the misreading "Gnosis" (cf. pp. 51 and 53).

[48] See, for example, *The Harbinger*, IV, 202; and V, 173.

[49] *Ibid.*, VI, 150-151. A passage in his commonplace book (MS. in the Widener Library) indicates that while at college Ripley was interested in the idea that German literature offered the best clue to an understanding of the modern world.

work offered "no points of contact with the American mind," he continued:

> The scholar may take pleasure in examining these remarkable processes of thought [those of Schelling, Hegel, etc.], as he would in studying the remains of the later Platonists, or the subtle speculations of the Oriental philosophers. They are wonderful specimens of intellectual gymnastics; they show the exceeding versatility of the constructive power which can give to "airy nothings" the semblance of a substantial system; but, as they do not even profess to be founded on ascertained facts, they can retain no permanent interest for the sincere and unsophisticated lover of reality. The attempt to explain the universe or the human soul by the mere force of thought, without the scientific analysis of facts, is as absurd as the attempt to leap over one's own head. But this is precisely the character of the leading German speculations since the time of the great intellectual analyst, Immanuel Kant.[50]

In view of the fact that Stallo's work was highly praised in *The Massachusetts Quarterly Review*,[51] Ripley's attitude is all the more striking. However, it appears that his speculative philosophy, like that of Brownson, was engendered largely by French idealism. Then, too, Ripley may have lost interest in transcendental metaphysics. That he did so later is proved by his letter to Theodore Parker, dated January 31, 1852, in which he refused the request to publish a translation from Schleiermacher made by himself, on the ground that no one would read the work, and that he had lost all "immediate interest in that line of speculation."[52]

Further material for the study of *The Harbinger's* relations with the New School is supplied in its attitude

---

[50] *The Harbinger*, VI, 110. While at Harvard Ripley may have first been brought in contact with the ideas of A. W. Schlegel, through George Ticknor, who regarded the German highly (*Life, Letters, and Journals of George Ticknor*, 1909, I, 128). In connection with this review, see J. H. Muirhead, "How Hegel Came to America" (*The Philosophical Review*, XXXVII, 226).

[51] *The Massachusetts Quarterly Review*, I, 263. Emerson's library contains a copy of Stallo's work.

[52] MS. in the library of the Mass. Hist. Soc.

toward *The Massachusetts Quarterly Review.* In the number for August 7, 1847, there appeared a preliminary advertisement of the new periodical, and three weeks later Ripley wrote of it as follows:

> We are glad to witness the announcement of the *Massachusetts Quarterly,* to be conducted by Emerson, Parker, Cabot, Howe, and other "disciples of the newness" in Boston and its vicinity. Judging by the names connected with it, it will be more distinguished for its adherence to the universal faith of Humanity than its attachment to canonical dogmas, and will be prepared to give a courteous reception to good and worthy ideas, although not dressed in the drab regimentals in which the scholars on duty in Cambridge and Boston so greatly rejoice. Of its soundness in matters of opinion and taste, according to our prevailing infallible standards, we entertain suspicions by no means slender; but that it will be conducted with great vigor, brilliancy, and literary integrity, we have the utmost confidence. The names of those associated with the senior Editor are a guaranty that the Review will not be characterized by the profound indifference to the great humanity movements of the age which forms such a signal defect in the philosophy, as well as the productions, of that gentleman.[53]

The reference to Emerson is one of the few indications of Ripley's attitude toward the idealist who would not become a reformer.

In several later numbers of *The Harbinger* brief notices of the new quarterly appeared. In one of them Ripley stated his belief that the periodical had fallen below its standard, and expressed a preference for *The North American Review, The Christian Examiner, Brownson's Quarterly Review,* and even *The Dial.* In connection with the last named periodical, he referred to "the naïve subjectivity and Orphic mysticism which gathered a crowd of youthful idolaters around the oracle of the illuminated *Dial.*"[54]

[53] *The Harbinger,* V, 192.   [54] *Ibid.,* VII, 150.

Margaret Fuller's name appeared in *The Harbinger* most notably in two connections. The paper contained a brief reply to an aspersion cast at her when she retired from the literary department of *The New York Tribune*;[55] and Dwight prepared for it a review of her *Papers on Literature and Art*. Her ideas, he thought, gave "a character to criticism," but her unrhythmical style and occasional grandiloquence struck him as better suited to a "converser" than to a writer.[56] Dwight tried to give a faint coloring of praise to his general estimate of her accomplishments, but cannot be said to have succeeded.

The interest in Emerson that the periodical manifested is, of course, significant. When the Brook Farmers were casting about to find contributors for their journal, Dwight wrote to Emerson for help. The reply he received was, in part, as follows:

Your letter was very kind and friendly, and one is always glad that anything is adventured in the midst of so much excusing and impediment; and yet, though I should heartily rejoice to aid in an uncommitted journal—not limited by the name of any man —I will not promise a line to any which has chosen a patron. . . . As far as your journal is sectarian, I shall respect it at a distance. If it should become catholic, I shall be found suing for a place in it.[57]

Apparently, Fourier was the bane of *The Harbinger* in more ways than one.

In a review of a work entitled *Studies in Religion*,[58] Dana referred to Emerson as "the Coryphaeus of the transcendental movement," who was "eminently a one-sided and unbalanced man, vainly endeavoring after equilibrium." Continuing, he wrote:

---

[55] *Ibid.*, III, 176.   [56] *Ibid.*, III, 249-252.
[57] G. W. Cooke, *op. cit.*, pp. 103-104. Emerson's reaction to Fourier's ideas is summed up in this sentence: "Our feeling was that Fourier had skipped no fact but one, namely, Life" ("Historic Notes of Life and Letters in New England").
[58] *The Harbinger*, I, 362.

The dogmatic and oracular mode of speech which fits him so well is insufferable when assumed by the callow youths and maidens, who deal so largely in self-reliance and spirituality, and who make nothing of seeing through and through all the divine and other things, wherewith the universe is indifferently furnished.

Although he admitted that transcendentalism had contributed "not a little" to the "general *elan* towards a broader mental freedom," he insisted that it lacked "real human sympathies" and that it was based upon "extreme individualism." Dana further decried the "calm arrogance" with which Emerson and his disciples spoke of modes of thought other than their own, and characterized their ideas as "the poetic and mystical expression of the Ego-ism which makes modern life so mean." He concluded by promising to resume his remarks on the subject at a later time, but, apparently, no fit opportunity ever presented itself.

For the second volume of the journal, W. W. Story furnished, among other contributions, an article on "Mr. Emerson's Lectures in Boston."[59] After an amusing elaboration of the reason for the popularity of lecturing in New England, which he believed to be due to the Puritan desire to make entertainment a means of instruction, he presented an objective summary of the contents of the series of discourses *(Representative Men)* under discussion. The lectures on Swedenborg and Plato received most consideration, the latter being termed "one of the finest exaggerations" which the critic had ever heard. Emerson's success on the platform, he believed, was an indication of "progress from facts to ideas, from utilitarianism to poetry."

On January 16, 1846, George Bush delivered at the Odeon, in Boston, a speech in reply to Emerson's remarks about Swedenborg, and when the work appeared in print,

---

[59] *The Harbinger*, II, 142.

Dana reviewed it in *The Harbinger*.[60] His critique made it clear that the arguments of Bush were, in his opinion, a very "plain and manly" attempt to meet "the assaults of Mr. Emerson's Pantheistic naturalism." However, he believed that the work was unequal to the task of combating the brilliant rhetoric it was designed to refute, and expressed the hope that another means would be sought whereby "the primary errors of Emerson's speculative thinking would be called into court and convicted." In this connection, it is of interest to note that as early as 1840 Dana believed that transcendentalism was "nothing more nor less than Pantheism."[61]

Two of Emerson's poems, "Forerunners" and "Give All to Love," were reprinted in *The Harbinger* for January 9, 1847. Soon after, Dwight reviewed the volume from which they were taken, along with the second series of poems by W. E. Channing, and a volume of verse by W. W. Story. The critique, which appeared in two unusually long sections occupied itself chiefly with Emerson, whom Dwight considered to be a "true poet," in spite of his frequent lack of a delicate musical sense. The chief fault with his poetry, according to the critic, was that it neglected humanity. As has been pointed out, Dwight made the same criticism of Poe, and in 1838, in an eminently noteworthy review of Tennyson's verse,[62] had charged the Englishman with divorcing his interest from the human. The truest poetry he believed to be "at once mystical and natural . . . transcendental and humane." But Emerson's verse was described as "more mystical than natural," a treatment of life viewed as "the retreating wave." With the gospel of self-reliance, according to Dwight, there should be coupled that of "a general mutual affiance, each to each, of a unity of system and organic

[60] *Ibid.*, II, 268. [61] J. H. Wilson, *op. cit.*, p. 27.
[62] *The Christian Examiner*, XXIII, 305.

solidarity, wherein no man can rely upon himself without the aid of all."[63] It is apparent that, like Ripley, Dwight also regarded Emerson's individualism as an essential weakness in his relations to humanity.

The foreign affairs department of *The Harbinger* also contained material dealing with the Concord lecturer and poet. This department of the paper, it should be said, was of unusual value in the eyes of Godwin, who sponsored it, for two reasons. First, *La Démocratie Pacifique*, a Paris daily journal controlled by the Fourierists,[64] had established connections with the American reformers, and supplied them with first-hand information about the political and economic hubbub with which France was then astir. Then, too, *The Harbinger* had secured as its London correspondent James J. G. Wilkinson, the noted translator and editor of Swedenborg, whom Emerson considered to be "a philosophic critic with a coequal vigor of understanding and imagination comparable only to Lord Bacon's."[65] When the Concord heretic journeyed to Europe late in 1847, Wilkinson met him, and soon afterward recorded his impressions of his new acquaintance in one of his letters to *The Harbinger*, dated April 11, 1848. The following excerpt is of interest:

I have now had many opportunities of seeing your remarkable Emerson. When first I met him, the impression was faint, but ever since then he has been coming out into clearer outline and more unique proportions. At present I reverence him for being no bigger than other men, while yet he is so much more precious. ... You feel that he is so candid, and so respectful, that communion of converse results even where the differences of nature and opinion are remarkable. ... We have had very much talk upon Association, and I tried to hint to friend Emerson, that that

---

[63] *The Harbinger*, IV, 106-108.
[64] For an account of the French periodicals connected with Fourierism, see Morris Friedburg, *L'Influence de Charles Fourier sur le Mouvement Social Contemporain en France*, U. of Paris diss., 1926, cap. I.
[65] "Swedenborg," *Representative Men*.

individuality which he would maintain so inviolate and so high as to make it even doubtful whether there be a Higher, was practically null in the present confusion, where there is no space between man and man, but would come forth with power and great splendor under the new social *régime*. He is quite willing to see whatever there is in this same Association, and I am sure, to help with his own earnest soul. He goes to Paris in a few days and will take a letter to Hugh Doherty.

On Sunday evening last we had a very edifying *reunion* at my house. Emerson, Thomas Cooper, and several others were present; and it was admirable to notice the topic of the evening into which all foreign subjects one by one immersed themselves, namely, the rights of labor, and the Association of man.[66]

Emerson, it seems, could not escape the reformers even when abroad.

The London correspondent also supplied *The Harbinger* with information dealing with the American's six lectures on "The Mind and Manners of the Nineteenth Century." The audience, he wrote, ranged in number from one hundred and fifty to three hundred. Further details he added in these words:

There sits Carlyle, with his weather-beaten, despairing visage, the unitary Priest of the God of Grievance, his lip curled up in perpetual adoration. And there sit all the talents of heterodoxy. . . . And there sits also an exception of aristocracy, a Duke and Duchess of Sutherland, with their daughter. . . .

At length the performer appears, coming forth from the folds of his red curtain. He is quiet, retiring, almost absent, in his bow and first words. He says "Ladies and Gentlemen," to himself, and the audience happens to overhear him. The whole lecture is rather overheard than heard.[67]

After a rhapsodic description of the effect of Emerson's rhetoric, the letter continues:

What is the central spring which requires this pabulum of experience, and puts in cunning action this machine of Series and Analogy? A few principles everlastingly true, and trite beyond

---

[66] *The Harbinger*, VII, 6.   [67] *Ibid.*, VII, 77.

any bare repetition; also many curious particulars of human nature, which it required a singularly conscious observer to fix, remarks which are obviously correct, but above, or beneath, beyond, or within, our previous recognition. Mixed with these there are some great negations, like huge air-bubbles in the field of the microscope, which waste the precious area of vision, and are mistaken by the novice for objects to be explored. . . .

There is a winning innocency about his manifold theological naughtiness. His heresies are *naive* and childlike, and you have a strong feeling that they are not wrong in *him*.

Such was the criticism offered by the man whom Emerson regarded as "the catholic, cosmic intellect" of England.[68] That *The Harbinger* gave space for the lengthy remarks that Wilkinson had to make about his American admirer indicates, possibly, that many of the reformers connected with the paper were still interested in the success of their countryman, who, content with his splendid emotional isolation, denounced them for being "sectarian."[69]

[68] "In England, Landor, De Quincey, Carlyle, three men of original literary genius; but the scholar, the catholic, cosmic intellect, Bacon's own son, the Lord Chief Justice on the Muse's Bench is Wilkinson" (Emerson's *Journals*, VII, 318-319). For Emerson's indebtedness to Wilkinson, see C. P. Hotson, "Emerson's Biographical Sources for 'Swedenborg,'" *Studies in Philology*, XXVI, 23. This article, however, does not discuss the personal relations of the two men.

[69] *The Harbinger* reprinted an extract from "Douglas Jerrold's Newspaper" dealing with Emerson's first appearance in London as a lecturer: "Precisely at four o'clock the lecturer glided in, and suddenly appeared at the reading desk. Tall, thin—his features aquiline, his eyes piercing and fixed; the effect, as he stood quietly before his audience, was at first somewhat startling, and then nobly impressive. Having placed his manuscript on the desk with nervous rapidity, and paused, the lecturer then quickly, and as it were with a flash of action, turned over the first leaf, whispering at the same time "Gentlemen and *ladies*." The initial sentences were next pronounced in a low tone—a few words at a time, hesitatingly, as if then extemporaneously meditated, and not, as they really were, pre-meditated and forewritten. Time was thus given for the audience to meditate them too. Meanwhile the meeting, as it were, was dragged up from under the veil and covering of the expression, and ever and anon a particular phrase was so emphatically italicised as to command attention. There was, however, nothing like acquired elocution—no regular intonation—in fact, none of the usual oratorical artifices—but, for the most part, a shapeless delivery (only varied by certain nervous twitches and angular movements of the hands and arms, curious to see and even smile at), and calling for much co-operation on the part of the auditor to help out its short-comings. Along with this there was an eminent *bonhommie*, earnestness, and sincerity which bespoke sympathy and respect—nay, more, secured veneration" (VII, 77).

Perhaps the most striking interest manifested by the journal of the Fourierists, other than its preoccupation with social problems, was not its connection with the transcendentalists, but its relationship with the Swedenborgians. The watchword of the paper—"All things, at the present day, stand provided and prepared, and await the light"—came from Swedenborg.[70] Of course, the fact that some of the contributors to the journal were members of the New Church had much to do with this particular aspect of *The Harbinger*. In addition to Wilkinson, Otis Clapp, the Swedenborgian publisher of Boston, and Henry James, Sr., are to be named particularly. C. A. Dana also had found in the great mystic a philosophical solace that led him to attend the meetings of the Church of the New Jerusalem when he removed to New York.[71] The members of the Brook Farm Phalanx were acquainted with the ideas of Swedenborg, since the reading of his works appears to have been a frequent diversion for Sunday afternoons;[72] and, in 1845, W. H. Channing proposed using "the Swedenborgian ritual or book of worship" at religious services in the community.[73]

The interest that *The Harbinger* displayed in the enunciator of the doctrine of correspondences is to be ascribed largely to the fact that many of his ideas were found to be akin to those of Charles Fourier. Then, too, the followers of the New School, like Coleridge, found in him a spiritual intensity that appealed to their native leaning toward the mystical. Emerson, of course, supplies the best illustration of this fact.[74]

[70] "Omnia hodie stant provisa, et parata, et expectant diem" (prologue to *Regnum Animale*, 1744, sec. 23).
[71] J. H. Wilson, *op. cit.*, pp. 27 and 451. Dana became interested in Swedenborg about 1840, the period in which he decided that transcendentalism was mere pantheism.
[72] A. E. Russel, *Home Life of the Brook Farm Association*, 1900, p. 93.
[73] *Letters from Brook Farm*, p. 123.
[74] Emerson's library, as it now stands, contains an eight-volume set of Swedenborg's works; Clissold's translation of his *Principia*, London, 1845;

When *The Harbinger*, following the tradition established by *The Phalanx*, devoted considerable space to the beliefs of the New Church and its founder, *The Perfectionist*, a theological paper published in Putney, Vermont, called the Brook Farmers to account for "the deference paid Swedenborg" in their journal. Dwight, in reply, stated:

> Swedenborg we reverence for the greatness and profundity of his thoughts. We study him continually for the light he sheds on so many problems of human destiny, and more especially for the remarkable correspondence, as of inner with outer, which his revelations present with the discoveries of Fourier concerning social organization, or the outward forms of life.[75]

Dana, soon afterward, qualified the paper's espousal of the cause of the Swedenborgians in these words:

> We believe that his [Swedenborg's] mission is of the highest importance to the human family, and shall take every fit occasion to call the attention of the public to it, though never in the spirit of religious or scientific sectaries.[76]

When Wilkinson began to bring out his translations of the posthumous tracts of Swedenborg, *The Harbinger* was enthusiastic in its commendation of them. Occasionally, however, the approval was not wholly unqualified. An interesting case in point is supplied by the reception of the Englishman's introduction to the *Outlines of a Philosophical Argument on the Infinite* (1847), in which the editor of the work had included in an exposition of transcendentalism a charge that the followers of the movement were mainly skeptics. Dwight, in his review, was emphatic in denying the justice of the accusation, but went on to state his full agreement with the opinion that tran-

---

Delights of Wisdom Concerning Conjugial Loves, Boston, 1843; and a presentation copy of Wilkinson's biography of the founder of the New Church.
[75] *The Harbinger*, II, 94.   [76] *Ibid.*, II, 269.

scendentalism was "afraid" of logic—of "mathematics, mechanics, of orders and degrees."[77]

Whether the enthusiasm evinced by the Fourierists toward Swedenborg was intended to win the support of the members of the New Church or not, one cannot say. However, a Swedenborgian publisher used the paper as a means of advertising his products, and, to judge from the letters of subscribers included in the later volumes, the periodical must have been read by certain members of the New Church. The letters to which reference has been made appeared in the paper in increasing numbers from the latter part of 1847 to the final issue. In spite of the friendly spirit that had been so marked in the earlier numbers of the weekly, Henry James, Sr., precipitated a controversy between the liberals and the conservatives among its Swedenborgian readers. His review of a tract, published in *The Harbinger* for November 13, 1847, had been attacked by a writer for *The New Jerusalem Magazine*, the chief organ of the followers of Swedenborg in America. James, who prided himself on his "rational reproduction" of the views held by the founder of his church, objected in stinging language to the "contemptible sectarianism" manifested by his critic.[78]

An issue was immediately raised, and Parke Godwin, at a loss to fill the pages of the journal with better material, announced that he would let the various correspondents involved express their opinions at length. At the same time, another group of readers used the paper as a means of airing their views about the charges made against

[77] *Ibid.*, IV, 327-328 (May 1, 1847).
[78] *Ibid.*, VI, 54 and 61. Although *The Harbinger* had reprinted material from *The New Jerusalem Magazine* and had praised it upon occasion, the organ of the New Church was eminently conservative. It early published articles against transcendentalism (cf. XIV, 137 and 380), and later attacked both *The Harbinger* and *The Massachusetts Quarterly Review* for expressing the belief that the views of the Associationists were supported by the adherents of the doctrines of the New Church (cf. XXI, 298).

Fourier's notions of sexual morality.[79] The result was inevitable, and *The Harbinger*, departing from one of the most worthy principles upon which it had been founded, ended its days in the midst of miserable wrangling.

[79] Emerson's view of the matter is contained in the following: "The Fourier marriage was a calculation how to secure the greatest amount of kissing that the infirmity of human constitution admitted. It was false and prurient, full of absurd French superstitions about women . . ." ("Historic Notes of Life and Letters in New England").

CHAPTER VI

THE SPIRIT OF THE AGE

Although the last number of *The Harbinger* had appeared on February 10, 1849, it was not until five months later that the reformers whose literary activities we have been considering, managed to bring out another journal wholly devoted to their projects. However, upon recalling the wretched end of their former periodical, despite the powerful array of its writers, one is rather surprised that any of the Fourierists had the temerity to try their luck again in the publishing world. But the evils of social conditions were still before their eyes, and the idealism that fostered the hope of their correction was still strong within the breasts of certain ones among the leaders at least. Brisbane and Ripley, for example, never repudiated their former principles as long as they lived.[1] But it was William H. Channing who once more assumed the rôle of editor, in another vain attempt to propagandize the nation in favor of what he considered to be "Christian Socialism."

The Spirit of the Age, his new journal, made its first appearance on July 7, 1849, from the publishing house of Fowler and Wells in New York. A prospectus provided the following information:

This weekly paper seeks as its end the Peaceful Transformation of human societies from isolated to associated interests; from competitive to coöperative industry, from disunity to unity. Amidst Revolution and Reaction it advocates Reorganization. It desires to reconcile conflicting classes and to harmonize man's various tendencies by an orderly arrangement of all relations, in the Family, the Township, the Nation, the World. Thus would it aid to introduce the era of Confederated Communities, which

---

[1] See *Albert Brisbane, A Mental Biography,* with a character study by his wife, Redelia Brisbane, Boston, 1893; and Theodore Stanton, "Some Unpublished Commentaries of George Ripley," *The Nation,* CVI, 736 (June 22, 1918).

in spirit, truth and deed shall be the Kingdom of God and his Righteousness, a Heaven upon Earth.

In promoting this era of peaceful transformation in human societies, *The Spirit of the Age* will aim to reflect the highest light on all sides communicated in relation to Nature, Man, and the Divine Being—illustrating according to its power, the laws of Universal Unity.

By summaries of News, domestic and foreign—reports of Reform Movements—sketches of Scientific discoveries and Mechanical inventions—notices of Books and Works of Art—and extracts from the periodical literature of Continental Europe, Great Britain and the United States—this periodical will endeavor to present a faithful record of human progress.

The Spirit of the Age is edited by William Henry Channing, with the aid of a large number of contributors. It is published every Saturday . . . being neatly printed on a super-royal sheet, folded into sixteen pages, and forming two large Octavo volumes a year. The subscription price is two dollars. . . .[2]

With the debacle of *The Harbinger* definitely in mind, Channing followed up the prospectus by a "Welcome and Warning," in which prospective contributors were cautioned against too arrant partisanship, and a few rules were laid down whereby dangers of controversy among their number might be avoided. Obviously, Channing had profited by his experiences among the reformers. At the same time, the editor announced that the services of several of the writers for the Brook Farm journal had been secured and that his periodical would be marked "by the independence, frankness, and freedom, which gave that paper its distinguished reputation."[3]

At first, the appearance of *The Spirit of the Age* was similar to that of *The Harbinger* in its later days, but gradually it declined into the hopeless mediocrity that characterized *The Univercoelum*,[4] a spiritual weekly

---

[2] *The Spirit of the Age*, I, 8.   [3] *Ibid.*, I, 10.

[4] *The Univercoelum and Spiritual Philosopher* had been edited in New York by William Fishbough. T. H. Chivers supplied several contributions (see, for example, III, 22, and 356).

whose subscription list had been bought up by the publishers of the new paper.

On January 5, 1850, a new volume was started and an introductory notice announced a new watchword, taken from Fourier; namely, "Transition." Among the "special ends" to be forwarded were various "transitional reforms," such as "abolition of the Death Penalty, and degrading punishments, Prison Discipline, Purity, Temperance, Anti-Slavery, Prevention of Pauperism, Justice to Labor, Land Limitation, Homestead Exemption, Protective Unions, Equitable Exchange and Currency, Mutual Insurance, Universal Education, and Peace."[5] However, the periodical never managed to devote much space to a consideration of any one of these important problems, for it went from bad to worse during seventeen more issues, and on April 27, 1850, ceased publication entirely. Channing had no compunctions about explaining the reason. "The paper," he wrote, "is discontinued because, in brief, I am brainsick—and it does not pay."[6]

Since the editor was still occupied with his duties as a clergyman and lecturer while *The Spirit of the Age* was in existence, his frequent absence from New York made it necessary to employ the generous aid of "a well known friend and brother." This was no other than George Ripley, who prepared the material for several departments of the paper: "European Affairs," "News of the Week," and "Town and Country Items."

At first Channing supplied most of the original articles that appeared in the journal, but soon he reduced his output to one lengthy editorial per week, and in the second volume even this was frequently missing. The nature of his lucubrations is to be seen in such a sample as the following:

[5] *The Spirit of the Age*, II, 8. [6] *Ibid.*, II, 264.

Indoctrinate the public thoroughly by *Criticism* of existing society so calmly just as to penetrate the most prejudiced and besotted mind, as sunlight peers through prison grates and daybreak glares upon the noisome chambers of debauch.

Hold up the glorious Oriflamme of God—the white and gold emblazoned banner, with its mighty motto, which symbolizes the Universal Unity of future society.

Attraction—Series—Harmony

Teach the all reconciling doctrine of *Transitions*. Thus! Oh Socialists! shall ye be redeemers of this weary, wicked, tried, tantalized generation; thus shall you be a means under God of subduing the War of Principles by the Principle of Peace.[7]

Of the former contributors to *The Harbinger* who also wrote for Channing's journal, none was more liberal in the use of his pen than Marx E. Lazarus, who supplied articles on various topics of a socialistic interest. The most impressive of the lot is an essay in which he demonstrates that by the application of Fourier's scheme of Groups and Series slavery would be made unprofitable.[8]

Henry James, Sr., supplied an appreciation of Blake's "The Little Vagabond" and a short sketch of Becky Sharp.[9] Moreover, some of his literary products were occasionally reprinted from other periodicals, among them being *The Massachusetts Quarterly Review*.[10] Charles A. Dana sent three essays to *The Spirit of the Age*,[11] and James J. G. Wilkinson furnished an address which he had delivered before the Swedenborg Association of London.[12] John S. Dwight wrote one article for the paper on "Objections to Association,"[13] and Parke Godwin contributed a short discussion of one of Fourier's doctrines,[14] which later prompted Channing to write a lengthy editorial on "Tendencies of Socialism," in which he stated very def-

---

[7] *Ibid.*, I, 121.   [8] *Ibid.*, II, 123.
[9] *Ibid.*, I, 113; and I, 49.
[10] See, for example, *ibid.*, II, 4, 19, 50; and I, 355.
[11] *Ibid.*, I, 97; I, 342 and 358; and I, 278, 324, and 371.
[12] *Ibid.*, I, 1 and 17.   [13] *Ibid.*, II, 88.   [14] *Ibid.*, I, 345.

initely that he differed from both Godwin and Henry James in believing that Fourier had been a pantheist.[15]

During the period in which *The Spirit of the Age* was struggling along, Albert Brisbane was passing into what he called his "second mental cycle,"[16] by which he meant a second adaptation of Fourier's methods to meet the exigencies of American life. Instead of fastening the social structure of his ideal community on the pattern of a Phalanstery, he had now decided that the township supplied the proper basis for reorganization. He first elaborated the usual notions of Utopian bliss in an article with the suggestive title, "A New Heaven and a New Earth,"[17] but did not explain his new project until several weeks had elapsed. Then, in a sketch of "The Mutualist Township,"[18] he tried to be as practical as an architect building a cottage. The township, he wrote, "would have a common oven, to which the farmers could send their bread to be baked. This would save 80 ovens and 80 heatings, a vast deal of useless labor and trouble to 80 housekeepers, and in addition, badly baked bread three times out of five."

J. K. Ingalls, a reformer who had been one of the mainstays among the writers for *The Univercoelum*, followed up Brisbane's article with a stirring account of his own efforts to establish such a "Mutualist Township" in Western Virginia.[19] This discussion is probably the most readable of all the material in the many articles that Ingalls wrote for Channing's paper.

Of the other contributors whom *The Spirit of the Age* acquired along with the subscription list of *The Univercoelum*, none is more interesting as a personality, if not as a writer, than Thomas L. Harris. For a time he was a

---

[15] *Ibid.*, II, 232-236.
[16] Albert Brisbane, *A Mental Biography*, pp. 247 ff.
[17] *The Spirit of the Age*, I, 33.
[18] *Ibid.*, II, 179 and 200.   [19] *Ibid.*, II, 202.

Universalist minister in New York, but later established a "Brotherhood of the New Life," of which the novelist Laurence Oliphant was a member, and finally ended in California as a successful grower of grapes. All the time, it must be understood, he posed as a kind of Messiah, with psychic powers of no mean order.[20] That such a man should have been one of the outstanding writers for the journal[21] indicates only too well the kind of associations that reform activity during the forties involved.

The most significant product of Harris's literary power was probably a very long poem entitled *An Epic of the Starry Heaven*, published at New York, in 1854. An introductory notice provides this explanation:

> The poem ... was spoken by Thomas L. Harris in the course of fourteen consecutive days, the speaker being in a trance state during its delivery. ... The precise time occupied in communicating the whole was twenty-six hours and sixteen minutes. ... During the progress of the work Harris was on several occasions magnetized by spirits, and gave a number of shorter poems, some of which were extremely beautiful in thought and versification.[22]

The introduction further gives the reader to understand that the spirit of Dante supplied the rhapsodist with his material. Perhaps this fact occasioned the interest of James Russell Lowell, who wrote in his own copy of the work some very amusing comments.[23]

---

[20] William Oxley, *Modern Messiahs and Wonder Workers*, London, 1889, pp. 60-78.
[21] See, for example, *The Spirit of the Age*, II, 9, 40, 104, 122, 216, etc.
[22] *An Epic of the Starry Heaven*, vii and xi.
[23] The volume in question, now in the Widener Library, contains such comments as these: "Swedenborg has been whispering in Dante's ear" (p. 38); "Dante has employed his time well. He has read also the New England version of the psalms" (p. 64); and "Dr. Watts may be suspected to have relieved Dante on this page" (p. 39). At the end of the twelfth section of the poem these words occur:

> "Here ends thy day on planet Jupiter;
> So speaks that Orphic sage.
> Ere long another planetary page
> Opens for thee, on, Spirit-traveler."

At the side of this stanza Lowell wrote "Alcott" (p. 152).

Another contributor to Channing's paper with claims to distinction as an oddity equal to those of Harris, was Charles Lane, who had contemplated raising silk worms at Fruitlands with his brother mystic, Amos Bronson Alcott. Lane sent along an essay on "Popular Music," and a couple of letters filled with news of socialistic activities in England.[24] One of these explains the reason for the failure of the educational institution which had been named after Alcott.[25]

Far more entertaining to the lover of oddity, however, is an article on "Human Pantheism," written by William B. Greene, a former Brook Farmer, who had become a Unitarian clergyman. After quoting from Emerson, the author began *in medias res* by asserting:

> There is but one soul, which is the 'Over Soul,' and this one soul is the animating principle of all bodies.... It is I who bark in the dog, grow in the tree, and murmur in the passing brook.... (We speak as Transcendentalist). I create the universe, and thou, also, my brother, createst the same; for we create not two universes but one, for we two have but one soul....[26]

By using more quotations from Emerson and comparing their fundamental idea with that of "Oriental philosophy" and the writings of Jacob Boehme and John Pordage, the author develops a theory of what he calls "Human Pantheism." The selection that has been given will be sufficient to assure a prospective reader that the philosophy contained is no "perpetual feast of nectared sweets."

In accordance with the tradition established by *The Harbinger*, *The Spirit of the Age* devoted considerable space to the works of foreign writers on socialistic topics. Pierre Leroux, Julien Le Rousseau, P. J. Proudhon, Victor Considerant, and J. G. Fichte were liberally represented. An essay by J. S. Mill "On the Probable Futurity

---

[24] *The Spirit of the Age*, I, 310, 321 and 353; I, 348; and II, 13.
[25] *Ibid.*, I, 281.
[26] *Ibid.*, I, 394.

of the Working Classes" was reprinted, as was also a story by Eugène Sue, "The Mysteries of the People."[27]

An attempt was made at times to balance the reform propaganda with material of a more literary interest. For example, several letters of Landor were reprinted from *The London Daily News,* and a sketch of Macaulay was reproduced.[28] Occasionally original verse appeared, including two poems by Phoebe Cary;[29] but most of the versifiers were from the ranks of the reformers, whose fervor was intense, but whose virtuosity approached the nadir as a limit. James Friswell's rendering of a stanza from "The Holy League of Nations" by Béranger will illustrate:

> Yes! free at last the world respires;
> Oh, throw oblivion o'er the past,
> And till your fields to tuneful lyres—
> The incense Art should offer Peace;
> And laughing Hope in Plenty's breast
> Again shall call the marriage feast
>   For jovial bands!
> Up, Nations, up! and form a League,
>   Give each your hands.[30]

Once in a while something better was reprinted from Whittier, Lowell, Tennyson, and even William Ellery Channing.

After Ripley's selected items ceased to appear, several new departments were started under the captions, "Literature and Art," "Reform Movements," and "Miscellany." Under the first heading a book review was printed now and then. The volumes chosen for criticism were for

---

[27] *Ibid.,* I, 85; and II, 81 and 145. For Brisbane's connections with Eugène Sue, see *Albert Brisbane, A Mental Biography,* p. 233. In December, 1844, Brisbane spoke very enthusiastically of Sue to the Brook Farmers (*Letters from Brook Farm, 1844-1847,* by Marianne Dwight, ed. Amy L. Reed, Poughkeepsie, 1928, p. 55).

[28] *The Spirit of the Age,* I, 134; and I, 166.

[29] *Ibid.,* I, 241 ("The Bride"); and II, 257 ("Labor").

[30] *Ibid.,* II, 240.

the most part of a socialistic nature, but occasionally better material was selected for comment. For example, there were an enthusiastic discussion of Shelley's verse and a very favorable notice of Sylvester Judd's *Philo*.[81] A proof of the catholicity of literary interest that *The Spirit of the Age* boasted is afforded by the selections from the *Desatir* and the *Bhagavad-Gita* that appeared during the earlier days of the paper's existence.[82]

Less exotic but equally indicative of a more or less unusual taste on the part of the writers for the journal, were several "psychometric observations" of Fourier, Priestley, Washington Allston, and Hiram Powers.[83] Character readings were, of course, a very popular amusement during the period, and several of the Brook Farmers appear to have had an ardent interest in the pastime.[84] A portion of a reading of Fourier's character, done by Anna Parsons, a friend of the members of the West Roxbury community, follows:

I don't believe this was a very gay person, though he gives me this inclination to laugh. Is there not a deep sadness in the character? He seems one who *sported* with misery.... He has a great power—power of putting aside what torments and troubles him and of being at ease for the time. Great activity of intellect. One who hates oppression. I am not certain that he would not be likely to oppress.[85]

Miss Parsons's method of analyzing a character, it seems, was to hold in her hand a letter written by the subject, or to put it against her forehead. After a brief pause for psychic activity to begin, she would start to speak, while an attendant jotted down her utterances.[86] Strange to say,

---
[81] *Ibid.*, II, 15; and II, 76. [82] *Ibid.*, I, 21, 36, 52, 67, 116, etc.
[83] *Ibid.*, I, 258 and 275; II, 139; II, 155; and II, 250.
[84] *Letters from Brook Farm*, pp. 13, 29, 35, and 38.
[85] *The Spirit of the Age*, I, 258. A variant of this reading is printed as an appendix to *Letters from Brook Farm*, pp. 181 ff.
[86] *Ibid.*, p. xiv. For Fredrika Bremer's experiences with Miss Parsons see *America of the Fifties: Letters of Fredrika Bremer*, New York, 1924, p. 318.

the particular reading from which a passage has just been quoted "satisfied and gratified" both Brisbane and Channing very much.[87]

Perhaps the most enthusiastic article to appear in *The Spirit of the Age* was an account of a Fourieristic festival held in Boston. *The Phalanx* and *The Harbinger* had occasionally described a celebration in honor of the French enunciator of Unity, but not one of them surpassed in fervor the assembly of the Boston Union of Associationists held in Cochituate Hall during the month of June, 1850.

The hall was beautifully decorated with a significantly connected series of banners, emblems, busts, and groups of statuary, flowers, and tables laden with refreshments.

At the upper end of the room was a dais in the middle surmounted by a canopy, from which was displayed as the presiding thought the circular white banner of "Universal Unity." This gave a keynote to the whole. . . .

Civilized Labor was typified on one side by the group of the Laocoön struggling in the serpents' coil; redeemed, coöperative, harmonious Labor, on the other, by the Apollo Belvidere, intimating that all labor shall become Fine Art.

A choir, under the direction of J. S. Dwight, opened the evening's exercises by singing a "Gloria" from one of Mozart's Masses. A trio from *Belisario,* a chorus from *Elijah,* and selections from Beethoven formed a background for the electric utterances of the speakers. Among the toasts were such as these:

To Woman! "The Earth waits for its Queen." The first home worthy of her sovereignty will be the Phalanstery; and that will offer the first perfect guarantee of purity and sanctity in Love and Marriage.

To Joy! To Liberty! To Childhood's mirth! To Youth's enthusiasm! To the warm Life-thrill of Attraction! Let rhythmic

---
[87] *Letters from Brook Farm,* p. 108.

feasts, and songs, and dances keep alive the prophecy of the Harmonic Times![38]

Despite the fiasco at Brook Farm, despite the charges of immorality and folly made against the doctrines of Fourier, at least the hundred and sixty people who took part in the celebration were convinced that Associationism was not a failure. Although the transcendentalists among their number sponsored no more organs of propaganda after *The Spirit of the Age* ceased publication, that fact is probably due to the growing interest in abolition, which gradually absorbed the activity of the reformers in America, and not to indifference or a conviction that social evils could not be rectified.

[38] *The Spirit of the Age*, II, 268-269. As late as January 31, 1857, Wm. F. Channing wrote to Parke Godwin that a few people in Boston were holding to the faith of 'Universality' "with larger acceptance than ever" (MS. in the Bryant-Godwin Collection of the New York Public Library).

Chapter VII
ELIZABETH PEABODY AND HER *ÆSTHETIC PAPERS*

Whatever the attitude of the transcendentalists as intimates of a domestic circle, *sub specie æternitatis*, so to speak, they were ardent believers in the rights of women. In this respect, perhaps, they were merely in harmony with the general trend of enlightened opinion during the nineteenth century. Indeed, so far as literature was concerned, even the unenlightened could not fail to appreciate the conquests made by the "damned mob of scribbling women," as Hawthorne dubbed them, or the "female poets" whose names appear in the collections of Griswold and others. When Poe delivered himself of such a eulogy as his essay on Mrs. Osgood, he may have shown himself to be, like any good journalist, a reflector of public taste, rather than a wholly misguided lover of female charms. Be that as it may, although many a young lady among the literary aspirants of the forties might have confessed with pride that she was a transcendentalist, the inner circle of the New School was blessed with an intimate association with only two Blue Stockings: Margaret Fuller and Elizabeth Peabody.

A romantic death and the services of friendly biographers have combined to make the first of these ladies a person of great importance to an age which finds a delight in "historical personalities who never existed." One who does not read Margaret Fuller's literary effusions might easily be led to believe that she was a critic of unusual discernment, simply because of the tradition which has been built up around her memory. Elizabeth Peabody has not been so kindly dealt with by posterity. Hers was the placid domestic life of a New England nun. Yet in her long career she managed to identify herself with most of the activities—philosophical, social, or religious—that the transcendentalists engaged in. In her later days she was familiarly spoken of as "the Grandmother of Boston." Emerson, who had taught her Greek, observed that her journals and correspondence would probably be "a complete literary and philosophical history of New England during her long life."[1]

Theodore Parker's journal contains a passage which contrasts the two women. In 1839, after receiving a call from Margaret Fuller, he wrote:

> She has outgrown Carlyle; thinks him inferior to Coleridge. I doubt this much. She says Coleridge will live and Carlyle be forgot. I am glad she has outgrown him,—I wish the world had. Miss Fuller is a critic, not a creator,—not a *vates*, I fear. Certainly she is a prodigious woman, though she puts herself upon her genius a little too much. She is not a good analyst, not a philosopher.

Several days later he was visited by Miss Peabody, and recorded his impressions as follows:

> She is a woman of most astonishing powers; has a manysidedness and a largeness of soul quite unusual; rare qualities of head and heart. I never before knew just with what class to place her; now I see she is a Boswell. Her office is to inquire and answer, "What did they say?" "What are the facts?" A good analyst of character, a free spirit, kind, generous, noble. She has an artistic gift also.[2]

As the sister-in-law of Hawthorne and of Horace Mann, Elizabeth Peabody was naturally thrown in contact with the leading figures in the New England renaissance. With the transcendentalists her connections were

---

[1] M. D. Conway, *Life of Nathaniel Hawthorne*, London, 1890, p. 10. Elizabeth Peabody lived from 1804 to 1894.
[2] F. B. Sanborn, *Recollections of Seventy Years*, Boston, 1909, II, 548. For Carlyle's reaction to Margaret Fuller, see *Carlyle-Emerson Correspondence*, ed. C. E. Norton, Boston, 1883, II, 125.

the closest of any woman.[3] In 1825 she lived in the home of the Apostle of Unitarianism, acting as his amanuensis, and recording many of his conversations, which she later included in a volume entitled *Reminiscences of Reverend William Ellery Channing, D.D.*, published in 1880. In 1826, the "first year of her intellectual life," according to her own statement, she became a transcendentalist. As she wrote to Brownson, she had never seen the word "transcendentalism" before that time except in Coleridge's *Friend*, through the perusal of which, "relying simply on her own poetical apprehension as a principle of exegesis," she became one of the New School.[4] She corresponded with all of the important exponents of the New Spirit, attended their club meetings,[5] and proved herself worthy of their friendship by a wholehearted devotion to their interests. She was Alcott's mainstay in his chief educational enterprise, and by writing *The Record of a School* (1835) and *Conversations with Children on the Gospels* (1836-1837) she gave to the world perhaps the most adequate expression of the rare genius of the mystic-pedagogue.

Alcott in turn honored her with one of his bleak poems:

> Daughter of Memory! who her watch doth keep
> O'er dark Oblivion's land of shade and dream,
> Peers down into the realm of ancient Sleep,
> Where Thought uprises with a sudden gleam
> And lights the devious path 'twixt *Be* and *Seem*;
> Mythologist! that dost thy legend steep
> Plenteously with opiate and anodyne,
> Inweaving fact with fable, line with line,
> Entangling anecdote and episode,

---

[3] A good sketch of her life may be found in G. W. Cooke's *Historical and Biographical Introduction to Accompany the Dial*, Rowfant Club Reprint, 1902, I, cap. IX.

[4] H. F. Brownson, *Orestes A. Brownson's Early Life*, Detroit, 1898, p. 227.

[5] See, for example, Emerson's *Journals*, IV, 292 (1837).

> Mindful of all that all men meant or said,—
> We follow, pleased, thy labyrinthine road,
> By Ariadne's skein and lesson led:
> For thou hast wrought so excellently well,
> Thou drop'st more casual truth than sages tell.[6]

As early as 1833 she offered a series of "conversations" to the public,[7] preceding Margaret Fuller by a half dozen years. In 1839 she opened a bookstore at 13 West Street in Boston, where the transcendentalists, and later the Brook Farmers, occasionally met. During the next year she started a "Foreign Library," with fifty subscribers, a number soon increased as her shop became the center of interest in foreign literature in Boston.[8] Thomas Wentworth Higginson, for example, came to her library to further his acquaintance with the writings of Cousin and Constant.[9] Her experiences with the bookstore soon led her into the publishing business, and she brought out numerous volumes, including several by Channing, Hawthorne, and herself.

The public at large, however, was never interested in her various activities until she became known as an educator. She was the founder of one of the first kindergartens in America, and, in later years, was recognized as the chief disciple of Froebel, whose system she elaborated in several tracts. Even the Concord School of Philosophy found a place for her opinions on "Childhood" during its sessions for 1882.[10] But in spite of all her practical pursuits Elizabeth Peabody managed to produce an occasional article of

---

[6] A. B. Alcott, *Sonnets and Canzonets*, Boston, 1882, p. 103.

[7] Other series of "conversations" were given by her in 1836, 1844 and 1845 (Henry Barnard's *American Journal of Education*, Hartford, XXX, 584 ff.).

[8] See a broadside, "New Bookstore and Foreign Library," August 1, 1840, in the library of the Mass. Hist. Soc. French magazines and books seem to have attracted more attention in this notice than their German counterparts.

[9] T. W. Higginson, *Cheerful Yesterdays*, Boston and New York, 1900, pp. 86-87.

[10] See the abstract of her lecture in *Concord Lectures on Philosophy*, ed. R. L. Bridgman, Cambridge, n.d. (1886).

merit, and to invite her soul into the realms of art and philosophy. Alcott's sonnet could not have been wholly subjective.

As may be remembered from previous chapters of the present volume, she was the distributor of *The Western Messenger* in New England, and wrote for *The Boston Quarterly Review* and, more notably, perhaps, *The Dial*, which she published for a time. To the later periodicals of transcendentalism she also contributed. But her chief importance in the history of the journalistic adventures of the New School is due to her attempt to establish a magazine for the literary epicures of New England. Only one number of the *Æsthetic Papers*, as the work was called, appeared—in May, 1849.

A prospectus,[11] with the customary idealism, announced that the editor desired to assemble, "upon the high æsthetic ground," removed from the regions of strife, the products of writers of different schools in order that the antagonistic views of philosophy and social culture prevailing in the fields of religion, science, and literature might be harmonized. "The white radiance of love and wisdom" was to be evolved from the union of "many-colored rays." "Good matter" was to be the prime requisite for the material published. More practical considerations were presented, rather ingenuously, in the following:

The plan of publication for this Work is like that of *The British and Foreign Review*, which has been the model of its form, size, and type; namely, that a number should appear whenever a sufficient quantity of valuable matter shall have accumulated to fill 256 pages. This will in no case happen more than three times a year; perhaps not oftener than once a year.

The terms of patronage proposed are peculiar to itself. No person is asked to subscribe for more than one number in advance;

[11] *Æsthetic Papers*, pp. iii and iv.

but whoever is so far pleased with the current number as to desire another is requested to send an order to that effect to the Editor, who is also Publisher, No. 13, West-street, Boston. When a sufficient number of orders are given to pay for the publication, including compensation to the authors, a new number will be printed; the Editor being content to receive such profit as may accrue from the sale of other numbers not subscribed for beforehand. The Publisher's subscribers will have the numbers at $1, payable on delivery. The price at the bookstores will be $1.25.

A letter from the editor's mother to Hawthorne's wife, written soon after the appearance of the Æsthetic Papers, mentions the fact that "one gentleman" had subscribed for three numbers of the next volume, and that Elizabeth Peabody would clear $400, should the entire edition be sold.[12] But in spite of the praise bestowed upon the work by various local papers,[13] only fifty subscribers were secured,[14] and most of the issue met the same fate as Thoreau's *Week*, which also undertook to supply the New England of 1849 with literature of artistic merit beyond that of journalistic accounts of the riots at the Opera House in New York or the woefully written epistles of immigrants to California.

In an introductory essay on "The Word Æsthetic"[15] the editor explained her idea of the philosophy of art. The "æsthetic element" she believed to be "a component and indivisible part in all human creations which are not mere works of necessity, in other words, which are based on idea, as distinguished from appetite." Since the German mind first approximated the "unpersonal principle that underlies the æsthetic view," Germany was hailed by her as the "discoverer of the æsthetic." All art, she believed, was, in its origin, national and religious. Feeling was of far greater importance than the vehicle whereby it

---
[12] Julian Hawthorne, *Nathaniel Hawthorne and His Wife*, Boston, 1885, I, 332.
[13] For example, the Boston *Daily Evening Traveller* for May 22, 1849; and *The Salem Gazette* for May 18, 1849.
[14] G. W. Cooke, *op. cit.*, I, 193.   [15] *Æsthetic Papers*, pp. 1-4.

is conveyed. In the first stage of art "the æsthetic element prevailed unconsciously," since neither taste nor artistic philosophy has any conscious place in an uncritical age. After numerous assertions of the nature of the examples already given, she expressed her purpose of using the word "æsthetic" as a kind of shibboleth, to designate "that phase in human progress which subordinates the individual to the general, that he may reappear on a higher plane of individuality."

Needless to say, this introductory disquisition was unlikely to attract popular interest for the periodical, and its decidedly heavy nature indicates clearly that a very unusual type of reader was expected from the outset. Upon comparing the sturdy qualities of the *Æsthetic Papers* with such a collection of drivel as *The Boston Miscellanies*, which held public attention during 1849, one is amazed at the extreme temerity which led Elizabeth Peabody to tempt fate.

The first article in the *Papers* was somewhat similar in nature to the introductory essay—a discussion of "Criticism" by Samuel G. Ward, the friend of Longfellow and Emerson, whose connections with *The Massachusetts Quarterly Review* will be discussed in the following chapter. He denounced the critics who vaunted American productions merely because they were American, and proceeded to descant upon the inventive spirit of the Greeks. He, too, believed that the Germans first manifested a "pure tendency towards criticism," and insisted upon the presence of a national element in all artistic productions. The essence of criticism, according to Ward, was merely

> To see what has taken place in the world under a new point of view; to find a point from which facts *arrange themselves* in a new and unexpected manner, so that circumstances, before isolated, are seen as part of a new whole.[16]

[16] *Ibid.*, pp. 12-13.

As a consequence, he argued, there is such a thing as creative criticism.

An aid to the transcendentalist confronted by the facts of science was suggested in the article. There are two distinct appearances of truth, its author asserted: "truths of exact science, and truths of faith." Accordingly, a different form of criticism must be distinguished for each.

A faith is the sum of the convictions of a man, or a nation, in regard to spiritual things; its form is based on the teachings of the past; and its criticism rests on inward, individual experience. When it criticizes facts, it is from an internal point of view, and because they disagree with inward experience; no fact becomes monstrous whilst it is the sign of an inward conviction.... Exact science ... rests on a correct observation of phenomena; its safety lies in admitting nothing which is not capable of demonstration or proof. It is based upon doubt.[17]

One may question whether Alcott would have agreed without a reservation. However, as future developments proved, such a comfortable dichotomy as Ward proposed would have saved many of the later members of the New School from the numerous perplexities in which they were involved when the criticism of science began to dissect the philosophy of intuition.

The second article was elevated to an equally lofty plane. It was entitled "Music," and was written by John Sullivan Dwight. As might have been expected of a man who had shown himself such an ardent member of the Brook Farm community, he could not avoid injecting Fourier's principle of "Unity" into his discussion of the art of Beethoven.[18] If any literary product can be said to apply the faith of transcendentalism to music, this essay certainly does. Moreover, its undeniable merit as a literary performance makes it one of the more significant

[17] *Ibid.*, p. 19.
[18] *Ibid.*, pp. 30-31. Ward also had mentioned a doctrine of Fourier in his article (*ibid.*, p. 18).

contributions of the man who is remembered as the first important musical critic in the United States.

Following the contribution of Dwight there appeared Emerson's lecture on "War,"[19] which had been obtained for the work "at much solicitation," since its author had not looked at it since the time of its first delivery, in March, 1838. The text is the same as that to be found in the eleventh volume of the Centenary Edition of Emerson's works.

The next contribution to the periodical was an extract from an unpublished course of lectures by Parke Godwin, bearing the title, "Organization."[20] This sociological treatise provided a kind of pseudo-philosophy upon which the superstructure of Fourierism might have been reared. Beneath most of its generalities one may see the idea of "Universal Unity," so familiar to the readers of *The Harbinger* or *The Spirit of the Age*. However, there is no direct advocacy of the scheme of the French reformer, and the whole lies in the realm of the ideal—a fact which no doubt accounts for its presence in the *Papers*.

Immediately after Godwin's article there was printed a lecture on "Genius"[21] by Sampson Reed, the Swedenborgian whose influence upon Emerson has been pointed out with no little emphasis. Indeed, Mr. G. Sutcliffe has asserted that until Emerson perused Reed's *Observations on the Growth of the Mind*, "nature had been for him suspected and pagan."[22] Dr. C. P. Hotson has declared that it was Reed who "gave the first definite impulse which led to Emerson's literary career."[23] The lecture on "Genius" had been delivered by its author as an oration at

[19] *Ibid.*, pp. 36-50.
[20] *Ibid.*, pp. 50-58.   [21] *Ibid.*, pp. 58-64.
[22] *Emerson's Theories of Literary Expression*, U. of Ill. diss., 1918, p. 129. For Brownson's reaction to Reed's book, see *The Boston Quarterly Review*, I, 385.
[23] "Sampson Reed, A Teacher of Emerson," *The New England Quarterly*, II, 249.

the commencement of 1821, when Harvard admitted him to the degree of Master of Arts.[24] It was probably at college that Reed made an impression upon Emerson, which remained for a surprisingly long time, since he frequently quoted from the works of Swedenborgian. For example, it has been asserted that six of the entries in Emerson's journals, "by quotation or direct reference," are based upon the oration on "Genius."[25] One might suppose that Emerson was responsible for its appearance in the *Æsthetic Papers*, if the general interest manifested by most of the transcendentalists in the doctrines of the New Church were not to be considered. Miss Peabody herself was keenly excited by Swedenborgianism, and one of the passages in Emerson's journal for 1835 consists of remarks about the great mystic which had first been written to her.[26]

An excerpt from the lecture will suffice to show why its utterance in 1821 must have seemed remarkable to the people who were shortly to be called the New School:

Science will be full of life, as nature is full of God. She will wring from her locks the dew which was gathered in the wilderness. By science, I mean natural science. The science of the human mind must change with its subject. Locke's mind will not always be the standard of metaphysics. Had we a description of it in its present state, it would make a very different book from "Locke on the Human Understanding."[27]

The next article to appear in the *Æsthetic Papers* was a lengthy essay on "The Dorian Measure, with a Modern Application," written by the editor herself.[28] This was an

---

[24] *The New Jerusalem Magazine*, New Series, IV (1880), 286.
[25] C. P. Hotson, *op. cit.*, p. 276. [26] *Emerson's Journals*, III, 530.
[27] *Æsthetic Papers*, pp. 63-64. Paulding expressed the usual attitude toward Locke during the early decades of the nineteenth century when he asserted that his chief work was "the only analysis of the human understanding which the human understanding was ever able to comprehend" (*Westward Ho!* 1832, cap. VI).
[28] *Æsthetic Papers*, pp. 64-110. In an unpublished letter to Parke Godwin, April 20, 1854, Miss Peabody referred to this essay as if it were her chief literary composition (Bryant-Godwin Collection in the New York Public Library).

elaborate exposition of Doric cultural and social ideas, based largely upon a reading of various works by K. O. Müller, a contemporary classicist. The application of these Hellenic principles to a modern system of education concluded the work. Miss Peabody, like Alcott,[29] insisted that gymnastics, music, drawing, and dancing should constitute a part of every educational curriculum. Her diffuseness of style, however, probably hindered an appreciation of her point of view, so novel as it must have been to the dusty formality of the pedagogues of her day.

Immediately following in the volume were two poems: "Crawford's Orpheus," and "A Spirit's Reply." The former, also written by Miss Peabody, is the closest approach to a discussion of plastic art to be found in the *Æsthetic Papers*.

Next came an explanation of the Swedenborgian doctrine of "Correspondences," by James J. G. Wilkinson, who, it may be remembered, had written foreign news for *The Harbinger*. His discussion is not marked by a particularly lucid explanation of the necessity for a belief in the doctrine which he was elaborating; and parts of it seem to be nothing more than an indication of the sad results of riding the horse of symbolism too far. One may well object to such nonsense as the following despite the dire seriousness with which it was written:

> Then the abdomen is the natural kitchen of the soul, raising to sublimity the processes of the gastrosophic art; preparing from all things in its indefinite stores one universal dish, lower than cookery, higher than philosophy, even the natural blood of life, to be served up day by day in repasts for the spiritual man: the viand of viands, solid and fluid all in one....[30]

A striking contrast to Wilkinson's effusion is presented by the contribution that followed it, written by the greatest

---

[29] She disagreed with Alcott on certain matters, however (cf. F. B. Sanborn, *op. cit.*, II, 559).   [30] *Æsthetic Papers*, p. 125.

master of symbolism in the history of American literature. In view of the close relationship that existed between Elizabeth Peabody and Hawthorne, it was only natural that one of his works should grace the pages of the *Æsthetic Papers*. In December, 1848, Hawthorne sent a story for the new periodical, apparently "Ethan Brand." But, if we are to trust his son's conjecture, the tale was "too lurid for Miss Peabody's aestheticism,"[31] and "Main Street" was substituted.[32] This exploitation of the history of Essex Street in Salem was without question the most highly praised contribution to appear in the volume.

Second to Hawthorne's sketch in its appeal to the reviewers of the *Æsthetic Papers* was an article on "Abuse of Representative Government,"[33] by S. H. Perkins, a Boston merchant who was a promoter of a variety of reforms, ranging from the amelioration of the condition of the poor to the pensioning of disabled soldiers. He had been sent to Germany to be educated under the guidance of Edward Everett, a fact which alone would have made him welcome to the transcendentalists.[34]

After *The Dial* had ceased to mark the spiritual hours of New England, Thoreau carefully avoided publication in any periodicals of a kindred sort. It has been pointed out that Parker and Lowell cherished a decidedly poor opinion of his literary ability, and their judgment may also have been responsible for the absence of material from his pen in the journals of the New School. However, not even the perversely disposed naturalist could refuse Elizabeth Peabody a favor,[35] and, as a consequence, her *Papers* included his lecture on "Resistance to Civil Government,"[36] which he had delivered in 1847. This is the

---

[31] Julian Hawthorne, *op. cit.*, I, 330. [33] *Ibid.*, pp. 174-188.
[32] *Æsthetic Papers*, pp. 145-174. [34] T. W. Higginson, *op. cit.*, p. 79.
[35] See her letter to Thoreau, dated Feb. 26, 1843 (F. B. Sanborn, *op. cit.*, II, 560).
[36] *Æsthetic Papers*, pp. 189-211.

work, later given the title "Civil Disobedience," which contains its author's account of his imprisonment in the Concord jail.

Two poems followed the contribution of the "born dissenter": "Hymn of a Spirit Shrouded," by Ellen Sturgis Hooper, one of the minor writers for *The Dial*, and "Meditations of a Widow."[37] Miss Peabody placed next her own remarks on "Language,"[38] which were prompted by a treatise of Horace Bushnell, who had shortly before received the full blast of 'orthodox' criticism on account of his views concerning the Trinity.

The last essay in the volume dealt with the "Vegetation about Salem, Massachusetts,"[39] and was written by an English resident of that village. It is important only in that it was one of the earlier efforts to interest the public in reforestation. At the very end of the *Æsthetic Papers* were two poems: "The Twofold Being," by Higginson, and "The Favorite," by his sister Louisa.[40] These verses, like the others in the work, scarcely emerged above the level of journalistic mediocrity.

Although Elizabeth Peabody had intimated in the prospectus of the *Æsthetic Papers* that she desired to bring together the literary offerings of different schools of thought, her purpose was not carried out, since, exclusive of herself, five of the writers for her periodical had earlier contributed to *The Dial*: Emerson, Thoreau, Ward, Dwight, and Ellen Hooper. As a consequence, very probably, her project failed, for public interest was never aroused over transcendentalism save as a matter of religious controversy. It is a bitter indictment of American

---

[37] *Ibid.*, pp. 211-214.
[38] *Ibid.*, pp. 214-224. With the exception of the introductory essay all of Elizabeth Peabody's work in her periodical is reprinted in her volume, *Last Evening with Allston and Other Papers*, Boston, n.d. (1886).
[39] *Æsthetic Papers*, pp. 224-245. This essay was reprinted in *The Salem Gazette* for May 19 and May 22, 1849.
[40] *Æsthetic Papers*, pp. 245-248.

taste during the forties that a journal containing important works by three of the outstanding figures in our literary history should have failed as soon as it made its first appearance.

CHAPTER VIII

THE MASSACHUSETTS QUARTERLY REVIEW

On April 4, 1844, Emerson wrote to his friend W. H. Furness:

> I have just done with *The Dial*. Its last number is printed; and having lived four years, which is a Presidential term in America, it may respectably end. I have continued it for some time against my own judgment to please other people, and though it has now some standing and increasing favour in England, it makes a very slow gain at home, and it is for home that it is designed. It is time that each of the principal contributors to it should write in their own names, and go to their proper readers. In New England its whole quadrennium will be a pretty historiette in literary annals. I have been impatient to dismiss it as I am a very *un*able editor, and only lose good time in my choosing and refusing and patching, that I want for more grateful work.[1]

Such was Emerson's attitude after his dismal experiences with *The Dial*. But it was not long before he and his more intimate associates were sketching plans for a new periodical, which, as Theodore Parker wrote to a friend, was to be a *tremendous* publication, "with ability in its arms and piety in its heart."[2]

An entry in Emerson's journal made during the month of May, 1847, provides information as to the identity of the chief movers of the project:

> Yesterday, Theodore Parker, W. H. Channing, Charles Sumner, Alcott, Thoreau, Elliot Cabot, Dwight, Stone, Weiss, J. F. Clarke, Stetson, and Mr. Arrington of Texas spent the day with me and discussed the project of the journal. George Bradford and I made fourteen.[3]

---

[1] *Records of a Lifelong Friendship, R. W. Emerson and W. H. Furness*, ed. H. H. Furness, 1910, pp. 33-34.
[2] John Weiss, *Life and Correspondence of Theodore Parker*, 1864, I, 266.
[3] *Journals*, VII, 268-269.

Perhaps an indication of the hopes entertained for the new periodical is a sentence which appears a few lines above the entry that has been quoted: "Look at literary New England; one would think that it was a national fast."

The account of the circumstances connected with the establishment of *The Massachusetts Quarterly Review*, as the new journal came to be called, is given best in the words of J. E. Cabot, who tells us in his memoir of Emerson:

> In the spring before he sailed there were meetings at his house looking to a new quarterly review which should be more alive than was the *North American* to the questions of the day. Theodore Parker and Dr. Samuel Gridley Howe, I think, were the persons most forward in the matter. Mr. Sumner came up, spoke approvingly of the undertaking, but doubted whether the time was quite ripe for it. Thoreau was there, but contented himself with asking whether any one present found difficulty in publishing in the existing journals anything that he might have occasion to say. On the whole, but little zeal was manifested, nor would anybody promise definite contributions. . . .
>
> A committee, consisting of Emerson, Parker, and Howe [was appointed], for the drafting of a manifesto to the public. This Emerson wrote, and he seems to have supposed his office thereby discharged. But when the first number of *The Massachusetts Quarterly Review* reached him in England, he found himself set down, with Mr. Parker and me, "assisted by several other gentlemen," as the editors. He did not like this, but suffered his name to stand upon the covers until, after his return home, the fourth number appeared with the announcement that he would now "of course" contribute regularly. Then he insisted upon withdrawing, and Mr. Parker became, what in fact he had always been, sole editor. Emerson had no part in it beyond writing the Editors' Address.[4]

The last sentence, it should be said here, is wholly untrue.

As has been pointed out, Theodore Parker, with his customary energy, was the most active of the transcenden-

---

[4] J. E. Cabot, *A Memoir of R. W. Emerson*, 1887, II, 497.

talists in furthering the cause of the quarterly. When casting about to find a suitable editor for the publication, he wrote to a friend:

> We don't want a man of the Middle Ages, but of the nineteenth century, for our work. I have written a letter to Emerson, asking him to undertake the matter. If he will, it will succeed. He is the better man, if he will take hold. He is a downright *man;* we never had such a jewel in America before. I think him worth two or three of Dr. Channing. How many young men do you know that could write in such a work? It should be literary, philosophical, poetical, theological, and, above all, human—human even to divinity.[5]

About the same time he wrote to Charles Sumner as follows:

> I think we want a new journal, devoted to letters, poetry, art, philosophy, theology, politics (in the best sense of that word), and humanity in general. You know better than I the *North American Review,* the *Christian Examiner,* etc. They are not *jusq' au niveau de l'humanité.* They will not be, cannot be. The better minds of the age cannot express their best thoughts therein. If there were such a journal, ably conducted, it would have two good influences: 1. It would strike a salutary terror into all the Ultramontanists, and make them see that they did not live in the Middle Ages—that they are not to be let alone dreaming of the garden of Eden, but are to buckle up and work; 2. It would spread abroad the ideas which now wait to be organized, some in letters, some in art, some in institutions and practical life. . . . Don't suppose I want to be one of the head and front of this movement; I want no such thing, but not to appear at all. I wrote to R. W. E. to ask him to take charge of such a work. If he fails, what say you to that?[6]

In another letter to Sumner he informed him that, after a conference with Emerson, the "council of the Gods" had pitched upon him to be the editor of the proposed magazine. In reply Sumner wrote:

[5] Weiss, *op. cit.,* I, 267.   [6] *Ibid.,* I, 267.

I do not think that the hour or the man has yet come for your journal. Most certainly I am not the man. I have not the time or the disposition for such a work. . . . Before such a journal is commenced its character and objects should be determined with reasonable certainty, and its supporters marshalled. There must also be a background of capital. I trust it must not wait an aeon to be born, but I am sure the time has not yet come.[7]

It is apparent from various letters written by Parker to his friends[8] that other men were considered as possible editors of the periodical; but, in the end, Parker himself, unwillingly, it seems, undertook the burden of the work, after Emerson had "rather weakly" consented to aid in the task, and J. E. Cabot had agreed to act as corresponding secretary and business manager.[9] Dr. Samuel G. Howe, the noted educator of the blind, also seems to have had a close connection with the management of the review, although for reasons of policy his name did not appear among the list of editors.[10] Although Emerson wrote to S. G. Ward on March 25, 1847, that he had refused to act as editor of the journal,[11] he must have changed his mind sufficiently to allow his name to appear, since some months before his departure for Europe the preliminary announcements of the magazine gave his name as one of its directors. In *The Harbinger* for August 7, 1847, for example, George Ripley inserted a notice which stated: "The Review will be conducted by R. W. Emerson, Reverend

[7] Parker MSS. in the library of the Mass. Hist. Soc.
[8] Cf. Weiss, *op. cit.*, I, 266.
[9] T. W. Higginson, "Memoir of J. E. Cabot," *Proc. Mass. Hist. Soc.*, second series, XX, 530.
[10] "Dr. Howe keeps still his interest in the work, but I thought his name had better not appear among the 'wise masterbuilders,' lest some should suspect that he was abandoning his duty to the blind who have no eyes, to attend to the blind who have eyes but see not" (Parker to S. J. May, Aug. 14, 1847, Weiss, *op. cit.*, I, 268).
[11] "Theodore Parker and others are considering just now, once more, the practicability of a new Quarterly Journal, and they seek me for an editor. They came to me and then to C. Sumner. I promised my best help, but no editorship (*Letters from R. W. Emerson to a Friend*, ed. C. E. Norton, 1899, p. 64)."

Theodore Parker, and J. Elliot Cabot, assisted by several other gentlemen."[12]

Just why the men responsible for the new journal desired an organ of their own has been suggested in part by Parker's letter to Sumner, in which he spoke of the conservative character of *The North American Review* and *The Christian Examiner*. A fair proportion of the literary ability among the transcendentalists was already absorbed by *The Harbinger* and *The New York Tribune*, not to mention the various antislavery periodicals to which certain members of the New School were contributing. But Parker, at least, seems to have been bent upon proving to the world that New England could support a journal open to every kind of reform,[13] but free from the sectarian interests of the Fourierists, radical yet solid—"*The Dial* with a beard*,*" as he expressed the idea.

Then, too, a magazine of liberal theology was felt to be sadly wanting. In this connection it is of interest to know that as early as November, 1846, Friederich Münch, a German liberal of Missouri, wrote to Parker:

> What do you think about establishing a periodical religious paper in English, devoted to the principles of Rational Christianity? . . . I have long wished to see some such paper started, but could find no one to assist me. I am still willing to offer what little I can do,—and many of my countrymen in New York, Philadelphia, and Cincinnati would cheerfully aid in such an undertaking.[14]

Very probably *The Massachusetts Quarterly Review* attracted some attention among the German liberals in the

---

[12] *The Harbinger*, V, 139.

[13] In his notebook of the period (MS. in the library of the Mass. Hist. Soc.) Parker made a list of the chief reforms of the day: Antislavery, Temperance, Association, Prisons, Education, Pauperism, Church Reform, Trade, etc. Under the heading "General Reform" the names of Emerson and Alcott appear.

[14] Parker MSS. in the library of the Mass. Hist. Soc. A sketch of Münch may be found in *Berühmnte Deutsche Vorkämpfer . . . in Nord-Amerika*, Cleveland, 1888, p. 218.

United States, since it provided its readers with a discussion of German thought. In England also a certain group of progressives were interested in the project, for James Martineau wrote to Parker, on October 3, 1847:

> Your promised Quarterly excites much expectation amongst us. May it last longer than *The Dial*, and be a little more acceptable to plebeian apprehensions like mine.[15]

Of the number and character of the subscribers to the journal little can be said. On July 24, 1848, a certain R. Redington wrote to the editor, informing him that the periodical was taken by "the first men" of Northern Ohio, and in another letter, written during the following month, stated that he distributed twenty-six copies of the publication.[16] As to the popularity of the work outside of the Western Reserve no direct evidence seems to be available. At the end of the first volume the editor inserted a notice which mentioned the fact that the vogue of the magazine was greater than had been anticipated. Moreover, the suspension of publication after the number for September, 1850, was not due to the lack of a sufficient subscription list, but to the failure of the printers, Coolidge and Wiley. Of them Parker wrote: "They made a little money on the Review, though *I* lost."[17]

The "Editors' Address," written by Emerson for the first issue, that for December, 1847, gives a fair indication of the subjects which seemed to him, and possibly his friends, to demand the consideration of the American people.[18] Beginning with the stock query of the magazine writers of the period—the query as to the source of works

---

[15] Parker MSS. in the library of the Mass. Hist. Soc. For the popularity of *The Dial* in England, see Margaret Fuller's *At Home and Abroad*, Boston, 1856, pp. 122-123.

[16] Parker MSS. in the library of the Mass. Hist. Soc.   [17] *Ibid.*

[18] *The Massachusetts Quarterly Review*, I, 1-7. Hereinafter cited as "M. Q. R." This is reprinted in the Centenary Edition of Emerson's works in the volume entitled *Miscellanies*, cap. XVIII.

of imagination equal to the breadth and activity of the nation—Emerson continued by asserting that the sponsors of the review would give advice on matters of politics, as lovers of the country, but "not always approvers of the public counsels." In regard to other topics of discussion he wrote:

A journal that would meet the real wants of this time must have a courage and power sufficient to solve the problems which the great groping society around us, stupid with perplexity, is dumbly exploring. Let it not show its astuteness by dodging each difficult question, and arguing diffusely every point on which men are long ago unanimous. Can it front this matter of Socialism, to which the names of Owen and Fourier have attached, and dispose of that question? Will it cope with allied questions of Government, Non-resistance, and all that belongs under that category? Will it measure itself with the chapter of Slavery, in some sort the special enigma of the time, as it has provoked against it a sort of inspiration and enthusiasm singular in modern history? There are literary and philosophical reputations to settle. The name of Swedenborg has in this very time acquired new honors, and the current year has witnessed the appearance, in their first English translation, of his manuscripts. Here is an unsettled account in the book of Fame; a nebula to dim eyes, but which great telescopes may yet resolve into a magnificent system. Here is the standing problem of Natural Science, and the merits of her great interpreters, to be determined; the encyclopedical Humboldt, and the intrepid generalizations collected by the author of the "Vestiges of Creation." Here is the balance to be adjusted between the exact French school of Cuvier, and the genial catholic theorists, Geoffroy St. Hilaire, Goethe, Davy, and Agassiz. Will it venture into the thin and difficult air of that school where the secrets of structure are discussed under the topics of mesmerism and the twilights of demonology? . . .

Mankind for the moment seem to be in search of a religion. The Jewish *cultus* is declining; the Divine, or, as some will say, the truly Human, hovers, now seen, now unseen, before us. . . . The moral and religious sentiments meet us everywhere, alike in markets as well as in churches. A God starts up behind cotton bales also.

With convictions in regard to such matters, Emerson concluded, "a few friends of good letters" had seen fit to establish a new journal which would rely not only on the talents and industry of "good men," but "much more on the magnetism of truth." This idealistic sketch of the problems of the day is of great importance to an understanding of the character of *The Massachusetts Quarterly Review*, for practically every point touched upon by Emerson—from the political disturbance occasioned by the "bad war" with Mexico, to "the thin and difficult air" of mesmerism—received attention in its pages.

From the outset Parker, of course, assumed most of the responsibility of getting suitable contributions. On June 21, 1847, he wrote to John P. Hale, the noted opponent of slavery in the United States Senate, to provide an article on the annexation of Texas and the Mexican War.[19] In his notebook[20] Parker made a list of "Subjects for the New Journal:"

- A. Political
    - Mexican War
    - Slavery
    - Character of politics in the U. S. A.
- B. Moral
    - Education of the people
    - Mission of U. S. A.
    - History and condition [sic] of society
- C. Theological
    - Condition of theology in Prot. and Cath.
    - Method of theol. A. Philosophical B. Historical
- D. Philosophical
    - State of philosophy in world. Methods. Results
    - Sketches of old masters, Pythagoras etc. down to Leibnitz etc.
    - Sketches of new masters

[19] Parker MSS. in the library of the Mass. Hist. Soc.
[20] Ibid.

E. Literary
    American literature, hist., facts, purpose
    English lit. as distinguished from Fr., Germ. etc.
    Modern Germ. lit. etc.
    Treatment of history. Democratic. Oligarchic. Despotic
    Ancient letters etc., etc.
Statesmen and politicians
Public education in Fr., in Eng., in Germ.
Advance of Fr. in pol. and jurisprudence etc. since 1700 [sic].

At another time he listed sixteen additional topics, some of which were followed by sources for reading:

Alexandrian school
Progress of France since Revolution
New rel. movement in Germany
Politics of Prussia [sic]
    [?] question
State of Ethnography [sic]
Condition of China
Articles on public ed.
Prison discipline
Constitution of New York
The Irish famine
Coleridge
Southey
Wordsworth
Shelley
Landor.

Of greater interest is his list of writers for the new periodical:

A. Certain and Valuable
    Emerson, Weiss, Cabot, W. H. Channing, Howe, Sumner [crossed out], Shedd [sic]
B. Valuable but not Certain
    Giddings, Palfrey, S. C. Philips, Ripley, Hawthorne, [?], J. P. Hale
C. Certain but not Valuable
    Wm. Ellery Channing, Thoreau, the two Downs [sic], et id genus omne, Margaret.

After the first number had appeared, Parker outlined in his journal a prospectus for a few succeeding issues,[21] but his plans failed to be materialized, and he soon found that he would be dependent upon his close friends and associates for the bulk of the material that was to fill the pages of the organ of "the Conservative Reformers," as they were called. Nothing could be truer than his statement, made in the "Editor's Farewell," at the end of the third volume, that the periodical never became what it was intended to be.

The final volume of *The Massachusetts Quarterly* contained printed slips with the names of the authors of the various articles included, but from the marginal notes made by the editor in his own copies of the earlier numbers[22] it is possible to give an almost complete list of the contributors to the magazine. A table of contents, with the names of the writers for the review, follows:

Volume 1

    December, 1847

Page
- 1. Editors' Address, R. W. Emerson
- 8. The Mexican War, Theodore Parker
- 54. Powers' Greek Slave, Samuel G. Ward
- 63. The Political Conditions and Prospects of Greece, George Finlay
- 96. The Life and Writings of Agassiz, J. Elliot Cabot[23]
- 120. Short Reviews and Notices

    March, 1848
- 145. Has Slavery in the U. S. a Legal Basis? Richard Hildreth
- 168. The Inductive System, J. Elliot Cabot
- 198. Education of the People, Theodore Parker
- 225. The Hebrew Monarchy, Theodore Parker

---

[21] Printed in O. B. Frothingham, *Theodore Parker, a Biography*, 1874, p. 396.

[22] In the Boston Public Library.

[23] Parker wrote "Desor" after this article, but reference is made within the essay to assistance received from Desor. A presentation copy in the Widener Library indicates that Cabot was the author.

240. Ballad Literature, Theodore Parker
256. Short Reviews and Notices

June, 1848
273. Has Slavery in the U. S. a Legal Basis? Richard Hildreth
293. Swedenborg as a Theologian, Henry James
308. Causes and Prevention of Idiocy, Samuel G. Howe
331. Discourse on the Death of John Quincy Adams, Theodore Parker
376. Short Reviews and Notices

September, 1848
401. The Philosophy of the Ancient Hindoos, J. Elliot Cabot
423. William Ellery Channing, Theodore Parker
456. Principles of Zoölogy, J. Elliot Cabot
463. Constitutionality of Slavery, Henry I. Bowditch
509. Apologetical and Explanatory, Samuel G. Howe[24]
512. Short Reviews and Notices

Volume 2

December, 1848
1. The Political Destination of America, and the Signs of the Times, Theodore Parker
32. Legality of American Slavery, Richard Hildreth
39. The Law of Evidence, John Appleton
63. The Works of Walter Savage Landor, James Russell Lowell
77. A New Theory of the Effect of Tides, Edouard Desor
82. Postal Reform, Samuel G. Howe
105. The Free Soil Movement, Theodore Parker
126. Short Reviews and Notices

March, 1849
137. The German Revolution of 1848, Bernard Roelker
183. The Eternity of God, Theodore Parker
187. Discovery of America by the Norsemen, J. Elliot Cabot
215. Character of Mr. Prescott as an Historian, Theodore Parker
249. Oxford Poetry, R. W. Emerson
253. Short Reviews and Notices

[24] This deals with remarks made in Howe's essay on Idiocy.

168 Periodicals of American Transcendentalism

June, 1849
273. The Methodology of Mesmerism, Samuel Brown
308. The Ocean and Its Meaning in Nature, Edouard Desor
326. Macaulay's *History of England*, Frederic Howes
356. Short Reviews and Notices

September, 1849
401. The Methodology of Mesmerism, Samuel Brown
414. The Poetry of Keats, Amory D. Mayo
428. Prichard's *Natural History of Man*, John Weiss
437. Prescott's *Conquest of Mexico*, Theodore Parker
471. Angelus Silesius, the Cherubic Pilgrim, Emmanuel V. Scherb
487. Recent Defences of Slavery, [Augustus R.?] Pope
514. Ruskin's *Seven Lamps of Architecture*, J. Elliot Cabot
520. Short Reviews and Notices

Volume 3
December, 1849
1. Senatorial Speeches on Slavery, James G. Birney
40. *A Week on the Concord and Merrimack Rivers*, James Russell Lowell
52. A Scientific Statement of the Doctrine of the Lord, or Divine Man, Henry James
67. Validity of Instruments and Contracts Executed on Sunday, Richard Hildreth
77. Mr. Colman on English Agriculture, Frederic Howes
93. The Financial Condition of Russia, Major Pelt
105. The Massachusetts Indians, Wendell Phillips
118. Mr. Polk's Administration, Theodore Parker
158. Short Reviews and Notices

March, 1850
161. Judicial Oaths, John Appleton
183. Specimens of German Lyrics, Theodore Parker and Julia Ward Howe[25]
191. Two New Trinities, John Weiss
200. The Writings of Ralph Waldo Emerson, Theodore Parker
255. Panslavism, Dr. Zille
262. The Postal System of the U. S. A., Charles M. Ellis
278. Short Reviews and Notices

[25] Marked "Anonymous" on the printed slip.

June, 1850

- 285. The Polish-Slavonian Philosophy, Anonymous
- 304. Causes of the Present Condition of Ireland, Frederic Howes
- 337. The Industrial Arts in Russia, Major Pelt
- 347. Browning's Poems, John Weiss
- 386. Hildreth's History of the United States, Theodore Parker
- 425. Short Reviews and Notices

September, 1850

- 431. Senatorial Opinions on the Right of Petition, James G. Birney
- 459. Geology of the Exploring Expedition, Edouard Desor
- 484. Hawthorne's *Scarlet Letter*, George B. Loring[26]
- 500. American and Alpine Botany Compared, John L. Russell
- 512. Different Christologies of the New Testament, Theodore Parker

According to Parker's marginal notes, all of the brief reviews and notices in the first volume were written by himself, with the following exceptions:

Page
- 120. A notice of three works dealing with phonotypy, etc., Elizabeth Peabody
- 129. A review of Ruskin's *Modern Painters*, J. Elliot Cabot
- 139. A notice of George P. Marsh's Phi Beta Kappa oration of 1847, "Human Knowledge," J. Elliot Cabot
- 256. A review of Tennyson's *Princess*, James Russell Lowell[27]
- 259. A notice of several foreign treatises on Idiocy, Samuel G. Howe
- 263. A critique of J. B. Stallo's *General Principles of the Philosophy of Nature, with an outline of some of its recent developments among the Germans*, J. Elliot Cabot[28]

---

[26] The slip is marked "Anonymous" for this article. For Loring's authorship see M. D. Conway, *Life of Nathaniel Hawthorne*, 1890, p. 130.

[27] Parker wrote "Dwight" after the review of Tennyson's work, but on March 26, 1848, Lowell wrote to C. F. Briggs: "The notice of Tennyson's 'Princess' in the last *Massachusetts Quarterly* was mine" (*Letters of J. R. Lowell*, ed. C. E. Norton, 1894, I, 124).

[28] Cf. Ripley's disparagement of Stallo's work in *The Harbinger*, VI, 110. In 1852, when informed by visitors from Cincinnati that the only men of thought in their section of the country were "one young Goddard and Stallo the German," Thoreau wrote in his journal (IV, 295): "The man of the West is not yet."

377. A summary of the contents of three histories of philosophical thought in France and Germany, J. Elliot Cabot
393. A critique of Q. A. King's *Twenty-Four Years in the Argentine Republic*, [?] Channing
397. A notice of J. G. Marvin's *Legal Bibliography*, J. Elliot Cabot
512. A critique of W. T. Thornton's *A Plea for Peasant Proprietors*, Samuel G. Howe
515. A review of Julius C. Hare's *Essays and Tales by John Sterling: with a Memoir of His Life*, R. W. Emerson
516. An announcement of John Carlyle's translation of Dante, R. W. Emerson

Unfortunately, Parker failed to write in the names or initials of the writers of the short reviews and notices in the second and third volumes of the periodical. However, it is possible to state that Samuel J. May supplied a critique of J. H. Allen's *Ten Discourses on Orthodoxy*,[29] and that T. W. Higginson[30] and J. S. Dwight[31] aided in the preparation of brief notices. George Ripley also may have furnished critical material, although his promise of a longer article was never fulfilled.[32]

A glance at the names of the contributors to *The Massachusetts Quarterly Review* is all that is needed to indicate the unusual character of the men who wrote for it. Among the foreigners in the list, the first is George Finlay, the historian of modern Greece, whose article must have been obtained through the efforts of Dr. Samuel Howe, who had been his comrade and fellow adventurer

---

[29] See Weiss, *op. cit.*, I, 379.
[30] See Parker's letter to Higginson, dated June 20, 1848, Frothingham, *op. cit.*, p. 397.
[31] In a fly leaf of one of his copies of the quarterly Parker jotted down the names of several contributors and the sums that they were to be paid. His closer associates, like Hildreth and Weiss, evidently received no money. Dr. Brown apparently was paid $101.52 for slightly more than forty-seven pages; Roelker, $50 for fifty-nine and a half. The regular remuneration, however, seems to have been one dollar per page. Dwight's name is included in the list as having written "3 plus 2" pages.
[32] See Ripley's letter to Parker, dated July 9, 1849, O. B. Frothingham, *George Ripley*, p. 293.

in the days when the American had won fame as the "Lafayette of the Greek Revolution."[33]

Edouard Desor was an eminent Swiss geologist who came to America as one of the chief assistants of Agassiz, and soon numbered himself among the close friends of Parker.[34] Samuel Brown, of Edinburgh, was a noted experimenter in the atomic construction of bodies. His essay on the "Methodology of Mesmerism" was probably obtained through the instrumentality of Emerson, who met him in 1848, and referred to him in terms of high praise.[35]

The slips that contained the list of the contributors to the third volume bore the word "Leipzig" after the names of Major Pelt and Dr. Zille. The latter appears to have been Moritz A. Zille, a man of considerable reputation in his day as a poet, theologian, and educator.[36] At least two other writers for the review were of German birth: Bernard Roelker and Emmanuel Scherb. The former, who became a tutor in Harvard during 1837 and later entered the legal profession, was most eminent as a writer of text books and a translator from German and Swedish.[37] Scherb, an exile or refugee from his native land, lived in Concord for about a year, and there, of course, became friendly with Emerson, whom he tried in vain to instruct in the doctrines of Hegel.[38] He seems to have made a

---

[33] For Howe's association with Finlay see *Letters and Journals of Samuel Gridley Howe*, ed. L. E. Richards and F. B. Sanborn, Vol. I (1906). Howe wrote an introduction for Finlay's *Hellenic Kingdom and the Greek Nation*, Boston and New York, 1837. Whittier, it may be remembered, celebrated one of Howe's adventures in "The Hero."

[34] See *Louis Agassiz, His Life and Correspondence*, ed. Elizabeth C. Agassiz, Boston, 1885, I, 282 *et passim*.

[35] See a letter to his wife in Cabot's memoir, II, 524. The essay from the journal is reprinted in Brown's *Lectures on the Atomic Theory and Essays Scientific and Literary*, Edinburgh, 1858. The same work contains an introductory biographical sketch of the author, written by his cousin, the famous Dr. John Brown.

[36] *Allgemeine Deutsche Biographie*, Leipzig, 1900, XLV, 225.

[37] A sketch of Roelker's life appears in *Appletons' Cyclopaedia of American Biography*, 1888, V, 304.

[38] Emerson's *Journals*, VIII, 69. See also Samuel Longfellow, *Life of Henry Wadsworth Longfellow*, 1891, II, 197, 307, and 395.

living while in America by lecturing on philosophical and literary subjects, an occupation that he plied with such skill and composure as to arouse the delight of the first citizen of Concord.[39]

Of the Americans who assisted the editors of the review little need be said here. The names of men like Hildreth, the historian, Howe, the pioneer in the education of the blind and insane, and Henry James, Sr., are still remembered. Samuel Ward, of course, was the young friend whom Emerson mentioned frequently in his journals, and whom he regarded as "beautiful," among "so many ordinary and mediocre youths."[40] John Appleton was a legal reformer, who later became the Chief Justice of Maine. His contributions to the periodical were perhaps due to the interest of F. H. Hedge, whose church in Bangor he attended during the period.[41] Charles M. Ellis was also a lawyer, of considerable eminence in Boston as an active opponent of slavery. It was he who defended Parker when the latter was arrested for aiding runaway slaves.[42]

Henry I. Bowditch was a physician who manifested a great interest in the theories of the Fourierists, although he never joined in their activities.[43] George B. Loring, who scandalized the "orthodox" by his review of *The Scarlet Letter*, was also a physician. His chief distinction, however, came as a result of political connections, which occasioned his appointment as United States Commissioner of Agriculture, and, later, as Minister to Portugal.[44]

---

[39] Emerson's *Journals*, VIII, 246.

[40] *Ibid.*, V, 530. For Emerson's letters to Ward see *Letters from R. W. Emerson to a Young Friend*, ed. C. E. Norton, 1899. Much material on Ward may be found in Samuel Longfellow's memoir of his brother, and the biographical sketch in *The Early Years of the Saturday Club*, ed. E. W. Emerson, 1918.

[41] For Appleton's legal reforms see *Great American Lawyers*, ed. W. D. Lewis, 1908, V, 41.

[42] *Proc. Mass. Hist. Soc.*, LV, 3-4.

[43] V. Y. Bowditch, *Life . . . of H. I. Bowditch*, 1902, I, 191-192.

[44] *The National Cyclopaedia of American Biography*, 1897, IV, 484.

James G. Birney is remembered chiefly because of his connection with the abolition movement. In 1837 he became the secretary of the National Anti-Slavery Society, and in 1840 and 1844 he was the Presidential candidate of the "Liberty Party."[45]

John L. Russell, a botanist, is of particular interest to the student of American literature because his remarkable knowledge of his chosen field made him a desirable companion to Emerson and the fastidious Thoreau when they felt inclined to receive instructions while enjoying a walk.[46] Amory D. Mayo, Augustus Pope, and Samuel May were Unitarian clergymen whose liberal views made them friendly to Parker.

One is at a loss to find a common denominator for such a varied assortment of men unless one is acquainted with the character of Theodore Parker, whose tremendous intellectual energy was responsible for his interest in men from every walk of life. His letters reveal a range of interest from theology to botany. To one man he writes about the latest developments in the United States Senate; to a second he entrusts his opinions as to the propriety of the scientific name of a plant; to a third he holds forth on the merits of a German treatise on philosophy.

However, it must also be said that, with a few exceptions, the Americans who wrote for *The Massachusetts Quarterly* had in common the devout purpose to abolish slavery by active means. Howe, May, Phillips, Bowditch, Parker, Hildreth, and Ellis, for example, were all members of the famous Vigilance Committee in Boston, which was formed when the excitement over the Fugitive Slave Act was at its peak.[47] But the natural conclusion that the periodical was primarily an organ of the opponents of

---

[45] *Ibid.*, II, 312.
[46] Cf. Emerson's *Journals*, V, 61; and Thoreau's *Journal*, VI, 446; and XI, 171.
[47] *Letters and Journals of Samuel G. Howe*, II (1909), 245; and *Proc. Mass. Hist. Soc.*, XLIV, 323.

slavery is not warranted by the facts, for a study of the contents of the review will prove that its chief interest was in science, history, and, including the shorter critiques, philosophy.

The periodical contained little poetry other than the illustrations quoted in the various critical articles, and that little consisted entirely of translations from the German. Of these perhaps the most striking is that of eighty-nine stanzas from the "Cherubic Pilgrim" of the seventeenth-century mystic Johann Scheffler, better known as Angelus Silesius. E. V. Scherb, who made the translation, provided also a short sketch of the author's life, and a brief, but ardent, exposition of the chief characteristics of mysticism, which he considered to be these:

1. The rejection of all outward authority.
2. The rejection of all mere historical belief in the great facts of Christianity.
3. The yearning for rest.
4. The placing of "a great stress" upon a perfect union with God.[48]

A few of the verses from the "Cherubic Pilgrim" follow:

1.
What I am and what I shall be.
I am a stream of Time, running to God, my sea,
But once I shall myself the eternal ocean be.

2.
The Dew and the Rose.
God's spirit falls on me as dew drops on a rose,
If I but like a rose to him my heart enclose.

3.
The highest good.
Rest is the highest good; and if God was not Rest,
Then Heaven would not be Heaven, and Angels not be blest.

[48] *M. Q. R.*, II, 475-477.

26.
   The greatest riddle.
I know not what I am, I am not what I know,
A thing and not a thing, a point, and circle too.

40.
   Divine passiveness.
Go out—God will go in; die thou and let him live;
Be not, and he will be; wait, and he'll all things give.

Despite the loss of effect in the translation, Scheffler's *Reimsprüche* must have appealed to the readers of the periodical who were capable of appreciating the mystical pantheism of Jacob Boehme and his followers. At any rate, Scherb's translations supplied the review with material that was very similar to the notorious "Orphic Sayings" of Alcott.

In the number for March, 1849, Parker printed his translation of "The Eternity of God," a German hymn whose author, according to a note pencilled in his own copy, he did not know.[49] Not content with his own version, Parker reproduced the original also. The same practice he followed in the case of a few of his translations of various German lyrics which he printed in the number for March, 1850.[50] Of the six poems included his notes assign "The Landlady's Daughter," from Uhland, and "Reconciliation," from Ida von Hahn-Hahn, to Mrs. Julia Ward Howe. After the verses entitled "Volkslied" the initials "T. P." appear, followed by a question mark. Before his translation of Gerhardt's "Evening Song" Parker presented a short introductory sketch in which he expressed his hope that his own poor version, with the original beneath it, would prompt someone to make a better translation, but because of the wooden character of his rendering one is not surprised that the slip with the names of the

---

[49] The note states that he found the poem in the *Bremen Hymn Book*, Bremen, 1814.   [50] *M. Q. R.*, III, 183-187.

contributors should have these effusions marked "Anonymous."

The interest that the quarterly displayed in German literature and philosophy in general is very marked. The first two numbers of the periodical contained a list of "Recent Publications in Continental Europe," which bristled with heavy German titles. In the brief critical notices, too, one finds a large number of German works mentioned. The department of "Short Reviews and Notices" in the issue for March, 1850, for example, contains the titles of six works, three of which are German. The other three, it is of interest to observe, are Latin. The example serves as a fair indication of the heavy quality which characterizes the review in general.

In a critique of the second number of *The Massachusetts Quarterly Review* which George Ripley wrote for *The Harbinger*, the fact is brought out that the work "exhibited more of the judicious composure of the venerable *North American* than the sparkling freshness" that one might expect of a new magazine.[51] Ripley ventured also to assert his belief that the persons accustomed to regard transcendentalism as the product of "mysticism, radicalism, and impiety" would be disappointed in the character of the periodical. In another criticism of the new journal written by Ripley for a later number of *The Harbinger*[52] the opinion was expressed that the articles coming from the "fertile pen" of the editor himself constituted "the chief attraction" of the work. In the main, this opinion appears to be just. Accordingly, it may be advisable to give consideration to the more significant articles written by Parker. Since his work included thirteen of the chief contributions, and the larger part of a fourteenth, he determined the general quality of the magazine in a way that few editors can be said to have done. Then, too, *The*

[51] *The Harbinger*, VI, 151.   [52] *Ibid.*, VII, 150.

Massachusetts Quarterly Review contains several essays which may well be considered the chief literary products of the "Paul of transcendentalism."

Of his articles dealing with the Mexican War, the life of John Quincy Adams, and the administration of Polk little need be said, except that his letters and notebook show that he made a great effort to find relevant material upon which to base his discussion. Frequently in all of his essays he made clear the source of his information, and occasionally added footnotes. It may be desirable also to pass by a consideration of his treatises on "The Hebrew Monarchy" and "The Different Christologies of the New Testament," since they are interesting to the reader without a theological penchant only in that they manifest the liberal attitude that made Parker the stormy petrel of the Unitarianism of his day.

His two articles on Prescott were written, apparently, because of the belief that the historian's works had not been subjected to the investigation of a "philosophical critic."[53] In typical fashion, Parker demanded that history should be written in the "spirit of humanity,"[54] and found fault with Prescott for merely "telling the fact for the fact's sake." However, he himself had acquired enough facts by dint of wide reading to point out an occasional error made by the historian.[55] Although time has added weight to the criticism that Prescott neglected what may be called the philosophy of history, yet the reader somehow receives the impression that Parker's close association with Bancroft and Hildreth must have made lukewarm any appreciation of the extraordinary merits of

---

[53] *M. Q. R.*, II, 215. Cf. Margaret Fuller's opinion of Prescott expressed in an essay on "American Literature," *Papers on Literature and Art*, London, 1846, II, 127.

[54] *M. Q. R.*, II, 247. Parker's ideas concerning historical methods are worthy of the attention of the student of American historiography.

[55] See *ibid.*, II, 458, for example.

the man whose genius far outshone that of his fellows. However, upon turning to the essay on "Hildreth's History of the United States," one finds that Parker charged his friend also with having neglected "the philosophical part of history."[56] Yet Hildreth fared better at the critic's hands than Prescott, since he wrote "in the spirit of democracy." In his discussion of his friend's work Parker devoted much space to the illustration of the bigotry of the early inhabitants of New England—their intolerance in theology, their lack of the democratic spirit, their cruelty and injustice to the Indians, and, above all, their attitude toward indentured servants.[57]

Evidently, the editor of the quarterly was much interested in the character of the so-called Puritans, for he had earlier written on the subject in one of his most entertaining contributions to the journal; namely, the essay on "Ballad Literature," which appeared in the issue for March, 1848. After a brief introduction dealing with the nature of popular ballads, "the field flowers of poetry," he commented on the "characteristic homeliness" of those developed among the English people, and then turned to a consideration of the ballad literature of America. A representative passage follows:

> They were struggling against poverty, against the wilderness, the wild beasts, and savage men—not to mention the difficulties which came from the other side of the water. Thus stood the fathers of New England. On the one side was Starvation; and Destruction on the other; and the Indians laying [*sic*] in wait and ready to hasten the advance of both. Under such circumstances few men would incline to sing anything very secular, or aesthetic. Besides, to the Puritan "common things" had a certain savor of

[56] *Ibid.*, III, 423.
[57] In March, 1849, Parker wrote to Whittier, asking for an article on the "white slaves," the servants of the New England fathers (printed in part in S. T. Pickard, *Life and Letters of John Greenleaf Whittier*, 1895, I, 342). Cf. Whittier's treatment of slavery in *Margaret Smith's Journal*, entry under date of August 1, 1678.

uncleanness about them, and were thought scarce worthy of being sung. Would a man be merry, he might indeed sing, for there was scriptural argument for his singing; but it must be—psalms. New England psalmody is a proverb amongst nations. We speak not of the melodies, so long-drawn and so nasal, but of the substantial words which endure while the volatile melodies have long ago been hushed into expressive silence. We give a verse from an old version of "The Psalms of David," assuring our readers that it is no invention of ours, but an undoubted original:

> The race is not to them that do the swiftest run,
> Nor the battell
> To the peopel
> That carries the longest gun.

Of psalm-singing there was no lack in New England. But that was not quite enough even for the Puritans. The natural heart of man wanted something a little more epic—some narrative of heroic events in a form slightly poetical, with a tinge of moral feeling, and a minute specification of time, place, person, and all particulars thereto belonging. This want was supplied—so far as we can learn—by the public prayers so abundantly made by the Puritans. They were as narrative as the popular ballads, about as long-winded, equally garrulous, it is said; only the rhythmic element was wanting; and that was supplied, we suppose, by the intonation of the orator, or by the repetition of particular phrases—as a sort of refrain, or "burden."[58]

Strangely enough, the same number which contained this humorous account included one of Parker's theological essays and a treatise on "The Education of the People." The last is of interest in that Parker scouted the "barbarous notion" of the inferiority of women, and advocated free schools for girls.[59] He further insisted upon the necessity of a "free public college";[60] and, after commenting upon the beneficial influence of the lectures delivered by Agassiz, Emerson, and James Walker, uttered a plea for the establishment of public libraries. As has been suggested by the passage quoted from the essay on ballads, Parker was

[58] *M. Q. R.*, I, 245-246.   [59] *Ibid.*, I, 209.   [60] *Ibid.*, I, 211.

capable of turning out neatly pointed sentences at times. As good an illustration as can be found, very probably, is provided by this one from his article on education: "Democracy is the government of all the citizens, for the sake of all the citizens, and by means of them all."[61]

Considered from the stylistic point of view, perhaps the most striking of the editor's contributions to his own journal is an essay on "The Political Destination of America, and the Signs of the Times," which appeared in the number for December, 1848. The most marked characteristic of the American people, Parker thought, was the love of freedom—"a genius for liberty." The problem of his day, demanding immediate action, he believed to be "the organization of the rights of man,"[62] a task which his friends among the Fourierists were trying to perform in their own way. Amid the hurly-burly tumult of national expansion and the multifarious activities of his day Parker thought that a few especially significant "signs of the times" were to be observed in American life: an impatience of authority, a philosophical tendency, a lack of first principles, a great intensity of purpose, and an excessive love of material things.

Like most of his countrymen who have undertaken to write about America, he criticized in no uncertain terms the conventional weaknesses of the national tradition.

There was once a man who said he always told a lie when it would serve his special turn. 'Tis a pity he went to his own place long ago. He seemed born for a party politician in America.[63]

"In education," he remarked, "the aim is not to get the most we can, but the least we can get along with."[64] Of our national pride, he wrote:

---

[61] *Ibid.*, I, 201. Lincoln is usually considered to have borrowed his famous definition from Parker, whose works contain several variants of the above.
[62] *Ibid.*, II, 5ff.   [63] *Ibid.*, II, 16.   [64] *Ibid.*, II, 20.

Jonathan is as vain as he is conceited, and expects that the Fiddlers, the Dickenses, and the Trollopes, who visit us periodically as the swallows, and likewise for what they can catch, shall only extol, or at least stand aghast at the brave spectacle we offer. . . . There was an African chief, long ago, who ruled over a few miserable cabins, and one day received a French traveller from Paris, under a tree. With the exception of a pair of shoes, our chief was as naked as a pestle, but with great complacency he asked the traveller, "What do they say of *me* at Paris?"[65]

American literature also came in for a share of his attention. Since the more studied and elegant literature of the United States seemed to him to be "mainly an imitation," the true spirit of the country he thought was to be found in speeches, pamphlets, and newspapers.

We dare not be original; our American Pine must be cut to the trim pattern of the English Yew, though the Pine bleed at every clip. This poet tunes his lyre at the harp of Goethe, Milton, Pope, or Tennyson. His songs might better be sung on the Rhine than the Kennebec. . . . Our Poet is not deep enough to see that Aphrodite came from the ordinary waters, that Homer only hitched into rhythm and furnished the accomplishment of verse to street-talk, nursery tales, and old men's gossip, in the Ionian towns; he thinks what is common is unclean. So he sings of Corinth and Athens, which he never saw, but has not a word to say of Boston, and Fall River, and Baltimore, and New York, which are just as meet for song.[66]

The fault of our writers in general, Parker thought, was that they were "too fastidious to be wise, too unlettered to be elegant—too critical to create." However, there was one man, "alike philosopher and bard," whom he excepted from his remarks, and about whom he promised to write more at a later time.

Before coming to a consideration of his essay on Emerson, the philosopher and bard alluded to, it seems desirable to present a brief summary of his opinions concerning Dr.

[65] *Ibid.*, II, 8-9. [66] *Ibid.*, II, 22-23.

William Ellery Channing. Although Parker believed that in the nineteenth century the clergy, quite rightly, possessed less power than ever before in the history of Christendom, he maintained that no clergyman of America had ever exercised such dominion among men as Dr. Channing, whose signal success, in his opinion, came not from the qualities that commonly attract mankind, but from "the supremacy of the moral and religious element" in his nature.[67] With his notorious "capacity for detraction," the Gadfly of Unitarianism continued:

> He had not the cool clear analysis of Dr. Barrow, his prodigious learning, his close logic, his masculine sense; nor the graceful imagery, the unbounded imagination of Jeremy Taylor, "the Shakespeare of Divines," nor his winsome way of talk about piety, elevating the commonest events of life to classic diginity.... He had not the power of condensing his thoughts into the energetic language of Webster—never a word wrong or too much—or of marshalling his forces in such magnificently stern array; no, he had not the exquisite rhythmic speech of Emerson, that wonderful artist in words, who unites manly strength with the rare beauty of a woman's mind.[68]

Yet, the critic continued, although Channing had never stood in the van of any reform, he was the aid of all the liberal movements that came within his range. His sermons and prayers were called "peerless," and his essay on Napoleon, "the fairest estimate of the man in the English language." But Parker could not forget that the great liberal clergyman had not offered assistance and counsel to William Lloyd Garrison, when the latter had suffered from insults and mob violence.[69] That failure to take advantage of such a notable opportunity appeared to be an indelible blot on the escutcheon of the man whose "one great idea," to the mind of his critic, was "respect for man."[70]

[67] *Ibid.*, I, 434.
[68] *Ibid.*, I, 433-434.
[69] *Ibid.*, I, 447.
[70] *Ibid.*, I, 454.

As one would expect, Parker had much more to say of Emerson. *Nature*, of 1836, "an early violet blooming out of Unitarian sand or snow,"[71] he regarded as the unsurpassed work of its author. The second series of *Essays* he esteemed to be inferior to the first, and *Representative Men* struck him as little more than rhetorical exaggeration. Emerson's influence upon young men and women he regarded as the greatest ever exerted by any man who wrote in the English language. When one puts these two opinions together—that concerning the power of Emerson's influence, and that concerning the superiority of his earliest writings—one is not at a loss to discover just what the great "Protestant of dissenters" had contributed to Parker's own intellectual and religious development. For after the initial impulse given by the early words of Emerson, his debt to the Sage of Concord appears to have been small. Like many another, Parker illustrated the point of Whitman's belief tht Emersonianism "breeds the giant that destroys itself."[72] As early as 1839 Parker wrote to Elizabeth Peabody, in regard to Emerson: "I find perhaps the most light from him when I most differ from him."[73] Soon after, he asked Convers Francis whether he did not believe Brownson to be more original than Emerson. The question was prompted by his having noticed that many of the ideas expressed by Emerson in his first lecture of the winter were "obviously" obtained from an article in *The Boston Quarterly Review*.[74]

With a few such facts in mind, the reader of the essay in *The Massachusetts Quarterly Review* is not surprised to find that Emerson is charged with having led "some youths and maidens astray" by his "extravagant estimate of ecstasy,"[75] with not understanding "the curious philos-

[71] *Ibid.*, III, 203.   [72] *Prose Works*, Putnams', 1902, II, 270.
[73] Letter of Jan. 8, 1839, in Parker MSS. in the library of the Mass. Hist. Soc.
[74] Letter of Dec. 6, 1839, in Parker MSS. in the library of the Mass. Hist. Soc.
[75] *M. Q. R.*, III, 233.

ophy" of the Orient from which he had borrowed "some hard names,"[76] and with perceiving beauty as merely "inanimate."[77] But more than the "vice" of the "Emersonidae" in affecting the "agony" of intuition, Emerson's lack of the power of orderly thought impressed the critic. A spiritual counterpart of this "greatest defect of his mind"[78] was believed to exist in "a certain coldness in his ethics," the coldness of a man "running alone, who would lead others to isolation, not society."[79] This last criticism, of course, was precisely the chief one made by Ripley and Dwight against their friend in Concord. But perhaps the climax of Parker's derogation of Emerson's accomplishments is reached in a discussion of his verse, which, with few exceptions, appeared to contain "his poorest, thinnest, and least musical prose."[80]

However, the essay goes to equal lengths in bestowing praise. Even "the most genial wit" is granted to be one of Emerson's virtues. But perhaps two quotations will best indicate the warmth of Parker's admiration:

In many things Goethe is superior to Emerson: in fertility of invention, in a wide acquaintance with men, in that intuitive perception of character which seems an instinct in some men, in regular discipline of the understanding, in literary and artistic culture; but in general harmony of the intellectual powers, and the steadiness of purpose which comes thereof, Emerson is incontestably the superior even of the many-sided Goethe.

To no English writer since Milton can we assign so high a place; even Milton himself, great genius though he was, and great architect of beauty, has not added so many thoughts to the treasury of the race; no, nor been the author of so much loveliness.[81]

---

[76] *Ibid.*, III, 211.   [77] *Ibid.*, III, 231.   [78] *Ibid.*, III, 232.   [79] *Ibid.*, III, 234.
[80] *Ibid.*, III, 245. Swinburne to Stedman, in 1875: "Again, whatever may be Mr. Emerson's merits, to talk of his poetry seems to me like talking of the scholarship of a child who has not learnt its letters. Even Browning's verse always goes to a recognizable tune (I say not a good one), but in the name of all bagpipes what is the tune of Emerson's?" (*The Life and Letters of E. C. Stedman*, ed. Laura Stedman and G. M. Gould, New York, 1910, II, 100).
[81] *M. Q. R.*, III, 234 and 252.

Evidently the nonsense contained in the passage just quoted did not pass without comment in its day, since *The Boston Evening Transcript* for March 15, 1850, contained an amusing article calculated to point out the folly of such extravagant praise of a mere "Great Transparent Eyeball." The comparison with Milton led the writer to observe, "Some person, with good lungs, is greatly needed to cry *Fudge.*"

Of Parker's contributions to *The Massachusetts Quarterly Review* in general it may be said that they constitute the bulk of his productions of a literary nature, and display an unusually wide range of interest. Although they are marked by occasional excess, and a tendency toward the rhetorical, natural to a man whose more effective medium was the spoken word, they are, nevertheless, not without merit.

Emerson's contributions to the review deserve little consideration. His biographer Cabot was of the opinion that the "Editors' Address" was the only product of his pen to appear in the journal, and his son expressed the belief that the only paper other than the initial one written by his father was "a notice of 'Some Oxford Poetry,' the recently published poems of John Sterling and A. H. Clough."[82] It is apparent that two separate contributions of Emerson have been confused, since the article "Oxford Poetry" deals only with Clough. The brief critique of J. C. Hare's *Essays and Tales by John Sterling*, and the notice of a "New Translation of Dante" have never been reprinted,[83] and, accordingly, are reproduced in an appendix to this volume. Except for the introductory address, Emerson's contributions to the periodical are entirely perfunctory.

[82] The Centenary Edition of Emerson's works, *Miscellanies*, p. 622.
[83] "Oxford Poetry" may be found in *Uncollected Writings by Ralph Waldo Emerson*, Lamb Publishing Co., New York, n.d. (1912), p. 23. This reprint lacks the quotations given by Emerson, as well as the sentences used to connect them.

Lowell's critique of Tennyson's *Princess*, while not as inept as Emerson's reviews for the journal, reveals little that deserves comment here. According to the plans sketched by Parker in his notebook,[84] W. H. Furness was to write on Landor, but for some reason that task devolved upon Lowell, who, after a delay, sent the editor his essay, along with a letter, which reads, in part, as follows:

> I am reluctant to send the article. I hardly know what is in it myself, but I am quite conscious that it is disjointed and wholly incomplete. I found it impossible to concentrate my mind upon it so as to give it any unity or entireness.[85]

The reader of the article soon finds that Lowell did himself no injustice in the statement quoted above. It may be of interest in this connection to remark that in a later, and better, essay on Landor, Lowell admitted that he was first attracted to that poet's works "by hearing how much store Emerson set by them."[86]

Of greater interest than the critiques of Landor and of Tennyson, no doubt, is Lowell's review of Thoreau's *A Week on the Concord and Merrimack Rivers*, although the critic appears to have been prejudiced because of the suspicion that the author was little more than one of the aspiring "Emersonidae." As early as 1838, while rusticated in Concord, Lowell wrote:

> I met Thoreau last night, and it is exquisitely amusing to see how he imitates Emerson's tone and manner. With my eyes shut, I shouldn't know them apart.[87]

Evidently, anything connected with Thoreau appeared "exquisitely amusing" to Lowell, for his essay is chiefly characterized by the attempt to be merry at the expense of

---

[84] Frothingham, *Theodore Parker*, p. 396.
[85] H. E. Scudder, *James Russell Lowell, a Biography*, 1901, I, 289.
[86] "Some Letters of Walter Savage Landor," *The Century Magazine*, new series, XIII, 511 (1888).
[87] *Letters of James Russell Lowell*, ed. C. E. Norton, 1894, I, 27.

the "bream Homer." Perhaps its most effective part is the glowing introduction dealing with the "humorsome" ingenuousness of the old voyagers. The literary diversions in the *Week* appeared to the critic to be "snags" to the placid drifting of the reader, and the discourse on friendship, an Emersonian preachment in the midst of a river-party. More trenchant is this observation: " 'Give me a sentence,' prays Mr. Thoreau bravely, 'which no intelligence can understand!'—and we think that the kind Gods have nodded." A few favorable comments are included, but, on the whole, the essence of the critic's attitude is summed up in the following:

If Mr. Emerson choose to leave some hard nuts for posterity to crack, he can perhaps afford it as well as any. We counsel Mr. Thoreau, in his own words, to take his hat and come out of that. If he prefer to put peas in his shoes when he makes private poetical excursions, it is nobody's affair. But if the public are to go along with him, they will find some way to boil theirs.[88]

Far more sympathetic than Lowell's review of Thoreau's work, and equally interesting, is the essay on *The Scarlet Letter*, written by Dr. George Loring, who was at the time a surgeon in the Marine Hospital at Chelsea. As a man who had also leaned "on the mighty arm of the Republic" he could well appreciate Hawthorne's account of his experiences in the Custom House, a treatise which he considered to be more in the vein of Charles Lamb than of Juvenal, although he feared that the general reception of the work would not justify his opinion. The novel itself he discussed as if it were an affair of real flesh and blood, and its characters the actual victims of a state of society in which "appetites were crimes." With singular boldness he wrote:

[88] *M. Q. R.*, III, 50. Lowell's more famous essay on Thoreau is, of course, slightly more respectful.

We naturally shrink from any apparent violation of virtue and chastity, and are very ready to forget, in our eager condemnation, how much that is beautiful and holy may be involved in it. We forget that what society calls chastity is often far the reverse, and that a violation of this perverted virtue may be a sad, sorrowful, and tearful beauty, which we would silently and reverently contemplate. . . .

Who that has recognized the deep and holy meaning of the human affections has not been frozen into demanding a warmhearted crime as a relief for the cold, false, vulgar, and cowardly asperity which is sometimes called chastity?[89]

One needs not marvel that the review was marked "Anonymous"!

More philosophical in its statements, but equally revelatory of the moral "Come-Outerism" that *The Massachusetts Quarterly Review* tolerated, is Henry James's article, "A Scientific Statement of the Doctrine of the Lord, or Divine Man." The peculiar beliefs held by the writer led him to assert that "man is the only competent revelation or image of God, because man alone possesses personality." As a consequence, "a divine instinct, in every soul of man, continually derides all our criminality as transient or unreal." Of morality in general James had to say:

I act morally only in so far as I act under obligation to others, being morally good when I practically acknowledge, and morally evil when I practically deny, this obligation. Thus morality displays me in subjection not to God, but to society or my fellowman, and thus equally with nature denies me proper personality.[90]

The perfect or "divine" man, to him, was "the aesthetic man or the Artist"—not the poet or painter, however, but "the man who is a law unto himself, and ignores all outward allegiance, whether to nature or society."[91]

---

[89] *Ibid.*, III, 496-497.   [90] *Ibid.*, III, 60.

[91] *Ibid.*, III, 63. The pernicious character of 'morality' was a favorite topic with James. Upon one occasion he was severely rebuked by Mary Moody Emerson for his beliefs ("Henry James," *The Early Years of the Saturday Club*).

In view of the close relationship which came to exist between Henry James and several of the more important transcendentalists, it may be desirable to present a brief account of his other contribution to *The Massachusetts Quarterly Review*, the essay on Swedenborg. The article in question aimed to do little more than point out "the leading theological import" of the writings of the founder of the New Church. The fundamental truth underlying all of the ideas of Swedenborg James considered to be "the actual humanity of God." The end of creation he thought to be "the eternal conjunction of the Creator with the Creature." In addition to these doctrines, the chief ideas of Swedenborgian theology were summed up in the following:

The *essential* Divine Humanity consists in Creative Love. The divine natural humanity consists in every varied form of Art, or productive use, and is conditioned upon a perfect society. This latter theme is the mystic burden of all sacred scripture since the world began, and we are now, according to this gifted seer, on the verge of its accomplishment.[92]

Of a more perplexing phase of the doctrines of the New Church, the theory of "correspondences," little is said in the essay. A brief suggestion is tendered in these words:

The universe, spiritually regarded, is a man: all creation flows through man: nature is but a type of man: these and a thousand similar maxims stand in the truth of the divine natural humanity.[93]

As a result, "the history of nature is to be sought only in the history of man."

---

[92] *M. Q. R.*, I, 306. Parker's attitude toward Swedenborgianism is to be seen in a letter written by him to Albert Sanford, on Aug. 24, 1853: "A wise man may get many nice bites out of him, and be the healthier for such eating; but if he swallows Swedenborg whole, as the fashion is with his followers, why it lies hard in the stomach, and the man has a nightmare on him all his natural life, and talks about "the word" and "the Spirit," "correspondences" and "receivers." Yet the Swedenborgians have a calm and religious beauty in their lives which is much to be admired" (Parker MSS. in the library of the Mass. Hist. Soc.).

[93] *M. Q. R.*, I, 307.

An explanation of Swedenborg's beliefs such as that made by Henry James is, of course, of great importance to an understanding of the unusual interest manifested in the subject by practically all of the transcendentalists. The "actual humanity of God" finds somewhat of a counterpart in the idea of the divinity of man, enunciated most notably by Channing. The belief in the conjunction of God and Nature appears to be typically Emersonian. The notion that Swedenborg conditioned his theology upon "a perfect society" is strikingly similar to the fundamental theory of the Fourierists. And the doctrine of "correspondences" is of course very near to the symbolism which is eminently characteristic of the mystical philosophy at the heart of transcendentalism.

To the student of American literature the most interesting of Cabot's contributions to the review—in number more than those of anyone except Parker—is his article on "The Philosophy of the Ancient Hindoos," a subject of no little interest to the members of the New School.[94] With the same desire for careful analysis that had marked his essay on the logic of John Stuart Mill,[95] Cabot undertook to point out a few of the leading principles of Hindu idealism. The chief one is taken to be a belief "that Reality is equivalent to pure abstract Soul or Thought, unexistent, and thus simple and unformed."[96] "Moral distinctions," since they appertain only to the individual, belong to the sphere of the body, and are to "be transcended by

---

[94] A good indication of the general interest in mystical writers manifested by the transcendentalists is to be seen in the following extract from a letter written by Convers Francis to Parker, on May 24, 1839: "We might have (Might we not?) what I should call a *World Bible*, which if we had now our choice to make would be better than the Jewish and Christian Bible,—I mean a combination of the essentially true and wise, which lies scattered among the sages of all times and nations, into a well-arranged mass. Confucius, Zoroaster, Pythagoras, Socrates, Plato, Moses, Jesus, Paul, Mohammed, Thomas à Kempis, Luther, Fenelon, Henry More, the German thinkers, etc. might each furnish their portion. Wouldn't it be a noble, a truly God-sent Bible?" (Parker MSS. in the library of the Mass. Hist. Soc.).

[95] *M. Q. R.*, I, 168.   [96] *Ibid.*, I, 403.

the wise man."[97] Cabot pointed out the fact that the failure of Hindu philosophy to give due consideration to Nature inclined it toward skepticism, which he, apparently, believed to be "the common meeting point" of all philosophy.[98] But the writer's observations occupy little space in the essay, for it consists mainly of numerous quotations from a variety of sources covering the chief documents of the religion of India, beginning with the Vedas and Puranas. A glance at the footnotes that accompany the article reveals the fact that its author had availed himself of an impressive number of translations from which to cull his illustrations.

No such treatment of the contents of *The Massachusetts Quarterly Review* as has been attempted in this chapter can be wholly satisfactory, but enough material has been discussed to show at least some of its outstanding qualities. The eminence of so many of its contributors, not to speak of its guiding spirits, gives it a place among the more notable journalistic adventures of its day. That it reflects the general tenor of the broad spirit of reform and inquiry so characteristic of the period, is obvious. Then, too, the periodical contains matter of unusual value to a study of the literary reputation of Emerson, Thoreau, and others. Moreover, as has been said already, it includes within its pages perhaps the best contributions made by Theodore Parker to American letters.

Apparently, *The Massachusetts Quarterly Review* had no immediate successor, but, in a way, it is connected with the establishment of *The Atlantic Monthly*. In the "Editor's Farewell to the Readers" Parker expressed the hope that a new journal would be started in the heart of New England, "in a more popular form," which would promote "the great ideas of our times by giving them an expression

---

[97] *Ibid.*, I, 406. [98] *Ibid.*, I, 422.

in literature."[99] But in a letter to James Birney, informing him that his last contribution would not be published in the review because of the failure of the publishers, Parker wrote: "We shall probably have some other journal to take its place, which will not be in my hands."[100] In December, 1850, Emerson wrote to Hawthorne:

> Mr. George Bradburn, better known, I think, in the sectarian and agitation than in the literary world, desires to try his luck in solving that impossible problem of a New England magazine. As I was known to be vulnerable, that is, credulous, on that side, I was attacked lately by Hildreth (of U. S. History) and urged to engage in it. I told him to go to Lowell, who had been for a year meditating the like project; that I wished a magazine, but would not think of an experiment and a failure; that if he would assure himself, before he began, of the coöperation of Hawthorne, Cabot, Thoreau, Lowell, Parker, Holmes, and whatever is as good—if there be as good—he should be sure of me. So I promised nothing. . . . A good magazine we have not in America, and we are all its friends beforehand.[101]

On February 19, 1850, Lowell wrote to Emerson:

> The plan seems a little more forward. I have seen Parker, who is as placable as the raven down of darkness, and not unwilling to shift his Old Man of the Sea to other shoulders. Longfellow also is toward, and talks in a quite Californian manner of raising funds by voluntary subscription.[102]

But the plans of Lowell, Parker, and others for a new journal were never carried out.

Some months later, however, Francis H. Underwood, a member of Parker's religious society, took up the task

---

[99] *Ibid.*, III, 525.
[100] Letter of July 16, 1850 (Parker MSS. in the library of the Mass. Hist. Soc.). Parker believed that since he was "the most hated man in America" he was not suited to be the editor of a successful journal. Already in November, 1849, he advised J. H. Allen to send an article to *The Christian Examiner* rather than to his own periodical because of the danger of being suspected of heresy (*ibid.*).
[101] Julian Hawthorne, *Nathaniel Hawthorne and His Wife*, 1885, I, 381-382.
[102] H. E. Scudder, *op. cit.*, I, 287.

where it had been left by others, and in 1853 announced that the new magazine, "reformatory and literary" in character, would soon appear. Hildreth was "very much interested in the undertaking," as were also Parker and Lowell.[103] Howe and Wendell Phillips were among those whom Underwood consulted. But again a postponement was made necessary—because of the failure of a publishing firm. However, in 1857 Underwood at last found his hopes realized in the establishment of *The Atlantic Monthly*, of which he was "still the initiating spirit."[104]

[103] Bliss Perry, "The Editor Who Was Never the Editor," *Park-Street Papers*, 1908, p. 223. All of the facts dealing with Underwood's project are taken from the letters printed in this essay.
[104] *Ibid.*, p. 205.

CHAPTER IX

THE DIAL (CINCINNATI)

It is altogether fitting, since *The Western Messenger*, the first of the transcendental periodicals, had appeared in the Ohio Valley, that one of the last journals devoted to the cause of the New Spirit and its adherents should likewise have been established in the same section of the country. *The Dial*, the magazine referred to, was founded and edited by Moncure Conway in Cincinnati during the year of 1860; and its twelve monthly issues constitute an important episode in the history of the transcendental movement. It may be desirable again in this connection to call attention to the fact that the development of the ideas of the New School in the Middle West was an integral part of the general evolution of the peculiar religious and literary philosophy that has now come to be identified chiefly with New England. The surprising interest in literary activities manifested by the people who followed the course of empire across the Appalachians supplied a ready soil for the seed that Emerson and his fellows were sowing by means of books and lectures.[1] Moreover,

---

[1] In 1814 a public library was opened in Cincinnati, and in 1821 the Apprentices' Library was founded. In 1826 the former contained 1300 "well selected" volumes, while the latter had 1200 (B. Drake and E. D. Mansfield, *Cincinnati in 1826*, Cin., 1827, pp. 46-47). In 1827 the Queen City had nine bookstores, and each of the military posts in the neighboring country had a library and reading room, where "regular files of the best newspapers published in the U. S." were received and read "with care" (Caleb Atwater, *Indians of the Northwest*, Columbus, 1850, pp. 6 and 179). In 1834 Charles Fenno Hoffman was astonished at a "literary soirée" in Cincinnati (*A Winter in the West*, 1835, II, 133). In 1840 the same city had twenty-five publishers of books and periodicals, and the value of their products was estimated at $518,500 (Charles Cist, *Cincinnati in 1841*, Cin., 1841, p. 56). Howells wrote of the hamlets of Northern Ohio as he knew them in his youth: "If our villages were not religious, they were, in a degree which I still think extraordinary, literary. Old and young, they talked about books . . . and any American author who made an effect in the East became promptly known in that small village of the Western Reserve" (*Years of My Youth*, 1916, p. 106). See also R. L. Rusk, *The Literature of the Middle Western Frontier*, 1925, I, 67ff.

the large German population concentrated in centers like Cincinnati and Columbus served to arouse a more or less general interest in the philosophy of intuition that, as far as formal elaboration is concerned, was esteemed to be essentially German in origin. It may be taken for granted that the philosophical interests of J. B. Stallo, for example, were not altogether unusual among the educated Germans of the Middle West.

Consideration is to be given also to the intellectual and spiritual aspirations of numerous individuals, of varying degrees of cultivation, who did not allow the isolation of frontier life to cut them off from contact with the steady march of religious liberalism in America, and who found in the writings of the transcendentalists a confirmation of ideas gleaned from a variety of sources. An apt illustration is supplied by two letters written to Theodore Parker in 1843, by a certain Isaac Lewis, of Harrison County, Ohio.[2] In one of them, dated June 21, Lewis naïvely asks, "Are you acquainted with Cousin's Philosophy?" and then proceeds to explain that it is an attack on the principles of Locke. He further writes:

> I am happy to report that your "Discourses" find even more admirers than I could have anticipated. I have it loaned out now one hundred miles from home.

In the other letter, dated January 22, he informs Parker: "There is no inconsiderable number in this section of the country who sympathize with the progress party in Theology in the East." Continuing, he describes his own connection with the cause. He had read Channing, then W. H. Furness, and, after seeing a notice in *The Liberator*, had subscribed for *The Boston Quarterly Review*, and had obtained a number of patrons for that magazine. He had bought a set of *The Christian Examiner* and the first

[2] MSS. in the library of the Mass. Hist. Soc.

volume of *The Dial*, and "intended to get the rest." His library, "much referred to in disputed matters," included "Emmerson's Essays," and Brownson's *New Views* and *Charles Elwood*. Yet, as he himself wrote, there was no Unitarian society in his section of the state.

To understand the part played by the Cincinnati *Dial* in spreading the views of the New School one must not only recall the fact that there really was such a thing as transcendentalism in the Middle West, but also give consideration to its editor's connection with the movement prior to the establishment of his journal. Moncure Conday, like O. B. Frothingham, belonged to what may be called the last rank of the transcendentalists—a notable rank chiefly because its members became the historians of the movement. It is unfortunate that none of the earlier progressives in the Unitarian church chose to record the various events that marked definite stages in the evolution of the reaction against the philosophy of sense,[3] because Frothingham and his contemporaries really came into direct contact with the New Spirit when it was on the wane —when its prominence in the public eye had yielded to the more practical question of abolition, and its delicate spiritual quality was being rapidly replaced by the rationalism induced by the absorption of the interest of the more intelligent liberals of America in scientific achievement. The career of Conway supplies a case in point.

A scion of a highly respected and influential family of the Old Dominion, Conway studied law for a short time after his graduation from Dickinson College, and in 1850, at the age of eighteen, became a Methodist minister. Oddly enough, "at the bottom" of his decision to enter

---

[3] George Ripley began an essay on "Philosophic Thought in Boston" for *The Memorial History of Boston* (Boston, 1881, IV, cap. III); but his death cut short his work. The essay was completed by George P. Bradford.

the church was the influence of Emerson.[4] But the long, long thoughts of youth, and his native leaning toward a kind of Jeffersonian liberalism made the acceptance of ecclesiastical dogmas irksome to his inquiring spirit. In his perplexing situation he resolved to write to Emerson,[5] whom already he seems to have regarded with all the affection and hero-worship that made the adulation of the "Emersonidae" so disgusting to Lowell and Parker. Under the influence of his idol, reinforced by the personality of Sylvester Judd[6] and the interest manifested by W. H. Furness and other progressive Unitarians, Conway confirmed himself in his rebellion, cultivated the society of the Hicksite Quakers who lived in his community,[7] and finally determined to enter the Divinity School at Harvard.

In 1853 he set out for Cambridge, where his extraordinary mental and social gifts, no doubt coupled with the unusual character of his earlier experiences, and above all, his pronounced antislavery views, made him *persona grata* to the leading spirits in and around Boston. During his first summer vacation, since his family refused to support him in his heresies, he was forced to stay in Massachusetts. Naturally, he established himself in Concord and thus confirmed the friendly relations that had already come to exist between himself and Emerson.[8] Needless to say perhaps, he lost few opportunities of forming contacts with as many of the transcendentalists as he could. He walked with Thoreau;[9] visited Parker, whom he regarded as "the standard-bearer of religious liberty";[10] and even sought out the mother of Margaret Fuller.[11] No better indication

---

[4] *Autobiography, Memories and Experiences of Moncure Daniel Conway,* Boston and New York, 1905, I, 91. This work will hereinafter be cited as *Autobiography.* Conway gives an account of his early contact with Emerson's ideas in the introductory chapter to his *Emerson at Home and Abroad,* Boston, 1882.

[5] Emerson's reply, dated Nov. 17, 1851, is printed in *Autobiography,* I, 109-110.

[6] *Ibid.,* I, 121.
[7] *Ibid.,* I, cap. IX and X.
[8] *Ibid.,* I, cap. XII.
[9] *Ibid.,* I, 141.
[10] *Ibid.,* I, 162.
[11] *Ibid.,* I, 178.

of the close attention that he paid to the casual utterances of Emerson can be found than one that he himself gives in his autobiography.[12] On one occasion when Emerson's son was ill, the father playfully remarked: "What, sonny, your mother says you are not well today. Now what naughty thing have you been doing, for when one is sick something *the devil* is the matter." Conway carefully remembered the expression and used it as the theme for a series of sermons on health, which he later condensed into an article for his *Dial*, on "The Moral Diagnosis of Disease."[13]

After his graduation from the Divinity School he became, in the fall of 1854, the minister of the Unitarian society in Washington, D. C., and served the charge in the capitol, apparently with notable success, until his unequivocal espousal of the abolition cause occasioned his dismissal.[14] In November, 1856, he became the pastor of the First Congregational Church of Cincinnati, where his attitude toward the problem of slavery was more in harmony with that of the influential members of his parish.[15] Of his subsequent career little perhaps needs to be said here. Although Conway later became identified with the spread of rationalism, and, like Frothingham, outgrew the faith of transcendentalism amid the changing fashions of nineteenth-century thought, he never ceased to adore Emerson, or to acknowledge the importance of the rôle played by the New School in his own spiritual progress or that of his age. At the time he edited *The Dial* he described his faith as "the theism evolved from pantheism by the poets"[16]—an expression which might pass current as a definition of transcendentalism.

[12] *Ibid.*, I, 172.
[13] *The Dial*, pp. 603 and 662.
[14] *Autobiography*, I, cap. XV.
[15] *Ibid.*, I, cap. XV.
[16] *Ibid.*, I, 305.

In regard to the establishment of his periodical Conway wrote:

> My theological and philosophical heresies reported in the Ohio journals excited discussion far and near. The papers teemed with controversial letters, and a magazine became inevitable. Its first number appeared in January, 1860, bearing the title, *The Dial: a monthly magazine for literature, philosophy, and religion....*"[17]

This statement, however, had best be taken as only a partial explanation. The fact of the matter seems to be that, like most of the progressives among the Unitarian clergy, he was possessed of the desire to appear before the public both as a writer and as a speaker. Even before he had applied for admission to the Baltimore Methodist Conference, he had written for various Virginia periodicals, and in 1851 had appeared among the contributors to *The Southern Literary Messenger*.[18] While in Cambridge he had frequently sent articles to *Dwight's Journal of Music*.[19]

According to Conway, his *Dial* was "well received, had a large subscription list—the Jews especially interesting themselves—and received good notices from the press throughout the State."[20] Among the press notices was one which moved him "deeply," written by William Dean Howells in *The Ohio State Journal* for February 15, 1860. It included the following words:

---

[17] *Ibid.*, I, 306. A search through several representative Ohio journals of the period indicates that the Cincinnati papers alone gave much consideration to Conway's opinions.

[18] *Ibid.*, I, 91. See *The Southern Literary Messenger*, XVII, 50, a Poesque tale entitled "A Webster Case in Europe." Cf. B. B. Minor, *The Southern Literary Messenger*, New York and Washington, 1905, p. 243.

[19] *Autobiography*, I, 177. Because of the absence of signatures these articles have not been identified.

[20] *Ibid.*, I, 307-308. Conway apparently forgot unfavorable criticism. For example, *The Cincinnati Daily Gazette* for Feb. 11, 1860, observed: "Thus far the Dial has disgraced the name of the respectable, if erratic, periodical which it is a clumsy attempt to revive."

That men should say what they think, outside of Boston, is of course astonishing. That they should say what they think, inside of Cincinnati, rather relieves the marvellousness of the first astonisher. . . . Until now Boston has been the only place in the land where the inalienable right to think what you please has been practised and upheld. . . . It [*The Dial*] numbers among its contributors some of the most distinguished thinkers of New England, and it seeks to bring out all the thinkers of the West. . . . The magazine is two dollars per year,—the editor to be addressed. But let no one who fears plain speech on the most vital subjects subscribe. It is the organ of profound thinkers, merciless logicians, and polished writers.

Howells, whose ambitions to become "Boston-plated" no doubt attracted him toward the new journal, supplied it with four poems,[21] but in later years spoke rather contemptuously of it as "a slight monthly magazine named after *The Dial* of Emerson at Concord, and too carefully studied from it."[22]

Of the more than two hundred articles published in his periodical Conway wrote thirty, besides seventy critical notices of new books.[23] In character his contributions ranged from fiction to essays on abolition and on science. Occasionally he revamped a sermon that had been well received and supplied it to the readers of his magazine.[24] To the student of transcendentalism three of his articles are of particular interest, largely because they reveal the debt which he, and his friends, owed to Theodore Parker. In one of them the writer affirmed: "When our class, the class of 1854, was about to graduate, the majority of us were radicals, and all of us had an admiration for Mr. Parker."[25] Another, entitled "Views of Theodore Parker," summarized, with numerous quotations, the tributes paid the memory of the noted clergyman by C. M. Ellis, Wen-

[21] *The Dial*, pp. 371, 555, and 709. [22] *Years of My Youth*, p. 176.
[23] *Autobiography*, I, 315.
[24] See, for example, *The Dial*, pp. 669 and 762.
[25] *Ibid.*, p. 444.

dell Phillips, C. T. Brooks, W. H. Channing, James Freeman Clarke, Emerson, and others.[26] The third, "The Nemesis of Unitarianism," sketched the history of the Unitarian church and pointed out the danger of its being dominated by the spirit of conservatism. Unitarianism is regarded as merely the "incorporation into a Christian Body of the negations" of Arius, Pelagius, and others; and, as a result, is considered to be in need of an "affirmation." The affirmation suggested is "simply, the entire sufficiency of the Human Spirit to attain the highest truth, and, by a fulfilment of spiritual laws, enjoy the highest communion."[27] Transcendentalism, "the first Catholic Power of American Intellect," is believed to have supplied a most necessary contribution to Unitarian spirituality; and hope is held out in the fact that the opposers of the New Spirit have lost ground, and that "twenty-five" ministers are to be regarded as occupying the ground which Parker alone held a few years before.[28]

Conway wrote to Emerson, asking for an article on Parker, but received a letter, dated June 6, 1860, which reads, in part, as follows:

I have nothing to say of Parker. I know well what a calamity is the loss of his courage and patriotism to the country; but of his mind and genius, few are less accurately informed than I. It is for you and Sanborn and many excellent young men who stood in age and sensibility hearers and judges of all his discourse and action—for you to weigh and report. I have just written to his society, who have asked me to speak with Phillips in the funeral oration, that I will come to hear, not to speak (though I shall not refuse to say a few words in honour). My relations to him are quite accidental and our differences of method and working such as really required and honoured all his catholicism and magnanimity to forgive in me.[29]

[26] *Ibid.*, pp. 616-627.
[27] *Ibid.*, p. 364.
[28] *Ibid.*, pp. 363-364.
[29] *Autobiography*, I, 313.

No better evidence for the assertion that transcendentalism in reality amounted to little more than individualism can be found than this letter of Emerson's. At the same time, another indication is afforded of the "coldness," the "aloofness," that the more active members of the New School found so distasteful in the man at Concord who could write glowing pages on Friendship and yet believe: "Every man alone is sincere. At the entrance of a second person, hypocrisy begins."[30]

The Abbé Miel, a convert from French Catholicism, brought Conway a note from Theodore Parker, and was of course received in Cincinnati with open arms.[31] He supplied *The Dial* with an article entitled "Are the Priesthood Sincere?"[32] The same number of the periodical that contained Miel's essay, that for November, included also a poem by Frances Power Cobbe, who had for years corresponded with Parker, and who later was to edit his works.[33] The September issue had contained lengthy excerpts from a letter of Edouard Desor addressed to Joseph D. Whitney, giving an account of Parker's last days, in which the writer declared: "Had he lived but two months longer I would have secured for him the Secular Doctorship at the Jubilee of the University of Basle."[34]

Like *The Massachusetts Quarterly Review*, the Cincinnati *Dial* manifested a great interest in science. For example, the March number contained an article on "Geology and the Bible," an enthusiastic notice of Darwin's *Origin of Species*, and a letter from Besançon signed "D," discussing a recent astronomical discovery.[35] The celebrated meteorologist, James Espy, who had been a member of Conway's society in Washington, sent his last philosophical essay to the periodical, on "The Nature of

[30] "Friendship," *Essays* (First Series).
[31] *Autobiography*, I, 276.
[32] *The Dial*, p. 701.
[33] *Ibid.*, p. 693.
[34] *Ibid.*, p. 567.
[35] *Ibid.*, pp. 181, 196, and 171.

Moral Accountability."[36]   Drs. F. Frédault and Marx E. Lazarus contributed articles on "Spontaneous Generation," "The Psychology of Opium and Hasheesh," phrenology, and "Ghost-craft."[37]

Lazarus, it may be remembered, had been one of the chief contributors to *The Harbinger* and to *The Spirit of the Age*. For a brief period he seems to have lived at Brook Farm.[38] Although a Jew, born in North Carolina, he was not only an ardent Associationist but an eloquent adherent of the cause of abolition. One of his essays for *The Dial*, entitled "True Principles of Emancipation," Conway often returned to as "a wonderful specimen of individual utopianism."[39] He had lived in Paris for a time, and there had become acquainted with Toussenel, the mystic and naturalist, from whose works he supplied the journal with various translations.[40] He also provided English renderings of selected passages from Benjamin Constant and Balzac.[41] In number and extent the contributions of Lazarus surpassed those of any other writer for the periodical save the editor himself.

In comparison with the great amount of space devoted to translations from the French,[42] the interest in German literature manifested by *The Dial* was little. An address on Schiller by W. H. Furness was printed in the journal,[43] and a sketch from Klinger, along with "a paramyth," "Blossoms and Leaves," by Richter.[44] A version of Goethe's "May Song," made by Joel Benton, and four

---

[36] *Ibid.*, pp. 102 and 157.
[37] *Ibid.*, pp. 471 and 536, 556 and 609, 345, and 281.
[38] See J. T. Codman, *Brook Farm*, Boston, 1894, p. 270.
[39] *Autobiography*, I, 313. *The Dial*, p. 219.
[40] See, for example, *ibid.*, pp. 188 and 248.
[41] *Ibid.*, pp. 293, 354, and 421; and 299, and 372.
[42] The great interest in French translations was probably due to Conway's lack of material other than the renderings made by Lazarus.
[43] *Ibid.*, p. 401.
[44] *Ibid.*, pp. 217 and 187.

brief renderings of poems by Rückert, Gleim, and Schiller, done by C. T. Brooks, also appeared.[45]

In a critical notice of Caroline Dall's treatise on *Woman's Right to Labor*, published at Boston in 1860, Conway observed that "Margaret Fuller's mantle did not pass into heaven with her."[46] Possibly his kind remarks occasioned the receipt of an essay on "The Late Lawsuit: Men and Women Versus Custom and Tradition," which he published in the number for May. In this article Caroline Dall of course paid her respects to Margaret Fuller in glowing terms of praise, boldly stating that from her "flowed forth the first clear, uncompromising, scholarly demand for civil rights for her sex."[47] It may be said here that the inordinate reputation that Margaret Fuller enjoyed among the later "Emersonidae," most of whom never knew her personally, has been largely responsible for the erroneous supposition that she was an influential member of the New School. Indeed, many cogent arguments have been adduced to prove that the lady of the "mountainous me," to borrow Emerson's expression, was not a transcendentalist at all.[48]

C. A. Bartol, although "difficult to classify under any school" was considered by Frothingham to have been a transcendentalist worthy of being remembered in the company of James Freeman Clarke and Samuel Johnson.[49] However, in a review of Bartol's *The Word of the Spirit to the Churches* Conway referred to the work as "a sublime pretense," and went on to say:

The writer shows affectation in every stroke of his pen, and only succeeds in revealing the passionless, bloodless nature of the church to which he adheres, by this effort at making his common-

---

[45] *Ibid.*, pp. 646, 660, 694, and 740.
[46] *Ibid.*, p. 70. [47] *Ibid.*, p. 291.
[48] F. A. Braun, *Margaret Fuller and Goethe*, New York, 1910, pp. 72ff., 146, and 242.
[49] *Transcendentalism in New England*, cap. XIV.

places pass under the image and superscription of Transcendentalism. It doesn't even require a banker to nail such false coin to the counter.[50]

Perhaps the most notable feature of *The Dial* as an organ of liberal theology was the disquisition on "The Christianity of Christ," by O. B. Frothingham, an instalment of which appeared in each number with the exception of those for August, October, and November. Acting upon the belief that "the religion of Jesus is the peculiar form which the religious sentiment took in the soul of Jesus," the writer employed the findings of the various Higher Critics of his day to demonstrate the methods whereby the increments of dogma and tradition had perverted the fundamental beliefs of Christ. The whole can scarcely be said to savor very strongly of transcendentalism; its appeal is intellectual rather than spiritual.

The original poetry that the magazine contained was of a high order. The contributions of Howells have already been mentioned. Frank Sanborn, whose adoration of Emerson most nearly approximated Conway's among the students at Harvard during the period when the Virginian was there, sent on at least two poems: "Walden Woods," and "Walden Water."[51] Since they were unsigned, Myron Benton, the brother of Joel Benton and likewise a contributor to *The Dial*, inferred from their subjects that Thoreau was their author. He wrote to the Concord naturalist to satisfy his curiosity about the matter, and received in reply what is probably the last letter dictated by Thoreau in his final illness.[52] Benton furnished a number of poems for the journal, most notably one entitled "Orchis," which appeared in the August number.[53]

---

[50] *The Dial*, p. 648.
[51] *The Dial*, pp. 101-102.
[52] Cf. "Thoreau's Last Letter," *Troutbeck Leaflets No. 5*, Amenia, N. Y., privately printed, 1925.
[53] *The Dial*, p. 470.

In regard to it Conway wrote the author, on January 9, 1861:

> Mr. Emerson, whose good opinion every poet must value, made very special inquiries as to the author of "Orchis," and afterward when I saw him, it was during the last summer, in a walk through the woods, he repeated a large portion of it which he had committed to memory.[54]

W. W. Fosdick, of Cincinnati, supplied two poems;[55] John A. Dorgan, three;[56] and J. M. Goodwin, at least one.[57] There were other contributors of verse, but their identity cannot be ascertained. Perhaps the fact should be mentioned that *The Dial* also contained a reprint of "Qui Laborat, Orat," by A. H. Clough, whom Conway had met while at Harvard.[58]

To the literary historian at least, the most important verse to appear in the magazine was contributed by Emerson: "The Sacred Dance (a song of the Spinning Dervish, translated from Von Hammer's *Redekunste*)," and twelve quatrains.[59] Occasionally Conway used a selection from Emerson as a "filler,"[60] and in the November and December issues of his journal he reprinted "The Story of West-Indian Emancipation," which Emerson had delivered as an address to the citizens of Concord in 1844.[61] The essay on "Domestic Life" was printed for the first time in *The Dial* for October.[62]

---

[54] "A Troutbeck Letter-Book, 1861-1867," *Troutbeck Leaflets* No. 9, Amenia, N. Y., 1925, p. 7.
[55] *The Dial*, pp. 216 and 295. A sketch of Fosdick's life may be found in W. T. Coggeshall, *The Poets and Poetry of the West*, Columbus, 1860, p. 471.
[56] *The Dial*, pp. 535 and 661.   [57] *Ibid.*, p. 615.
[58] *Ibid.*, p. 156. *Autobiography*, I, cap. XIII.
[59] *The Dial*, p. 37 (Jan.). The quatrains were "Cras, heri, hodie," "Climacteric," "Botanist," "Forester" (*ibid.*, p. 131, Feb.), "Gardener," "Northman," "From Alcuin," "Nature," "Natura in Minimis," "Orator," "Poet," and "Artist" (*ibid.*, p. 195, Mar.). For variations in the titles of these poems see the Emerson bibliography in *The Cambridge History of American Literature*.
[60] See, for example, *The Dial*, p. 279.   [61] *Ibid.*, pp. 649 and 716.
[62] As printed in *The Dial* the essay began: "In proportion to the intelligence of the inquirer, the objects of inquiry are near and familiar. To a student of

Although the journal advertised the writings of Emerson, Parker, Furness, and other transcendentalists,[63] and carried flattering reviews of the works published by various members of the New School during the period,[64] its series of "Catholic Chapters" perhaps best reveals the broad interests of the New School. The first of these chapters was headed "Religion," and contained excerpts from Schiller, Swedenborg,[65] Emerson, Hegel, Charles Emerson, Richter, Coleridge, and others.[66] The second, entitled "Worship," consisted of cullings from the *Desatir* and from Plato.[67] The "Catholic Chapter" for the April issue contained "The Laws of Menu,"[68] while that for the following month was devoted almost entirely to "The Sayings of Confucius."[69] Selections from Saadi and other Orientals appeared in various numbers, along with selected portions from the works of Carlyle, Hare, Sterling, and others.[70] The September number had as its feature chapter twenty-two of Alcott's "Orphic Sayings."[71]

---

realities, the study of fossils, the history of meteors, the genesis of nebulae, is less interesting than the system of life into which he was born, the society of beings whose lineaments resemble his own, and the objects which stick close about him. These usual things, which he can never get out of sight of, most pique the curiosity. Could anybody tell him what the meaning of them is? Can any topic take precedence in a reasonable mind of the topic of Domestic Life?" (*ibid.*, p. 585). At the end of the first suggestion, relative to the establishment of art museums, the essay as it appeared in *The Dial* included these words, which also do not appear in the Centenary Edition of Emerson's works: "In Europe, where the feudal form of society secures the permanence of wealth in certain families, those families in each town buy and preserve these things and throw them open to the public. That is the reason why our countrymen of taste and education desire to go to Europe—to visit the galleries and libraries that are there preserved in a hundred palaces. But in America, where democratic institutions regularly divide every great estate into small portions again after a few years, it is necessary that the public should step into the place of these permanent proprietors, and a lyceum, a public library, a public gallery, should exist in every town and village for the education and inspiration of all the individuals" (*ibid.*, p. 601).

[63] See, for example, *The Dial*, p. 329.
[64] Cf. *ibid.*, for example, pp. 199 and 778.
[65] *The Dial* contained an article on "The Swedenborgian Heretic," in which Conway espoused the cause of a minister of the New Church who had been expelled for his belief in the "non-eternity of Hells" (p. 547).
[66] *Ibid.*, pp. 49-52.
[67] *Ibid.*, pp. 131-134.
[68] *Ibid.*, pp. 252-257.
[69] *Ibid.*, pp. 321-323.
[70] See, for example, *ibid.*, pp. 193 and 385.
[71] *Ibid.*, pp. 575-581.

Of course, Conway borrowed the idea for his "Catholic Chapters" from the Boston *Dial*, which had devoted considerable space to its "Ethnical Scriptures." It is of interest in this connection to recall a conversation which Conway held with Thoreau when Emerson introduced the two men. The naturalist asked what the young Virginian and his fellows were studying at Harvard, and upon being informed, "The Scriptures," immediately questioned, "Which?" Emerson genially remarked, "You will find our Thoreau a sad pagan."[72]

As the editor of *The Dial* himself wrote, his journal is a fair "mirror of the movements of thought" in the Middle West during a period of "extraordinary, generous seeking."[73] But perhaps its chief value to the student of American literature lies in the fact that it reflects also the spirit of the last group of transcendentalists. The names of Emerson, Parker, and Margaret Fuller appear in it like the names of the apostles in a history of the Christian church. Yet many of its pages, such as those devoted to Frothingham's treatise on "The Christianity of Christ," reveal the growth of a critical attitude toward the things of the spirit; and its marked interest in scientific discussion indicates that the time was not far off when a progressive young Unitarian was to be a rationalist rather than a transcendentalist. In spite of its name, the magazine is more nearly like *The Massachusetts Quarterly Review* than the Boston *Dial*; and despite its editor's veneration of Emerson, the spirit of Theodore Parker is most manifest in its contents.

According to Conway, his journal was "slain" by the approaching war, whose premonitory turmoil made impossible further literary and philosophical discussion in Cincinnati.[74] However, in the letter to Benton already quoted, he wrote:

[72] *Autobiography*, I, 140-141.   [73] *Ibid.*, I, 312.   [74] *Loc. cit.*

You have doubtless observed that my plan is to change *The Dial* to a quarterly.... Subscribers are coming in very slowly.... I do wish I could interest the rising thinkers and singers of this generation in the great importance of having a free and bold quarterly which shall be the organ of thought elsewhere suppressed.

But the plans for a quarterly at Cincinnati were never matured, for in the summer of 1862 Conway left that city for Concord, his removal being occasioned by his acceptance of the editorship of a new weekly paper which was to advocate immediate emancipation.[75] In a sense, this new periodical, *The Commonwealth*, as it was called, may be considered a successor to *The Dial*, since it possessed a literary department to which various members of the New School occasionally contributed.

[75] *Ibid.*, I, cap. XXII.

CHAPTER X

THE RADICAL

So far as religion was concerned the earlier transcendentalists had contented themselves for the most part with voicing a protest against the supernaturalism inherited by their era from the days of the Mathers. In his *Divinity School Address* Emerson insisted that revelation was not a phenomenon peculiar to a past age but a vital element of human nature. Content with insinuating this disturbing doctrine into the consciousness of the orthodox, and perhaps fearing the *odium theologicum*, he retired from the scene of controversy and addressed his attention to those who sympathized with his opinions. In regard to theological argument Emerson was adroit. George Ripley succeeded him as the protagonist of the transcendental view of religion, and after an unsuccessful attack upon the dogma of miracles, gave place to Theodore Parker, who attempted to carry the implied principles of the New School to their logical conclusion. Parker's unbounded energy, hampered as it was by ill health and the turmoil of the abolition movement, was probably most responsible for the diffusion of radical religious opinions among the intellectual ranks of America.

But the transcendentalists really did not discard altogether the supernaturalism which they attacked so vehemently. In the final analysis, they merely substituted a subjective supernaturalism for an objective supernaturalism. They transferred the miraculous from the sphere of the concrete and the material to a psychological state. John Winthrop found a Remarkable Providence in the fact that mice gnawed at the Book of Common Prayer but left the Greek Testament and the Psalms untouched. Emerson found a heavenly dispensation in the "untaught sallies of the spirit."[1] In explaining the psychological basis of the doctrines of the New School, C. A. Bartol observed:

> Transcendentalism relies on those ideas in the mind which are laws in the life. Pantheism is said to sink man and nature in God, materialism to sink God and man in nature, and Transcendentalism to sink God and nature in man. But the Transcendentalist, at least, is belied and put in jail by the definition, which is so neat at the expense of truth. He made consciousness, not sense, the ground of truth. . . .[2]

The immediate effect of the psychological approach to religion was rather slight. The orthodox who were aware of the existence of a New School denounced its adherents as fanatics or infidels,[3] while the conservative Unitarians hastened to disclaim any connection with their views and to facilitate their withdrawal from the church.[4] Two years after Emerson's address to the divinity students, Longfellow wrote that there was no more transcendentalism in the theological school at Cambridge, and that "rigid Puseyism" was holding the attention of the prospective clergymen.[5] After Parker was dismissed from the Unitarian conference, at least a portion of the church of Chan-

---

[1] *Nature*, 1836.
[2] *Radical Problems*, Boston, 1872, p. 83. Bartol continued: "The Transcendental school must, however, encounter one criticism. Part of it led into the doctrine of Divine Impersonality. Emerson followed Cousin. The objection to Personality was its supposed limitation" (*ibid.*, p. 85). James Martineau mentioned Emerson's indebtedness to Cousin in a letter addressed to Alexander Ireland, on December 31, 1882: "I well remember addressing some question to him after his first lecture on 'Representative Men,' in 1847, about one of his citations, or statements of opinion, and his reply that, life being too short to allow of seeking knowledge at the fountain-head, he was thankful for such an interpreter of Plato as Victor Cousin, on whom he had depended" (*The Life and Letters of James Martineau*, ed. James Drummond, New York, 1902, II, 313).
[3] See, for example, *The New York Review*, VIII (1841), 509; *The New York Beacon*, I (1846), 88; and *The Southern Quarterly Review*, Charleston, II (1842), 471.
[4] See, for example, G. E. Ellis, *A Half Century of the Unitarian Controversy*, Boston, 1857, pp. 412ff.
[5] Samuel Longfellow, *Life of Henry W. Longfellow*, Boston and New York, 1899, I, 378.

ning settled back, as Coleridge had done, into an increasingly conservative position.[6]

But when the disbanding of the armies at the close of the Civil War left the New England reformers without an immediate project upon which to focus the energy which had previously been absorbed by their opposition to slavery, the leaders of thought, maintaining the Puritan tradition of venting intellectual disquiet in religious argument, promptly returned to the task which Parker had left unfinished at the time of his death. Combining forces with the constantly increasing number of materialists, the transcendentalists renewed their attack upon the conservative element of the Unitarian church. It was the later group of the New School, of course, who were most active in the opposition.

The Radicals, as the leaders in the protest were called, demanded that the surviving relics of Christian supernaturalism, such as the authority of Jesus and the Bible, be discarded by the Unitarian Association, and that the liberal clergy unite in nothing short of a Free Religion which was to embody the spiritual intuition of humanity at large. They desired "freedom, and the broadest assertion of individuality."[7] Their genius was essentially critical; they set forth no new theological principles. In spite of a firm belief in the reality of intuition the transcendentalists among them thought that they were transferring the religious sentiment from a supernatural to a scientific basis.[8]

[6] Cf. I. N. Tarbox, "The Present Condition and Prospects of Unitarianism," *The New Englander*, New Haven, XXVI (1867), 191ff.

[7] G. W. Cooke, *Unitarianism in America*, Boston, 1902, p. 210. Years earlier others had held a similar position—for example, Karl Follen. On September 30, 1836, Catherine Sedgwick wrote to Bryant: "He [Follen] is a thorough democrat too, and of course passes by the theocracy of the Jews and the hierarchy of Christians to the attempt to establish, or rather improve, a religion in accordance with the spirit of our institutions—a religion free and universal . . ." (MS. in the Bryant-Godwin Collection of the New York Public Library).

[8] See, for example, *Autobiography, Memories and Experiences of Moncure Daniel Conway*, Boston and New York, 1905, II, 358.

A fair example of their position may be obtained from the chapter on "Radicalism" in the volume entitled *Radical Problems*, written by C. A. Bartol. After expressing the opinion that their platform was "against any final wording," the author nevertheless proceeded to point out several ideas upon which the Radicals agreed. Their protest, he believed, was directed against the notion that God's word was confined to the Bible, against the authority of any religious leader, and against any "contradiction of science."[9] It may be seen from Bartol's explanation that they were contending for negations and that, after all, they were merely reviving the opinions of Theodore Parker.

The dissatisfaction of the reformers with the conservative attitude of the Unitarian church manifested itself not only in books and lectures, but in a Free Religious Association, whose history will be discussed in the following chapter, and in various Radical Clubs, the most famous of which met at Boston in the home of John T. Sargent, a clergyman who had been ousted from his charge because of his sympathy with the views of Parker. Mrs. Sargent, whose social genius contributed much toward the success of the club, wrote concerning its origin:

The Radical Club may be said to have had its origin, in the spring of the year 1867, in the growing desire of certain ministers and laymen for larger liberty of faith, fellowship, and communion. In this respect it was akin to the Transcendental movement of earlier date. It was designed to meet a demand for the freest investigation of all forms of religious thought and inquiry. . . . Thirty persons were present at its first meeting; and at the closing sessions, in 1880, nearly two hundred were in attendance.[10]

Needless to say, perhaps, practically all of the transcendentalists read papers or took part in the discussions at its

[9] C. A. Bartol, *op. cit.*, pp. 110ff. Cf. in this connection *Freedom and Fellowship in Religion*, edited by a committee of the Free Religious Association, Boston, 1875.
[10] *Sketches and Reminiscences of the Radical Club of Chestnut Street, Boston*, ed. Mrs. John T. Sargent, Boston, 1880, Introduction.

various meetings. Emerson, however, came but rarely, rebelling at the presence of newspaper reporters.[11]

The accounts of the proceedings at the Radical Club as reported in various journals[12] were not the only means whereby the reformers brought their opinions before the magazine readers of the day, for one of their number, Sidney H. Morse, now remembered as a sculptor and a friend of Walt Whitman, had previously established a periodical called *The Radical*, which was the chief organ of the heterodox of New England from September, 1865, to June, 1872. While Morse, who was both editor and proprietor of the journal, and his associate for a time, Joseph B. Marvin, did not belong to the New School themselves, they placed their publication at the disposal of the transcendentalists, who did not neglect the opportunity thus presented.

Although the title page of the monthly bore the legend "Devoted to Religion," the editor wrote in his introductory article:

In devoting our Magazine to Religion, have we drawn any exluding line to bar our entrance into whatever field, so that we cannot well consider all questions of public interest? ... On the contrary, we include all departments of thought and work which have furnished mankind any real worth or significance.[13]

In the number for March, 1867, he further stressed the liberal attitude which the periodical sought to maintain:

The Radical is a medium for the freest expression of thought on all religious and social topics. No subject important enough to be discussed at all in its pages is to be pronounced settled, and arbitrarily closed in deference to the popular sentiment. The alarm-bells of ignorance, bigotry, sentimental piety, wherever

---

[11] T. W. Higginson(?), "The Passing of a Salon," *The Boston Evening Transcript* for June 4, 1904.

[12] See particularly the department "Our Boston Correspondence" in the later numbers of *The National Anti-Slavery Standard*.

[13] *The Radical*, I, 4.

heard, it will allow to swing out their force unheeded. It does not believe that the world is to be upset, nor the providence of nature set on fire, or balked, by the frank expression of any man's or woman's opinion, on even the most delicate subjects; but quite the contrary. . . . The contributors to *The Radical* are responsible each for his or her own productions, but for no others.[14]

A writer for the journal, George Stearns, expressed his approval of the editor's policy in these words:

A capital feature of *The Radical*, and that which, conjoined with its national spirit, commends it to the patronage of all comprehensive thinkers, is its ostensible *devotion to Religion* in a sense quite distinct from that of the organ of any religious sect. It is the fact that without advocating faith and worship according to any projected form, it addresses itself to the work of discussing the merits of all ecclesiastical creeds and ordinances.[15]

However, the attacks on "the faith of the fathers" which the magazine contained were not calculated to make a financial success of the project, for, in spite of the fact that it had subscribers in "nearly every state of the Union,"[16] the journal was forced to suspend publication with the number for July, 1870. In January of the following year it was revived, with a slight change of policy. A variety of topics touching upon contemporary problems was included in each issue, and occasionally a little fiction. As Morse wrote, the intention was "to satisfy the taste as well as stimulate thought." Nevertheless, subscriptions were again insufficient to pay the costs of publication; and to meet the situation efforts were made in 1872 to establish a Radical Publishing Association, which was to be incorporated in Massachusetts with a capital stock of fifty thousand dollars, to be issued in shares of one hundred dollars each.[17] In June, 1872, Morse announced that

[14] *Ibid.*, II, 448.   [15] *Ibid.*, III, 309.
[16] *Ibid.*, VII, 66. One half of the subscribers were in the West or Middle West, according to Morse.
[17] *Ibid.*, X, 160 and 319.

there was little indication that the amount of stock necessary to complete the proposed corporation would be sold, and that since he himself was unable to continue "the experiment" further, the journal would no longer be published.[18]

During the first few years of the existence of the magazine most of the contributions were written by Samuel Johnson, David Wasson, and John Weiss—three staunch followers of the precepts of Theodore Parker.[19] These men practically controlled the journal at the outset, even writing most of the book reviews which appeared in the earlier numbers. Johnson's most significant contribution appears to have been a series of "Discourses Concerning the Foundations of Religious Belief," which he had delivered before the Free Church of Lynn, Massachusetts.[20] In these disquisitions he maintained that "positive certainty" must exist "somehow" in the soul, which was to be considered of "more value than many Bibles and many sciences";[21] and in his assault upon "The Fallacies of Supernaturalism" he insisted that a transcendental intuition alone could "establish the existence of God, the reality of Duty, and the truth of Immortality."[22] "Natural Religion," to his mind, was more adequate to meet the demands of the spiritual nature than "the Bible, the Church, the word of Jesus, or the alleged miracles."[23] Of his numerous other sermons which appeared in later volumes of *The Radical* perhaps two should be mentioned here: "American Religion," and "Free Religion and the Free State." In the former he paid a generous tribute to the

---

[18] *Ibid.*, X, 468.
[19] See the introductory memoir in Samuel Johnson, *Lectures, Essays and Sermons*, ed. Samuel Longfellow, Boston and New York, 1883; and David A. Wasson, *Essays, Religious, Social and Political*, ed. O. B. Frothingham, Boston, 1889, pp. 92ff.
[20] *The Radical*, I, 73, 113, 154, 233, 313, and 401.
[21] *Ibid.*, I, 83.   [22] *Ibid.*, I, 165.   [23] *Ibid.*, I, 233.

"speculative boldness" of the German mind in the West, and observed that the old faith of New England was "but a rocky ledge of the land of promise."[24] In the latter he stressed the importance of the intellectual ferment which the Civil War had brought in its aftermath.[25]

Wasson's most noteworthy literary efforts to appear in the magazine were numerous poems, and an occasional discussion of some aspect of religious liberalism.[26] Weiss not only wrote most of the reviews for the earlier issues of *The Radical*, but supplied several poems of merit, and numerous sermons, ranging from matters of politics to the more esoteric topics of interest to dissenters. An idea of the attitude toward Christ prevailing among the Radicals may be obtained from his discourse on "The Essential Jesus."[27] His Divinity School address delivered at Cambridge in 1869, with the title "The Task of Religion," is of interest in that he boldly urged his hearers to "appropriate the subsidies of science," and even asserted that there was a unity of science and religion.[28] In view of the fate that transcendentalism was to suffer at the hands of the followers of the scientific method, the unquestioning attitude of Weiss and his fellows is all the more striking. Dominated in their speculative thought by a firm conviction of the reality of intuition, they seem never to have questioned the tenableness of their own position in the light of science.

In addition to Johnson, Wasson, and Weiss, the names of Moncure Conway, C. K. Whipple, and C. A. Bartol should be mentioned among the more frequent contributors to the periodical. At first Conway sent numerous letters from England, giving an account of religious de-

[24] *Ibid.*, II, 257.
[25] *Ibid.*, VI, 282ff. Cf. in this connection the introductory chapter to F. L. Pattee, *A History of American Literature Since 1870*, New York, 1917.
[26] *The Radical*, I, 63, 177, 330; II, 467; IV, 261; V, 471; and VII, 1, for example. [27] *Ibid.*, III, 459. [28] *Ibid.*, VI, 177.

velopments abroad, and later he supplied a number of addresses.[29] Whipple, a prominent abolitionist who owed his religious beliefs to the preaching of Parker,[30] furnished several essays on subjects which might have been expected to interest a man who had passed from the most bigoted type of Calvinism to the emancipated faith of the Parkerites. Bartol allowed several of his sermons to appear in the journal, one of them being an address to the divinity students in Harvard.[31]

Samuel Longfellow also provided a number of pulpit discourses for the magazine. In his treatment of "Some Radical Doctrines," he frankly stated: "Our theology bases itself upon faith in man,"[32] a principle which was also at the bottom of an elaborate treatise which he wrote on "The Unity and Universality of the Religious Idea."[33] His treatment of the subject of "Theism" is an unusually thoughtful manifesto of the transcendental view of the Deity. God, he wrote, is "not a deduction of the understanding, but a conviction of the reason."[34]

T. W. Higginson did not appear so frequently among the contributors to *The Radical* as the other transcendentalists of the later group.[35] Of particular interest, however, is his brief article contending that the dissenters in New England during Colonial times had occupied a position similar to that of the Radicals of his own day. He made a transcript of the Covenant of the first church organized at Salem, in 1629, and asserted that "but for a few phrases" he could subscribe to every word of this "original Declaration of Independence."[36] Another writer

---

[29] For example, see *ibid.*, I, 110, 146, 256, 291, 426, 486; V, 22; and VIII, 46 and 233.
[30] Charles K. Whipple, *A Chapter of Theological and Religious Experience*, Boston, 1858, p. 34.
[31] *The Radical*, III, 65.
[32] *Ibid.*, II, 516.
[33] *Ibid.*, III, 433.
[34] *Ibid.*, X, 180.
[35] For examples of his work see *ibid.*, II, 283; III, 283; V, 385; and VIII, 1.
[36] *Ibid.*, III, 484-485.

for the journal, J. S. Patterson, whose opinion that the New England fathers were responsible for the supernaturalism of the orthodox had occasioned Higginson's article, promptly made the obvious rejoinder that no true liberalism could come from a society which persecuted High Churchmen, Roman Catholics, Anabaptists, and Quakers.[37]

O. B. Frothingham, with his customary ardor, supplied numerous contributions, most of which dealt with such topics as "The Radical's Attitude towards the Bible," "The Historical Position of Jesus," and "The Religion of Humanity."[38]

Although the second, or later, group of transcendentalists wrote most frequently for the journal, particularly during its earlier years, they were generously aided by several important Unitarians who likewise felt that the last vestiges of supernaturalism should be eradicated from the doctrines of their church. Among these were Robert Collyer, Daniel Bowen, J. V. Blake, J. W. Chadwick, F. E. Abbott, F. M. Holland, W. J. Potter, J. T. Sargent, and C. D. B. Mills. All of these men were, of course, imbued with the spirit of Theodore Parker.[39]

Various other writers whose names have been mentioned in connection with the earlier periodicals of the transcendentalists contributed to *The Radical*. For example, Henry James, Sr., wrote for the magazine several letters exhibiting his customary argumentative disposition.[40] Wendell Phillips supplied a brief political article,[41] and W. H. Furness, one of his sermons.[42] Myron Benton furnished several poems and reviews,[43] and Elizabeth Pea-

---

[37] *Ibid.*, III, 636.
[38] *Ibid.*, I, 449; IV, 81; X, 241, 321 and 401.
[39] Cf., for example, F. M. Holland, "How I Turned 'Parkerite,'" *ibid.*, I, 143.
[40] *Ibid.*, I, 66, 97; and II, 84.
[41] *Ibid.*, I, 295.   [42] *Ibid.*, I, 126.
[43] For example, *ibid.*, I, 96, 205; II, 100; and VIII, 181.

body,[44] F. B. Sanborn, and Mrs. C. H. Dall contributed material of various kinds, none of which, however, claims special mention. S. D. Robbins was represented by one poem.[45]

James Freeman Clarke sent on a couple of letters which took issue with Samuel Johnson on his attempt to minimize the significance of Jesus and the Bible to the Christian church. In the first he stated that he himself had always wished to see a periodical devoted to the discussion of important subjects of religious controversy and had once proposed such a publication, to be called *The Arena*.[46] In the course of his remarks concerning the extreme position of the dissenters he observed:

> The radical certainly considers Christ and the Bible as a source of truth—only he does not go to them so much as to others. He goes to science; he goes to the Vedas (when he can find them); he goes to Emerson and Thoreau; he goes to Theodore Parker, and Miss Cobbe.[47]

Johnson, in his reply to Clarke, admitted that his opponent was "at heart" a radical like himself, but went on to declare with emphasis that "the soul" alone was to be regarded as the authority in matters of religion.[48] Clarke again took him to task for his opinion, so subversive of all church organization, and argued that he had gone far beyond the mere opposition to the letter of the Word. If religion is to be "all soul," Clarke contended, then Brahminism is an example of it—a faith which, "ascending the highest spiritual elevation in its flight to God, resolutely trampled on the rights of men."[49] This attempt to demonstrate the practical effect of unmitigated individualism in religion, despite the fact that it came from one of the

[44] *Ibid.*, II, 191, 745; III, 28; and VI, 316.
[45] *Ibid.*, VIII, 110.
[46] *The Radical*, I, 148.
[47] *Ibid.*, I, 150.
[48] *Ibid.*, I, 218-226.
[49] *Ibid.*, I, 347.

transcendentalists, did not give Johnson pause in reiterating his views.[50] The result of the controversy was that Clarke found himself called a "supernaturalist" who could never be "scientifically a radical."[51]

No member of the New School was held in greater regard by the writers for the journal than Theodore Parker. Parts of his works were occasionally reproduced in the magazine, and a number of his letters to Higginson were printed for the first time.[52] A poem in his honor, written by Frances P. Cobbe, appeared,[53] as well as several discussions of various aspects of his life and work.[54]

Emerson allowed Morse to reprint his *Divinity School Address*, which appeared in *The Radical* for October, 1865.[55] Referring to it later, the editor wrote:

> Emerson made little ado in assaulting the outer works, but entered quietly within the gates of the city, and built his temple without noise of hammer.... His Address remains as fresh today as it was thirty years ago. It covers the entire ground of all present controversies.[56]

When Emerson's *May-Day and Other Pieces* was published, Wasson reviewed the volume in flattering terms, asserting that in places the verse was more "aboriginal" than the products of Walt Whitman.[57] His introduction for an edition of Plutarch's *Morals* was also praised, by Higginson.[58] A selection from *English Traits* dealing with "The Religion of England" was reprinted, as well as several of his poems.[59] "Fillers" from his various lectures and essays occasionally appeared in the journal.

---

[50] *Ibid.*, II, 116-123.
[51] John Weiss, "The Policy of the American Unitarian Association," *ibid.*, IV, 45.
[52] *Ibid.*, VIII, 244-248. [53] *Ibid.*, VII, 127.
[54] See, in particular, *ibid.*, VI, 89; and VIII, 428.
[55] *Ibid.*, I, 34-48. [56] *Ibid.*, II, 749.
[57] *Ibid.*, II, 760. [58] *Ibid.*, VIII, 104.
[59] *Ibid.*, II, 230-233; II, 621 ("Character"); III, 217 ("Sursum Corda"); and IX, 52 ("Fame").

Of particular interest is an article on "A Portrait of R. W. Emerson, By David Scott," from the pen of Mrs. E. D. Cheney, containing passages from the painter's journal which record his reactions to his subject.[60] In an editorial note the following reference to Emerson is to be found:

> "We cannot afford to spare Jesus," Mr. Emerson is quoted as saying. This is construed into a mild rebuke of certain younger men whose zeal, perhaps, outruns their wisdom. But with the next breath we hear the same voice melodiously singing of the "sufficiency of the moral sentiment." Put the two texts together, and the meaning is plain enough.[61]

Whether Emerson wholly approved of the attitude of the "younger men," it is impossible to say. However, he may have implied a caution in his remarks on "Religion" made to the Radical Club in May, 1867: "I think we should not assail Christianity or Judaism or Buddhism, but frankly thank each for every brave and just sentence or history that is furnished us."[62]

The Radical contained one disparaging reference to the "Emersonidae." In one of his letters James Freeman Clarke observed: "When Mr. Emerson says, 'The soul knows no persons,' he seems to contradict all experience; but his devout scholar does not criticize or question this saying. If Paul had said it, his first thought, perhaps, would be to show its error."[63]

No one helped more in giving *The Radical* a lofty character than Alcott. In his later years, it seems, his ideas commanded a greater respect among the transcendentalists and their friends. Theodore Parker's reaction to the Platonist is well shown in the following words of George F. Hoar:

---

[60] *Ibid.*, VII, 22-27. [61] *Ibid.*, VI, 157.
[62] Mrs. J. T. Sargent, *op. cit.*, p. 6. In his discourse Emerson spoke of Christ as "a saint of Nazareth," and referred to a "religion which does not degrade," whose adherents would not "wonder that there was a Christ, but that there were not a thousand." [63] *The Radical*, I, 150.

Emerson told me once: "I got together some people . . . to meet Alcott and to hear him converse. I wanted them to know what a rare fellow he was. But we did not get along very well. Poor Alcott had a hard time. Theodore Parker came all stuck full of knives. He wound himself around Alcott like an anaconda; you could hear poor Alcott's bones crunch."[64]

Convers Francis, in an account of a meeting of the Transcendental Club, expressed his disapproval of Alcott's views in these terms:

You did not attend our meeting on Wednesday at George Ripley's, for which we (especially I) were sorry. The talk was animated, and on the whole the meeting was interesting and edifying. We conversed about the position and character of Jesus in the world's history—whether we ought to call him *Saviour* or not;—and towards the close the question about man's struggle with sin came up. Alcott sang the same monotone which he always sings—absolutely ignoring everything but his own view, but "musical as is Apollo's lute." How divinely he sometimes expresses himself; but the more I hear him, the wider I think my difference from him. He and Emerson denied the fact of any such thing as a struggle, or combat with sin, in the phenomena of human consciousness. I cannot understand such an opinion except from their subjective peculiarities.[65]

As has been seen, comparatively little of Alcott's work had appeared in the earlier periodicals of the transcendentalists. Accordingly, Morse's journal in giving considerable space to his thoughts may indicate that the earlier opposition to his ethereal utterances had given place to at least a sympathetic effort to understand what he said. Three of the idealist's poems appeared in the magazine,[66] a selection from his *Conversations on the Gospels*,[67] and several of his short critiques of various philosophers and writers, such as were later included in his book entitled

---

[64] George F. Hoar, *Autobiography of Seventy Years*, New York, 1903, I, 74.
[65] Francis to Parker, May 24, 1839, MS. in the library of the Mass. Hist. Soc.
[66] *The Radical*, I, 303 ("The Patriot"); I, 414 ("The Chase"); and II, 59 ("Misrule"). [67] *Ibid.*, IV, 223-231.

Concord Days.[68] Twenty of his Orphics, with the new name "Tablets," were printed,[69] and the volume bearing the same name was reviewed with sympathy by John Weiss.[70] Stenographic reports of his "conversations" on "Woman," "Plato," and "Personal Theism" were included in the material which Morse used for his journal,[71] as well as various notes concerning his activities as a lecturer, and his remarks made at the meetings of the Radical Club.[72]

Of all the contributions of Alcott perhaps the most interesting are the "conversations," not because they offer new material on the topics which they were intended to discuss, but because they reveal the serene manner in which he disentangled himself from the logic of his inquisitors.[73]

Other than the transcendentalists the only writer for *The Radical* whose work is likely to interest the student of American literature was Edward Rowland Sill. An early volume of the periodical contained a reprint of his verses entitled "The Future," as well as a short critique of the book from which they were taken, *The Hermitage and Other Poems*.[74] Weiss, the reviewer, mentioned the fact that the author had forsaken his studies in the Divinity School at Harvard and expressed the opinion that his "singing robe was more convenient than a surplice." One might be tempted to suppose that this bit of encouragement in a time of doubt was responsible for the eight poems which Sill contributed to later numbers of the magazine,[75] were it not that one of them, addressed "To *The*

---

[68] *Ibid.*, III, 105 ("Wendell Phillips"); III, 495 ("Plutarch"); III, 571 ("Montaigne"); IV, 133 ("Plotinus"); IV, 294 ("Coleridge"); IV, 347 ("Berkeley"); V, 44 ("Boehme"); and VI, 487 ("Hermes Trismegistus").
[69] *Ibid.*, I, 328; II, 177; and III, 374.
[70] *Ibid.*, IV, 479. [71] *Ibid.*, V, 89; V, 177; and VI, 22.
[72] For example, *ibid.*, I, 351; V, 67; and VIII, 286.
[73] See, for example, *ibid.*, V, 195ff. [74] *Ibid.*, III, 292 and 512.
[75] *Ibid.*, VI, 113 ("Dare You?"); VI, 361 ("In Reply"); VII, 456 ("The Secret"); VIII, 57 ("The New Year"); VIII, 152 ("To *The Radical*"); IX,

Radical" upon the occasion of its renewed publication, hailed the journal as "Our first free voice mid servile tongues and secret sneers and bigot wrongs." Perhaps the poet entertained an opinion of the religious views of the dissenters akin to his high regard of Emerson.[76]

An unkind fate prevented the magazine from containing verse from the pen of a more notable poet, for according to a letter from Richard J. Hinton, Walt Whitman thought of sending *The Radical* a contribution.[77] Morse's journal, however, contained a reprint of "Thick-Sprinkled Bunting," and a noteworthy criticism of *Drum Taps*, written by Myron Benton, who also reviewed Burroughs's *Notes on Walt Whitman as Poet and Person*.[78] But the attention given by the Radicals to the Good Gray Poet is best indicated by the fact that their organ first published Mrs. Anne Gilchrist's article, "A Woman's Estimate of Walt Whitman."[79]

The interest of the reformers in the emancipation of women from their traditional place in society grew apace as new standards were being established during the period following the Civil War. A *Woman's Journal* was founded, with Julia Ward Howe, Lucy Stone, Garrison, and Higginson among the editors.[80] That *The Radical* should have devoted itself to the advocacy of equal rights for the sexes was only natural, in view of the liberal attitude of the transcendentalists, and the large number of female contributors whose products appeared in its pages. Alcott's "conversation" on "Woman" has already been

---

19 ("A Foolish Wish"); IX, 128 ("A Drifting Soul"); and IX, 265 ("Tranquillity").

[76] Sill called Emerson "a perfect old telegraph line from the Infinite"—worth "the whole nursery" of old-fashioned poets (Wm. B. Parker, *Edward Rowland Sill, His Life and Work*, Boston and New York, 1915, pp. 109-110).

[77] *The Radical*, III, 486-487. [78] *Ibid.*, I, 311, and III, 189.

[79] *Ibid.*, VII, 345. This is reprinted in Herbert Gilchrist, *Anne Gilchrist: Her Life and Writings*, London, 1887; and *In Re Walt Whitman*, ed. Traubel, Bucke and Harned, Philadelphia, 1893.

[80] See a notice in *The Radical*, VII, 157.

mentioned. Similar to his ideas were those of Frothingham, expressed in an article dealing with "Woman in Society," and those of J. S. Patterson, who wrote on "Woman and Science."[81] John Weiss made an eloquent plea for "Woman's Suffrage," and various ladies, such as Eliza Archard and Elizabeth Stanton, added their literary efforts to the cause.[82]

In connection with this subject, Margaret Fuller's activities in behalf of her sex received whole-hearted commendation. Examples may be found in an address by Anna C. Brackett, and an article by Mary R. Whittlesey, as well as in a couple of poems honoring the memory of the Countess Ossoli.[83] The absurd nature of much of this material is well shown in a review of her works written by Morse, who declared: "Her farewell address to the young ladies of her private school belongs as much to standard work as one of Cicero's orations."[84]

Much of the literary criticism in the journal, however, was worthy of the intelligence which characterized the magazine in general. Various volumes by the better known American authors,[85] such as Thoreau and Whittier, were reviewed, in addition to books dealing with the problems confronting religious nonconformists. Occasionally a critique was expanded into a full-length essay. Of this type were, most notably, a discussion of Swinburne's *Laus Veneris*, by Tom Davidson; a treatise on Blake, by W. A. Cram; another on Milton, by B. W. Ball; an essay on "Jefferson's Rip Van Winkle," by Samuel Johnson; and an extended treatment of Browning's *Sordello*, by Mrs. C. H. Dall.[86]

German literature, especially poetry, was well rep-

---

[81] *Ibid.*, II, 598; and VII, 169 and 287.
[82] *Ibid.*, V, 445; II, 715; and III, 18.   [83] *Ibid.*, IX, 354; VI, 1, 21, and 320.
[84] *Ibid.*, VII, 164.
[85] For example, *ibid.*, I, 32, and 397; II, 512; and VIII, 79.
[86] *Ibid.*, III, 316, 378, 718; VI, 133; and X, 289, 372 and 445.

arouse an appreciation for the religious instinct of all races and creeds, their interest in the literature of the East seems somewhat forced. Their opposition to the orthodoxy of America, particularly among the later group, led to excess when they sought to find a substitute for what they regarded as the bulwark of supernaturalism; namely, the Bible. Nowhere is that excess better illustrated than in *The Radical*.

In one of his lectures on "Transcendentalism" Joseph Cook maintained that the followers of Theodore Parker had not been wholly consistent with the principles for which the earlier transcendentalists had stood. "Rationalistic Transcendentalism," he contended, "is not Transcendentalism, but, in the last analysis, Individualism."[98] If one considers the problem in its religious aspect, and is willing to accept the paradox presented in the expression "rationalistic Transcendentalism," there can be little doubt that the faith of the "soul" which Johnson and his fellows believed in, like the genuine Puritanism of early New England, resolved itself into a reassertion of the ageless notion of the direct relation existing between God and the individual. Whether the later transcendentalists differed from the earlier ones in this respect is another question.

As a magazine of religion *The Radical* is most important in that it reveals the fact that the later members of the New School could not remain content merely with enjoying their own belief in the efficacy of intuition, but, following the example of Theodore Parker, undertook to destroy the Fundamentalism of their day. Its contents, in essence largely critical, offer the strange anomaly of a potential mysticism combined with an active spirit of reform.

[98] *Boston Monday Lectures*, Boston, 1878, p. 40.

Chapter XI
THE INDEX

Before coming to a recital of the chief facts relating to the establishment of *The Index*, in many respects a fellow journal of *The Radical*, it seems desirable to present a brief account of the founding of the Free Religious Association of America, an organization whose connections with the later history of transcendentalism appear to be unusually important.

As has been indicated from time to time, the members of the New School were all aroused by the prospect of a world religion which should eschew the paltry parochialism of sects and creeds, and base itself upon a fundamental religious instinct. One after the other—Emerson, Ripley, Dwight, Cranch, and others—had found even the limitations imposed by Unitarianism irksome in the extreme. Thoreau, perhaps as little a transcendentalist as any who bear the name, had found intellectual comfort at least in the religion of the Orient; Convers Francis had written to Parker of the glorious idea of a catholic bible, to consist of cullings from the various sacred literatures known to man; W. H. Channing had forsaken all creeds to embrace the larger faith of "Christian Socialism." With the widespread discussion of comparative religion aroused by the ethnological investigations of the nineteenth century, the catholicity of spiritual interest that had so early marked the transcendental movement in America received a stimulus of a very effective character. The selections from various "Ethnical Scriptures" that had appeared in the journals controlled by the members of the New School were merely precursors of such works as Conway's *Sacred Anthology* (London, 1874), and the volumes on India, China, and Persia published by Samuel Johnson, at Boston, in 1872 and afterward, under the title of *Oriental Religions and Their Relation to Universal Religion*. And when an association was finally projected to provide a means of coöperation among the Americans "who were longing for a generous communion in religion with no fetters of church or creed or nation,"[1] the transcendentalists were zealous in furthering its cause.

In the spring of 1865 the Unitarians called a convention in New York City to which many liberals outside the church were invited. A contest between the progressive and conservative elements ensued, out of which came "a closer denominational organization of the Unitarian societies than had ever before existed." During the next year, at a meeting of the newly organized National Conference, held at Syracuse, a more systematic attempt to gain wider liberty within Unitarian ranks was again emphatically defeated. A few days after the sessions of this conference, several younger men interested in "a spiritual Anti-Slavery Society" met at the home of C. A. Bartol. They were Samuel Johnson, John Weiss, Sidney Morse, George A. Thayer, Francis Abbot, Henry W. Brown, Edward C. Towne, and Wm. J. Potter, most of whom, as may be remembered, were contributors to *The Radical*. Although some of these men were not willing to join a new association, they arranged plans for further gatherings at the home of Bartol, called in O. B. Frothingham and others to consult with them, and finally made plans for a public meeting, to be held at Horticultural Hall in Boston, on May 30, 1867.[2]

At this meeting were to be seen the leaders of dissent and reform. O. B. Frothingham, as chairman, made an enthusiastic speech, as did also E. C. Towne, Henry

[1] *Reminiscences of Ednah Dow Cheney*, Boston, 1902, p. 147.
[2] W. J. Potter, *The Free Religious Association, Its Twenty-Five Years and Their Meaning*, Boston, 1892.

Blanchard, Lucretia Mott, Robert Dale Owen, John Weiss, Oliver Johnson, Francis Abbot, D. A. Wasson, T. W. Higginson, and Emerson. Incidental to the question of organization remarks were added by Alcott, F. B. Sanborn, Mrs. C. H. Dall, and others.[3] Out of the enthusiasm and oratorical display of this assembly there came the Free Religious Association, whose purpose has already been suggested. The primary idea, to repeat, was to provide for a non-sectarian religion to which any intelligent person could subscribe despite conditions of race and birth. The new movement was so shaped that there was no secession from Unitarianism or any other ecclesiastical body, although a large number of those present at the initial meeting were, or had been, connected with the Twenty-eighth Congregational Society of Boston, Parker's old church.[4]

Emerson, whose name was the first on the list of members, and who acted as one of the vice-presidents of the association for years, expressed at least a significant idea back of the project in his speech delivered at the second annual meeting of the organization:

> I object, of course, to the claim of miraculous dispensation,—certainly not to the doctrine of Christianity . . . . I submit that, in sound frame of mind, we read or remember the religious sayings and oracles of other men, whether Jew or Indian, or Greek or Persian, only for friendship, only for joy in the social identity which they open to us, and that these words would have no weight with us if we had not the same conviction already. I find something stingy in the unwilling and disparaging admission of these foreign opinions,—opinions from all parts of the world—by our

---

[3] *Report of Addresses at a Meeting Held in Boston, May 30, 1867, to consider the conditions, wants, and prospects of Free Religion in America*, Boston, 1867. Emerson's speech is reproduced in the volume of his works entitled *Miscellanies*.

[4] W. J. Potter, *op. cit.*, and *The Index* for Jan. 1, 1870. Cf. also O. B. Frothingham, *Recollections and Impressions 1822-1890*, New York and London, 1891, cap. IX.

churchmen, as if only to enhance by their dimness the superior light of Christianity.[5]

Alcott, later, suggested that in the Free Religion God should not be named at all, and went on to say:

If you have had Jesus, have also Mohammed, have also Zoroaster, have also Plato, and have the rest of the great leaders of the world, and know what thought has done and what civilization has done throughout the world.[6]

At the first annual meeting of the association he revealed to his auditors a belief which many others at that time, and later, also held. After advocating the use of music and journalism in spreading their views, Alcott continued:

A friend said to me today: "Mr. Emerson! O, Yes, a lovely man, but what has he done?" *Who brought us here?* Who is the father, or, if not the father, the cousin, at least, of the thought that brought us here? You know who, so far as any one person is concerned. This meeting is transcendentalism. This is the fruit of forty years of earnest, private, self-respecting modest thought. . . . So fine, so sublime a religion as ours, older than Christ, old as the God-head, old as the soul, eternal as the heavens, solid as the rock, *is and only is;* nothing else is but that; and it is in us, and is us; and nothing is our real selves but that in the breast.[7]

Orestes Brownson, fulminating from *The Catholic World*, also saw the shaping influence of Emerson's maxim, "Obey Thyself," in the religion of the association, but characterized its adherents in no uncertain terms:

This Free Religious Association appears to be composed of men and women who, some thirty years ago, were, or would have been,

[5] *Proceedings at the Second Annual Meeting of the Free Religious Association*, Boston, 1869, pp. 43-44. This speech also is reproduced in the volume entitled *Miscellanies*.
[6] *Proceedings at the Fifth Annual Meeting of the Free Religious Association*, Boston, 1872, pp. 44-45.
[7] *Proceedings at the First Annual Meeting of the Free Religious Association*, Boston, 1868, pp. 77-78.

called *come-outers* in Boston and its vicinity, but who are now generally called radicals, a name which they seem quite willing to accept. They are universal agitators, and see or imagine grievances everywhere, and make it a point wherever they see or can invent a grievance, to hit it; at least, to strike at it. They were conspicuous in the late abolition movement, are strenuous advocates for negro equality—or, rather, negro superiority—stanch women's rights men, in a word, reformers in general. They claim to have a pure and universal religion; and though some of them are downright atheists, they profess to be more Christian than Christianity itself, and their aim would seem to be to get rid of all special religion, so as to have only religion in general.[8]

The usual caustic quality of Brownson's remarks about his erstwhile associates and friends is here given a further irritating power by the admixture of more than a modicum of truth.

Keeping in mind the brief account of the origin of the Free Religious Association here presented, one may perhaps understand more fully the nature of the relations existing between the transcendental movement and a journal which, on the surface, may well appear to have little in common with the principles of the New School. The periodical under consideration, *The Index*, was a weekly paper which weathered the storms of American journalism from January 1, 1870, to December 30, 1886.

Its founder, Francis Ellingwood Abbot, already mentioned as one of the prime movers of the Free Association, was a Unitarian minister whose radical views and dismal experiences in connection with his church at Dover, New Hampshire, had led him to resolve never again to connect himself with any "Christian Society." But the ineluctable urge to preach and propagandize, usually characteristic of a man with strong opinions, soon led him to try once more his oratory and logic upon the church-going public. To be far away from the scene of his late troubles, Abbot, in

[8] *The Catholic World*, X (1869), 195.

September, 1869, considered an offer from the Toledo Unitarian Society, delivered there a series of lectures setting forth the contrast between Christianity and Free Religion, and prevailed upon that church to change its name to that of an "Independent" society, and to make him its pastor.[9]

Prominent among his parishioners in Toledo was the so-called humorist, David R. Locke, better known, during Civil War times at any rate, as Petroleum V. Nasby. It was Locke who first suggested a paper to present to the public such views as Abbot held, and, together with a certain Albert E. Macomber, he offered to be responsible for all the expenses of such a journal during one year, to the amount of three thousand dollars—provided that Abbot would undertake the task of editing it for that period, the understanding being that the three men should be joint and equal proprietors.[10]

The rather unexpected success of the project from the start, due in part, no doubt, to the valuable experiences of Locke as editor and owner of the Toledo *Blade*, occasioned the renewal of the initial arrangements for a second year. But plans were immediately made for expansion, and to this end an Index Association was legally incorporated in April, 1871, by E. P. Bassett, C. Cone, P. H. Bateson, F. E. Abbot, and H. E. Howe—all of Toledo.[11] This organization, using "modern" business methods, proceeded to sell shares of stock to the amount of one hundred thousand dollars. When the first half of this amount was subscribed, on October 26, 1871, the Index Association, of which T. W. Higginson was president for a time, assumed

---

[9] *The Springfield Republican* for Sept. 4, 1869; and the Boston *Commonwealth* for Sept. 11, 1869. Cf. also *The Dictionary of American Biography*. The lectures delivered by Abbot were printed in the early numbers of *The Index*.

[10] F. E. Abbot, *The Inside History of the Index Association, a report on the recent "Index Troubles" made to the stockholders of the Index Association at their second annual meeting in Toledo, Ohio, June 7, 1873*, Cambridge, 1873, p. 1.

[11] *Ibid.*, p. 2.

publication, and continued to be responsible for the paper until July 1, 1880, when it became the property of the Free Religious Association, not by purchase, but by a "purely voluntary and gratuitous donation." According to Abbot, the journal cost the stockholders for the ten and a half years over forty thousand dollars.[12] *The Index* continued to be published by the Free Religious Association through an incorporated board of trustees until January, 1887, when its place was taken by *The Open Court*, despite the charge of its first editor that such a transfer was in direct violation of the principles of the agreement under which the paper had become the property of the Free Religious Association.[13]

Of the patronage of the periodical little can be said. On June 10, 1871, the total number of paying subscribers was 1,574; and on March 1, 1873, the number had increased to 3,817, in spite of a change in its price from two to three dollars per annum.[14] A notice to the readers printed in the issue for November 26, 1870, stated that seventy-seven Unitarian clergymen were on the mailing list. Efforts were continually being made to increase the number of subscribers, the works of Emerson, Alcott, Parker, Thoreau, and John Weiss being offered as premiums. An announcement on the back of the numbers printed early in 1873 stated:

The Index begins its fourth volume under the most flattering auspices. Steadily working for the religious emancipation and noblest culture of humanity at large, and more immediately, of the American people, it has received from the liberal public a most generous support.

During the year 1872 Abbot had ardently fought a proposed amendment of the constitution of the United

---

[12] See Abbot's final communication to *The Index*, published in its last issue (XVIII, 324).   [13] *Loc. cit.*
[14] F. E. Abbot, *The Inside History of the Index Association*, pp. 2 and 41.

States which would declare Christ the ruler and the Bible the "control" of the nation's life. He used his paper as a means of organizing local resistant groups, and in 1876 founded a National Liberal League, of which he was the first president, and Robert Ingersoll an influential member.[15] In 1877 *The Index* became the official organ of the league, a fact which must have enlarged its subscription list materially, since the periodical supplied a ready means of focusing the widespread hostility to the amendment upon active means of opposition. While Abbot's efforts as a propagandist seem to have been successful in promoting the sale of the paper, the better type of patrons, such as the transcendentalists, became disgusted. Samuel Johnson, for example, wrote to his friend Samuel Longfellow, on June 29, 1879, complaining of the drift of "American radicalism into organization, reliance on numbers, utilities, outward forces, experience included, as contrasted with personal, interior, ideal values."[16]

But the very fact that Abbot was able to continue publishing his paper for so many years, despite the obviously limited scope of its appeal, attests to the success of his policy. At the time of the transfer to the Free Religious Association the value of the donation was reckoned at slightly more than four thousand dollars.[17] Although the subscription list was larger at the time the paper ceased to appear than it had been in 1880, *The Index* during its last few years was by no means self-supporting.

The prospectus of the journal, as it appeared in the first number, stated that the periodical would be devoted to "the cause of Free Religion," which was to be advocated with all the "moral earnestness" possible. Further re-

---

[15] "The Liberal League movement, as a definite, organized endeavor to accomplish the total separation of Church and State in this country, had its beginning in *The Index* . . . (*Equal Rights in Religion*, Boston, 1876, p. 7).

[16] Samuel Johnson, *Lectures, Essays, and Sermons*, with a memoir by Samuel Longfellow, Boston, 1883, p. 127.   [17] *The Index*, XVIII, 325.

marks concerning its character were included in the following:

> Without limiting itself to any of the great reformatory movements of the time, it proposes to work for them all in the most efficient way, by fostering the *spirit of reform*, and by uprooting every conservative prejudice by which reform is checked. Uncompromising, fearless, radical, it will put faith in ideas, and work for them openly, regardless of all consequences. Its only policy will be strong thought and plain speech. It will neither seek nor shun to "shock" the religious nerve.... It will pay no deference to the authority of the Bible, the Church, or the Christ, but rest solely on the authority of right reason and good conscience.

A brief notice in the first number also announced that the new journal would be the co-worker of *The Radical* "in the same general movement."[18]

The Index, at first, not only reprinted material from *The Radical* and frequently advertised that magazine, but further allied itself with the projects in which the transcendentalists were interested by devoting a portion of its space each week to a "Department of the Free Religious Association," for which T. W. Higginson, O. B. Frothingham, and W. J. Potter did most of the writing. At the end of the first year, however, this department was abolished, on the ground that the purely official matters of the association were not sufficient to fill up the allotted space. Abbot very probably had hoped that the association would make the journal its official organ.

When the Free Religious Association at length assumed responsibility for the publication, the various practical objects which the paper had sponsored were no longer stressed, since they were not in harmony with the broad generalizations upon which the organization had been founded. The name of the journal was changed, for a

---

[18] *The Index* for Jan. 1, 1870, p. 6. There are tables of contents and contributors in each volume of *The Index* except the final one. The pages of the first volume are not numbered consecutively.

time, to *The Free Religious Index*, and a watchword from Lucretia Mott appeared on the title-page: "Truth for authority, not authority for truth." A new prospectus announced:

> The objects of *The Index* may be defined by the objects of the Free Religious Association; namely, 'To promote the practical interests of pure religion, to increase fellowship in the Spirit, and to encourage the scientific study of man's religious nature and history'; in other words, Righteousness, Brotherhood, and Truth. ... It would seek to emancipate Religion from bondage to ecclesiastical dogmatism and sectarianism, in order that the practical power of religion may be put more effectually to the service of a higher Morality and an improved Social Welfare.

With the exception of a short period in 1873, when forced out of his office by an internal conflict among the members of the board of directors, Abbot edited the paper until July, 1880. During the days of his forced retirement the direction of affairs fell into the hands of the assistant editor, A. W. Stevens. After September 1, 1873, the editorial and publishing offices were removed to Boston, where *The Index* continued to be brought out until it gave place to *The Open Court*. The change in location was due in part to Abbot's removal to Cambridge and to the fact that most of the important material to appear in its pages came from men who were living in New England. During the summer of 1877, the former editor of *The Radical*, Sidney Morse, who had been previously a frequent contributor of prose and verse, assumed charge. When the paper became the organ of the Free Religious Association, W. J. Potter, the secretary of the organization, acted as editor, assisted by David H. Clark. The latter, however, was soon replaced by Benjamin F. Underwood, who appears to have performed most of the labor of editing during the later days of the journal's existence, Potter contenting himself with a bare weekly editorial.

During most of its years *The Index* devoted a considerable portion of its space to letters from various correspondents, who discussed the usual variety of subjects of interest to "radicals" and free-thinkers. The problem of immortality came in for its share of attention,[19] as well as the faith of the Quakers, the actual message of Jesus, the religion of India,[20] the ideas of Tom Paine,[21] and, later, evolution, Mormonism, and Ethical Culture. Of the writers of these epistles little need be said except, perhaps, that they included the names of the chief contributors to *The Radical*, and, less frequently, others who have been mentioned in connection with the periodicals discussed earlier in this work. Among the latter, for example, were John Orvis,[22] E. P. Grant,[23] Elizabeth Peabody,[24] Frances Power Cobbe, W. H. Channing,[25] Henry James, Sr.,[26] Lydia Maria Child,[27] C. P. Cranch,[28] and M. E. Lazarus.[29]

More important than these, however, were the editorial contributors, among whom were the following: T. W. Higginson, Moncure Conway, R. P. Hallowell, J. V. Blake, W. H. Spencer, C. A. Bartol, Mrs. E. D. Cheney, C. D. B. Mills, Elizur Wright, J. L. Stoddard, and Elizabeth Stanton. After 1880, the list of regular or occasional contributors that appeared in *The Index* included the names of Felix Adler, Francis Abbot, John Albee, J. W. Chadwick, Mrs. Cheney, Rowland Connor, F. M. Holland, Albert W. Kelsey, C. D. B. Mills, M. J. Savage, W. H. Spencer, Elizabeth Stanton, B. F. Underwood, and Sara A. Underwood.

---

[19] One of the subscribers wrote: "Can some of your readers give me any reliable information about the problem of immortality? Out here in Wisconsin we are anxious to know more about it."
[20] Cf., for example, *The Index*, V, 328; and XIV, 562.
[21] A previously unpublished letter of Paine's should be noted (*ibid.*, XIII, 356).
[22] *Ibid.*, XV, 32, for example. [24] *Ibid.*, XVII, 297 and 302.
[23] *Ibid.*, Nov. 5, 1870. [25] *Ibid.*, II, 109 and 197.
[26] *Ibid.*, VII, 26, 134, 138 and 172, for example.
[27] *Ibid.*, IX, 608. Cf. also *ibid.*, IX, 374 ff.; and XII, 254.
[28] *Ibid.*, IX, 391. [29] *Ibid.*, XV, 45, 141, 166, and 268, for example.

From abroad came not only Conway's numerous articles and letters, and the contributions of Frances Cobbe, but communications and essays from Max Müller, the noted authority on comparative religions,[30] Charles Voysey and George Jacob Holyoake, English radicals, and F. W. Newman, the brother of the famous Cardinal, and the translator of Homer with whom Matthew Arnold took issue.[31] Newman, it may be added, translated a portion of *Hiawatha* into Latin.

The poetry that was printed in the journal came largely from undistinguished persons. Perhaps it should be mentioned that among the number were several ardent "Emersonidae," such as Emma Lazarus,[32] Elizabeth Oakes Smith,[33] B. W. Ball, Horace Traubel, and W. S. Kennedy. The two men last mentioned—known to students of American literature largely through their connection with Whitman—also wrote meritorious essays for the paper during its later days.

Of the general contents of *The Index* little need perhaps be said here, except that under the auspices of the Free Religious Association it became more of a literary magazine. Its department of criticism, for example, was expanded somewhat, under the guidance of Mrs. Cheney and others, and the paper as a whole was better written. It lost the element of propaganda which had led Samuel Johnson to complain of Abbot's efforts at "organizing the Eternal Truth into 'Liberal Leagues.'"[34]

However, attention should be called to a letter from W. H. Herndon, dated February 18, 1870, in which Lin-

---

[30] *Ibid.*, IV, 7; V, 62; and VII, 280, for example.
[31] In connection with these men, see A. W. Benn, *The History of English Rationalism in the Nineteenth Century*, London, 1906; and *A Biographical Dictionary of Modern Rationalists*, compiled by Joseph McCabe, London, 1920.
[32] *The Index*, III, 399.
[33] For Mrs. Smith's relations with Emerson, see chapter IX of *Selections from the Autobiography of Elizabeth Oakes Smith*, ed. Mary A. Wyman, Lewiston, Maine, n.d. (1924).
[34] Samuel Johnson, *op. cit.*, p. 134.

coln's former law partner furnished the readers of *The Index* with an account of the Emancipator's religion.[35] About 1834, Herndon claimed, Lincoln came across the writings of Tom Paine and others, which so aroused him that he set about writing a treatise on "Infidelity," intending to have it published. The store-keeper in New Salem, Illinois, however, destroyed the manuscript before it could be printed. Herndon denied that his friend had believed in a special creation, the authority of the Bible, or the divinity of Christ. However authoritative this document may be,[36] it is of interest to the student of transcendentalism for this sentence: "I used to loan him Theodore Parker's works; I loaned him Emerson sometimes and other writers, and he would sometimes read and sometimes would not, as I suppose—nay, know."

Although lectures, articles, and letters by John Weiss, Samuel Johnson, T. W. Higginson, David Wasson, and others of the later transcendentalists appeared in *The Index*, it should be remembered that most of the material printed in the journal, particularly up to 1880, came from men like Abbot or W. J. Potter, who were never connected with the New School. Indeed, the paper owes its significance in the history of the periodicals of the transcendental movement principally to the opposition to, and criticism of, idealism.

Leaving to later consideration the discussion of the conflict between the intuitionalists and evolutionists that makes *The Index* notable, it may be desirable to illustrate the minor connections of the periodical with the members of the New School and their writings, before proceeding

---

[35] *The Index* for April 2, 1870.
[36] For the place which this letter holds in the controversy over Lincoln's religion, see John W. Starr, "What Was Abraham Lincoln's Religion?", *The Magazine of History with Notes and Queries*, extra number 73, Tarrytown, 1921, pp. 39ff.

to an outline of the journal's reaction to Parker and Emerson.

James Freeman Clarke's opinions as to the character of Jesus led to a rehearsal of his views.[37] A speech delivered by F. H. Hedge was reported, important only because in it the author ascribed all his intellectual life to his contact with German thought.[38] Abbot, in a lecture on "Modern Principles," harked back to the chief "transcendental" concept of the philosophy of the Fourierists in a glowing tribute to the "Unity of the Universe" which is "repeated in miniature in the ideal Unity of Mankind."[39] Holmes's description of Margaret Fuller was reprinted.[40] Volumes by Alcott, Elizabeth Peabody, and Thoreau were favorably reviewed.[41] Some verses written by Jones Very were reprinted, later followed by a letter from Samuel Longfellow recommending to the readers of the paper the poet's "pure theism" and "devotional sentiment" as complementary to their radicalism.[42]

Such examples might be multiplied, but sufficient illustration of the point at issue has perhaps been given. However, the connection of *The Index* and the Concord School of Philosophy should be noted. Since many of the contributors to the journal were among the lecturers who held forth at the gatherings in Concord,[43] it is only natural that it should have given some of its space to notices of meetings, and reports of discourses held at the school.[44] Of interest is a communication from A. N. Olcott, of Fred-

[37] *The Index* for April 23, 1870; and VI, 218.
[38] *Ibid.*, Aug. 27, 1870.
[39] *Ibid.*, II, 17. The material included in this discourse was later published in a tract which excited the interest of Charles Darwin (*ibid.*, II, 404).
[40] *Ibid.*, V, 377.
[41] *Ibid.*, XII, 568; and VI, 128, for example.
[42] *Ibid.*, XIII, 450; and XV, 10.
[43] D. A. Wasson, Ednah Cheney, John Albee, E. D. Mead, John Fiske, and Francis Abbot, among others (Austin Warren, "The Concord School of Philosophy," *The New England Quarterly*, II, 199ff.).
[44] Cf., for example, *The Index*, XVI, 70, 74, 80; and XVII, 75.

ericksburg, Ohio, who had attended all the sessions held at the institution for a period of four weeks. He concluded that the object of the school seemed to be "to stimulate philosophic thought and to proclaim no finalities."[45] He was so impressed by his experiences that he proposed that the Free Religious Association should sponsor a similar school, the aim of which would be to exhibit the "several systems of philosophy which have formed the basis of the great religions," including that of the Egyptians and even the Scandinavians.

More entertaining, however, is an account of a day spent at Concord by Sara Underwood,[46] who was fortunate enough to attend the School of Philosophy at a time when two of its lecturers had waxed a bit earnest in their arguments. Alcott, vaguely fearing that something was wrong, began to deprecate the apparent misunderstanding, when both speakers exclaimed that they did not know what he meant. The worthy dean subsided into his seat with the words, "Well, I don't know as I know what I mean myself," adding, as the audience laughed, "I am a 'mystic,' you know." Mrs. Underwood found herself further amused at a subsequent discussion, in which Alcott gave his opinion that by right living man could prolong his present life to a term of one, or even two, hundred years.

Since many of the people interested in forming the Free Religious Association had been among Theodore Parker's parishioners, and since he had been the most "radical" of all the major transcendentalists, *The Index* was not slow in honoring his memory. Indeed, the most highly esteemed editors and biographers of the bold clergyman were among the writers for the journal: Weiss, Frothingham, Chadwick, and Frances Cobbe. Some of the letters printed in the periodical recorded their writers' efforts to honor the memory of Parker by pilgrimages to

[45] *Ibid.*, XIII, 135.   [46] *Ibid.*, XIII, 78-79.

his old church in West Roxbury or to his grave in Florence. Through the activity of Theodore Stanton, a fund was raised by the paper to provide the proper care for his tomb. "The Channing and the Parker Type" was discussed, as well as his connections with Sumner and the abolitionists.[47] His intellectual relations with Emerson also claimed attention, most notably in an article by Edwin D. Mead, who asserted: "Emerson was Parker writing books. Parker was Emerson's truth in the pulpit."[48] The second editor of *The Index*, William Potter, summed up the importance of Parker to himself and his friends by contending that the author of *The Transient and the Permanent in Christianity* was the apostle in the history of religious belief, of "natural law in opposition to the idea of miracle."[49] In general, it may be said that the journal exhibited an interest in Parker similar to that of Conway, Wasson,[50] and their contemporaries, who regarded him as "the standard bearer of religious liberty."

Emerson, of course, attracted more attention in the paper than any other transcendentalist. "Fillers" from his writings were used; notices of his lectures were occasionally reprinted from various sources, as well as the lectures themselves; poems honoring him appeared; and various phases of his religious and philosophical beliefs were discussed, particularly after his death, in 1882.

Attention should perhaps be called to a couple of letters from a party of American travellers who had been in company with Emerson when he made his last trip abroad. The first of these, originally published in an obscure periodical called *The Golden Age*, was dated February 19, 1873, and contained the following:

[47] *Ibid.*, V, 81 and 209.
[48] *Ibid.*, XIV, 79. Cf. E. D. Mead, *The Influence of Emerson*, Boston, 1903.
[49] *The Index*, XV, 266.
[50] Cf. D. A. Wasson, *Essays Religious, Social, and Political*, Boston, 1889, p. 92.

On board the steamer from Alexandria to Naples.... Among our first-cabin passengers are R. W. Emerson and his daughter. Their 'dahabiah' was lying at Luxor when we arrived in the steamboat. The old gentleman has escaped sea-sickness. He busies himself with one of the Latin classics, and with letter-writing. He smokes after each meal, and at all times is very affable.[51]

The second letter, written from Naples on March 2, 1873, supplies further information:

In the evening, when we were again at sea, Mr. Emerson gave us a pleasant little entertainment in the shape of some readings from the poets, making selections from several with whom we were not familiar. The old gentleman is as totally different from the grave philosopher I had painted him as you can well imagine; and the childlike affections and sympathy between himself and his daughter is [sic] something quite touching. The easy, simple style of his conversation is in marked contrast with the heavy tone of his books, over which we remember laboring (while boys) as we would have done over so many pages of the higher mathematics. As I expected, he does not place Longfellow among the foremost poets of the age, but speaks admiringly of Whittier, Lowell, and Holmes, and says many kind things of Bret Harte's graver pieces. To Tennyson he freely awards the palm. Speaking of Bayard Taylor's intended life of Goethe, he took no pains to conceal his opinion that Taylor was not the right man for the work.[52]

But the chief value of the discussion of Emerson that *The Index* contains does not lie in its addition of biographical details, or its enthusiastic praise of "the purest piece of Orientalism that ever grew in the West," as one of the contributors to the paper called him. More important, rather, are the numerous articles which deal with his religious views. The most finished production among these, perhaps, is a discourse on the Sage of Concord delivered by John W. Chadwick in Brooklyn, on April 30, 1882.[53] This lecture contains an excellent biographical sketch,

---

[51] *The Index*, IV, 210.
[52] *Loc. cit.*
[53] *The Index*, XIII, 535-538.

spiced with personal reminiscences, and expresses its author's belief that Emerson is to be considered "a prophet of the ultimate synthesis of our most radical science with an idealist philosophy and a religion drenched with the consciousness of an omnipotent and omnipresent God." William J. Potter, the editor of the periodical during its later years, in discussing "Mr. Emerson's Religious Position," maintained that the great preacher of self-reliance "more than any other, may be called the father of the Free Religious movement,"[54] thus reiterating the statement made years previously by Alcott.

Soon after Emerson's death a dispute arose over his attendance at church during his last days. In an address to the Concord School of Philosophy C. A. Bartol had remarked: "Emerson feared the excesses of radicalism, and went to meeting regularly in his last days. I count it a spiritual assent in him, not an intellectual assent."[55] *The Catholic Review* and other similar journals made much of this assertion, coming from a man who, supposedly, had good grounds for his statement. The editor of *The Index* acknowledged the fact that Emerson had gone to church "quite regularly" during his last months, but contended that he had not resumed the habit until his memory had become so weakened that he was not responsible for his actions.[56]

When Matthew Arnold expressed his opinion of Emerson's worth as a literary artist, *The Index* joined in with the numerous papers that registered their disapproval of his views.[57] Similarly, when the idea prevailed in Boston that the Concord lecturer had been slow to espouse the

---
[54] *Ibid.*, XIII, 519.
[55] Cf. Bartol's lecture on "Emerson's Religion" in *The Genius and Character of Emerson*, lectures at the Concord School of Philosophy, ed. F. B. Sanborn, Boston, 1885, cap. V. Edward Emerson denied that his father "recanted" (*Emerson in Concord*, 1889, pp. 253ff.).
[56] *The Index*, XIV, 134. See the preface to G. W. Cooke, *Ralph Waldo Emerson*, Boston, 1882. [57] *Ibid.*, XV, 290 and 293.

cause of the abolitionists, several correspondents arose to his defense, among them being T. W. Higginson, H. I. Bowditch, and Elizabeth Peabody.[58]

Sufficient illustration has perhaps been given to show that the writers for the journal, particularly after it had become the organ of the Free Religious Association, hailed Emerson as the "unfrocked priest of the human mind," the literary exponent of a theism in which most of them could have confessed a belief. But, one must hasten to say, the heightened enthusiasm for his memory induced by the *nil nisi bonum* attitude must also be given consideration, particularly when it is remembered that the amount of material relating to him that appeared in the paper during the early days of its existence is not impressive.

But more important to the present study than the reaction of *The Index* to the transcendentalists is its reaction to transcendentalism itself—or, better, to "the philosophy of Concord," which the serene snobbery of a Henry Adams could regard as nothing more than an eccentric offshoot of the pulpit.

The first editor of the paper, according to his latest biographer,[59] was "a philosopher of parts," whose misfortune was to have been twenty years ahead of his time in launching a vigorous attack upon idealism. Though intimately connected with the Free Religious Association, as has been mentioned, he did not hesitate to criticize most adversely the philosophy of intuition, in spite of his realization that many of his friends in New England would take offence. Among his utterances of note in this regard was a lecture on "The Scientific Method of Religion"

---

[58] *Ibid.*, XVII, 101, 248 and 297.
[59] Francis A. Christie, in *The Dictionary of American Biography*. Abbot was strongly recommended by Emerson and others for the chair of Intellectual Philosophy in Cornell (see his *Testimonials*, privately printed, Boston, 1879); and, in 1888, served as a substitute for Josiah Royce at Harvard.

which he delivered before the Association in Boston, on March 11, 1877, and which was reported soon after in *The Index*. Abbot first explained the origin of transcendentalism as a protest against the narrowing tendencies of Unitarianism.

> The authority of the Church, of the Bible, of the Christ, no matter how plausibly disguised, was seen by the Transcendentalists to be what it really is—an external, arbitrary limitation of spiritual freedom; and they raised their voices against it, in all its forms, in the name of Intuition. Certain great ideas—God, Immortality, Duty—they claimed to be facts of consciousness, part and parcel of the human mind, truths wrought into the very structure of the human soul and wholly independent of experience, testimony, or demonstration. Channing demanded freedom in the name of Christ; Parker demanded it in the name of God,— the one simply as a Christian, the other as a Christian theist, a Transcendentalist, an Intuitionalist. The "religious element in man" was assumed by the Transcendentalists to be a "primary faculty," immediately cognizant of external realities which "transcended experience," hence their name.[60]

Continuing, he quoted from Parker and Max Müller, concluding from these authorities that transcendentalism involved "another inward limitation" of its own in what the former called the "Intuition of Reason" and the latter, a special "faculty of faith." His argument proceeded:

> By this philosophy the ideas of God, of Immortality, of Duty, are elevated above the reach of legitimate doubt or question or examination; they are pronounced to be primordial truths, facts given in consciousness, absolute certainties, original revelations of God to the Soul; they are too sacred to be tested or even scrutinized by the discursive reason or "understanding," and must be accepted by it unreservedly, unquestioningly, submissively.[61]

As a consequence, all thought, he believed, must approach these tremendous problems "self-fitted with foregone con-

---

[60] *The Index*, VIII, 134-135 (March 22, 1877).
[61] *Loc. cit.*

clusions," and, as a result, it follows that the transcendental "creed" becomes the "last ditch of dogmatism."

The position held by Abbot was of course the same as that of any of the more competent critics of the fundamental idea of the New School; but this attack, with its charge of "dogmatism" made against the element of American liberalism that proudly vaunted itself as being "unorthodox," and delivered from within the ranks of the reformers, came as a thunderbolt upon the New England intelligentsia. Many of the readers of *The Index*, no doubt, were ready to agree with Abbot, not knowing what the issue involved, and loving any criticism of older forms of thought. But the transcendentalists who were capable of argument hastily set about defending themselves.

Higginson, who had been thoroughly acquainted with Abbot's views previously, wrote a letter to the Boston *Commonwealth* for March 31, 1877,[62] in which he asserted that the intuitionalists were practically read out of the Free Religious Association by the speech. Abbot promptly defended his position by claiming the right to interpret for himself the generalities which made up the constitution of the organization. W. J. Potter, striving to throw oil upon the waters of discord, argued that so long as the intuitionalists did not attempt to impose their philosophy upon others, they had as much right to be numbered among the *Free* in religion as anyone. C. D. B. Mills, an ardent Emersonian,[63] sent a letter to *The Index*, for April 19, 1877,[64] in which he undertook to explain the fundamental position of the transcendentalists and then to defend them. His chief point is contained in the following:

[62] Reprinted in *The Index*, VIII, 171.
[63] See *Charles D. B. Mills, 1821-1900*, In Memoriam, n.pl., n.d., p. 15.
[64] *The Index*, VIII, 182.

Either the validity of truths resident and luminous in the consciousness must be maintained and held as good against all beside,—and this will carry us to the main postulate of Transcendentalism, the intuitional vision, the authority of the ideal; or, these denied, we hew away from under our feet all ground upon which it is possible to base an affirmation in religious thought, and this brings to the destruction of all religion, free, as well as every other.

Abbot replied to this line of reasoning in an editorial entitled "Free Religion Versus Transcendentalism."[65] After disposing of Potter's suggestion by contending that the essential attitude of the transcendentalists made it impossible for them to concede the "equal mental rights" of their opponents, he stated his full agreement with the definition of the philosophy of intuition which Mills had given, but insisted that if God is a mere "subjective truth of the soul," he is a dream. The existence of God, to his mind, must be "an objective truth of the universe." He returned to the rankling suggestion of orthodoxy:

But the essence of the dogmatism which we find in Transcendentalism lies in its refusal to allow the *scientific intellect,* or what it calls the "understanding," to submit the alleged deliverances of Intuition, or what it calls the "higher reason," to the ordinary tests of science.

In the issue for May 10, 1877, Samuel Longfellow involved himself in the discussion, but merely claimed that the members of the New School never considered their spiritual intuition to be "infallible," and that certain classes of truth could be arrived at only through the imagination and "feeling."[66] In a lengthy reply Abbot stated his conviction that the only recourse the transcendentalists had was to the "claim of divine revelation," and quoted F. H. Hedge to prove that they really did hold faith in a "super-

---

[65] *Ibid.,* VIII, 186-187 (April 19, 1877).
[66] *Ibid.,* VIII, 222.

natural divine revelation as the only possible alternative of objective atheism."[67]

The arguments continued on both sides, Abbot maintaining that a finite consciousness could not contain the idea of an Infinite Spirit without a supernatural revelation, and that transcendentalism had become effete, a fact borne out by the number of apostates to its cause. C. P. Cranch contributed his opinions in an article on "Matter and Spirit," in which he said:

> Grant that science limits herself to experience of facts. But the world of facts is a very wide world. It does not follow that she is bound to exclude all experiences save that of the senses, or even of the pure intellect. . . . It is high time for truth-seekers to protest against these ultra-materialistic tendencies of science.[68]

Cranch at least understood the nature of the opposition.

Samuel Johnson added his protests to those of his friends. In one of them he denied the suggestion that religious societies had been founded on "the transcendental idea," and went on to explain:

> As I understand the Transcendental Idea, it is not the ground of special religious organizations; it is the *rationale of mental movement*, the self-affirmation of mind concerning its own necessary forms and processes, as the organic methods of all sane-thinking, the fundamental conditions of all experience. It considers mind, in its essential functions as the active (not passive) internal force, to which all empirical phenomena appeal, and by which they are lifted above themselves into ideas and laws. It not only accepts every fact of experimental science, allows every form of honest doubt concerning the contents of its own ideal forms, and hails all progressive reconstruction of beliefs: it is *itself* the necessary ground, the inevitable condition of every such fresh experience.[69]

---

[67] *Ibid.*, VIII, 223. Cf. Hedge's *Reason in Religion*, Boston, 1865, Introduction, cap. II.

[68] *The Index*, IX, 391. The same number of the paper contains a portion of one of Cranch's poems.

[69] *Ibid.*, XII, 388 (Feb. 10, 1881).

He concluded his attempt to broaden the psychological basis of transcendentalism by an acknowledgement of the futility of his efforts to make an impression on the "present phase of the radical mind."

However, Johnson was unwilling to retire from the conflict. W. J. Potter argued that the failure of the religious societies established by various members of the New School proved the inability of their philosophy to withstand the progress of science. Johnson was quick to resent the idea.

> I prefer to reply that the old free societies did *not* grow, wholly or even chiefly, out of the Transcendental movement, but out of a great revival of free inquiry and moral conviction which was leavening the community in those days with aspirations that no such special application of philosophy to religion . . . could explain. They did not, I must beg leave to suggest, spring from the example of Parker, nor from the philosophy of Emerson, nor from the logic of Brownson. That these were without influence in this direction, no one will pretend. But that they were to be regarded as other than portions of a great *renaissance* of American principles and demands is, to my mind, equally inconsistent with a broad view of the phenomena of the time.[70]

The force of the distinction which Johnson made between transcendentalism proper and the general progress of New England thought disappeared when he tried to prove that the New School did not lack coöperative purpose. The best he could say on the subject was that W. H. Furness had ministered for a half century to a single religious society and that the Fourieristic associations in America owed their existence to the transcendental movement. The latter assertion is a "vulgar error" which still survives.

The junior editor of *The Index* during its last years, B. F. Underwood, summed up the whole controversy in an editorial with the significant title "Transcendentalism at

---

[70] *Ibid.*, XII, 436 (March 10, 1881).

Bay."[71] After quoting from Frothingham's history of the movement in New England, he observed that few of the members of the New School were left. The intuitionalism and sensationalism defended by their respective adherents in his youth he regarded as now absorbed in a "deeper synthesis," in which the error of each was lost—a synthesis "entirely consistent with evolution," of which Herbert Spencer was to be considered the chief sponsor.

Higginson made a last "Transcendentalist's Plea for Life,"[72] charging the opposition with using "evolution" as a loophole in much the same manner as the earlier Christian sects had used "inspiration." He confessed his own belief in evolution, but that of Charles Darwin—not Spencer—and maintained that both transcendentalism and agnosticism were legitimate forms of Free Religion. He was convinced that his philosophy would always appeal to a certain class of minds, particularly youthful ones, and that the hostility of the Free Religious Association would merely drive the younger idealists into the church of Phillips Brooks and the Concord School of Philosophy.

There is no need to extend the account of the conflict of opinions. It is apparent that the assault of Abbot was continued throughout the history of the periodical, despite the veneration for Parker and Emerson shown by the evolutionists who controlled the journal. That *The Index* maintained such a sturdy opposition even after it had passed from Abbot's guidance indicates only too well the fate that transcendentalism met. As Samuel Johnson expressed the idea, it had become a "prevailing habit" to call the movement a half-way step, a school outgrown, good and needed in its day, but belonging to the past. The New School was no longer new.

In allying itself with each intellectual protest that was made in America during the later nineteenth century tran-

[71] *Ibid.*, XIV, 160 (Oct. 5, 1882). [72] *Ibid.*, XIV, 195 (Oct. 26, 1882).

scendentalism finally completed the circle and turned against itself when it showed itself friendly to the protest of science. Evolution, in so far as it was based upon materialism, denied its fundamental postulate of intuition and relegated it, despite its acknowledged catalytic effect, to the realm of the discarded. In 1843 Emerson noted in his journal,[78] "We come down with free thinking into the dear institutions, and at once make carnage amongst them." Forty years later the same principle held true.

[78] *Journals*, VI, 470.

APPENDIX

TWO UNCOLLECTED EMERSON ITEMS
I. [JOHN STERLING]

Essays and Tales by John Sterling: with a Memoir of His Life, by Julius Charles Hare, London, 1848.

John Sterling, during his short life, was a valued ornament of the best literary circle, and the friend of Coleridge, Arnold, Carlyle, Mill, Hare, Tennyson, French, Maurice, and other noted scholars. He was the son of Edward Sterling, well known to politicians as "the thunderer of the Times," on account of certain powerful contributions to that newspaper. He was educated at Cambridge. To a fine literary talent he added extraordinary powers of conversation, a scholar devoted to the best books, a reader of Plato, of Aeschylus, of Simonides; of Dante, Calderon, Montaigne, Leibnitz; and of Goethe, Schiller, and the criticism of modern Germany. He had also, what is rare in the brilliant society in which he lived, a military love of action, which carried him over that bound which a scholar can rarely pass without ridicule or ruin, and drew him into various resolutions of charity and patriotism; mixed him up with anti-slavery in St. Vincent's in the West Indies; made him the strenuous friend of public education; put him forward in a disastrous Spanish insurrection in 1830, which ended in the death of his friend, General Torrijos. The same conscience and desire to serve men led him to take orders in the church, though the progress of his mind, more than the state of his health, withdrew him from it afterwards. His hospitable mind was continually exploring books most distasteful to his countrymen, Schelling, Hegel, Schleiermacher, Strauss, and the neology of Germany and the socialism of France. He had a great range of friends and correspondents. Whatever belonged to thought or religion was sure of his sympathy, and he loudly complained of the torpor of the English mind, whilst the real strength of the nation seemed to him to be all of the brute mechanic sort. "Think," he says, "if we had a dozen men to stand up for ideas, as Cobden and his friends do for machinery!"

The Essays indicate the ardor and activity of his mind; they embrace a range of interesting topics, and furnish often the best insight into the spiritual condition of England. Ill health made him a traveller, and he learned, at least, from his journeys in other countries, to look at his own with some advantage. Of the tales, "The Onyx Ring," from Blackwood, long since well known in this country, is the best.

In his last illness, Sterling appointed Mr. Carlyle and Mr. Hare his literary executors. Mr. Hare, in writing his biography, has wisely drawn it in great part from his letters. From Mr. Hare's commentary, it is easy to see how distasteful was the task, and how much praise he deserves for printing what he did. We must not be ungrateful for good meaning; but the heroic Sterling shows so ill in these faint and deprecating paragraphs, that every one will wonder at the silence of Mr. Hare's colleague, and regret that the greatest portraying hand of this age did not draw the picture. [Seven lines from *Lycidas* follow.]—*The Massachusetts Quarterly Review* (Sept., 1848), I, 515-516.

2. NEW TRANSLATION OF DANTE

Dr. John Carlyle is publishing, in London and in New York, a translation of Dante's *Inferno* into English prose. Dr. Carlyle brings rare qualifications to the task, and having, in a residence of six or seven years in Italy, devoted himself to the study of Dante, is probably better acquainted with the *Divine Comedy* than any man living. He has collated with great care his text from all the best editions. The Italian text stands above, the version below, with a few indispensable notes at the bottom of the page. We are not ungrateful to Cary, who has been our English helper so long, and whom we esteem for spirit, conciseness, and accuracy, the best of metrical translators; but it is very certain that all the tribe of English metrical versions of the great poets, the miserable Potters and Franklins and Wests, who have lulled their dullness by the august names of Aeschylus, and Sophocles, and Pindar, must give place to exact versions word for word, without rhyme or metre. So only can the real curiosity of the student be satisfied. Dr. Carlyle is no careless workman, but has executed his task with a biblical fidelity, selecting his phrase with scrupulous judgment, and italicizing every word added in English to complete the abstemious sentence of the author.

We assure the book a warm welcome in this country, where we have long observed, as a good sign of the times, the increasing study of Dante.—*The Massachusetts Quarterly Review* (Sept., 1848), I, 527.

INDEX

Abbott, F. E., 219, 230, 233 ff., 247 ff.
Adams, Henry, 247
Adams, John Quincy, 83-84, 167
Adler, Felix, 239
Æsthetic Papers, chapter VII
Agassiz, Louis, 163, 166, 171, 179
Albee, John, 239
Alcott, Amos Bronson, 3, 9, 14, 29, 30, 31, 32, 40, 41, 42, 48, 52-53, 63-64, 65, 67-68, 90-91, 138, 145, 150, 157, 161 n, 207, 222-224, 231, 232, 235, 242, 243
Alcott, W. A., 52
Allen, John, 103, 109
Allston, Washington, 32, 113, 140
American Literature, 76-77, 181
Appleton, John, 167, 168, 172
Arius, 201
Arnold, Matthew, 78, 246
Atlantic Monthly, The, 191-193
Ball, B. W., 226, 240
Balzac, 203
Bancroft, George, 20, 40, 48, 80 n
Bartol, C. A., 9, 204-205, 211, 213, 217, 218, 230, 239, 246
Bassett, E. P., 234
Bateson, P. H., 234
Benton, Joel, 203, 205-206
Benton, Myron, 205-206, 219, 225
Birney, J. G., 168, 169, 192
Blackwood's Edinburgh Magazine, 93, 93 n
Blake, J. V., 219, 239
Blake, William, 115, 226
Blanchard, H., 231
Boehme, Jacob, 3, 138, 175, 224 n
Boston Daily Advertiser, The, 24, 59 n, 61
Boston Morning Post, The, 47, 74
Boston Quarterly Review, The, 27 n, chapter III

Boston Reformer, The, 40
Boston Transcript, The, 185
Bowditch, H. I., 172, 247
Bowen, Daniel, 219
Bowen, Francis, 45
Bremer, Fredrika, 140 n
Brewster, B. H., 48
Brisbane, Albert, 13, 48, 67, 71, 88, 101, 102, 107, 108, 109, 111, 132, 136, 139 n, 140, 142
British and Foreign Review, The, 92, 147
Brook Farm, 11, 13, 41, 88 n, 89, 90, chapter V, 140, 142, 146, 150
Brooks, C. T., 29, 117, 204, 227
Brooks, Phillips, 253
Brother Jonathan, 6
Brown, H. W., 230
Brown, Samuel, 168, 171, 171 n
Brown, Thomas, 38
Browning, Robert, 169, 226
Brownson, H. F., 48
Brownson, Orestes A., 9, 11, 15, 25, 29, 33-34, 34 n, chapter III, 84, 93 n, 97, 120, 145, 183, 196, 232, 252
Brownson's Quarterly Review, 46, 121
Bryant, W. C., 20
Burroughs, John, 225
Bush, George, 85 n, 123-124
Butler, Mann, 35

Cabot, J. E., 157 n, 158, 160, 161, 165, 166, 168, 169, 170, 190-191
Calvert, George H., 109, 110
Carlyle, John, 256
Carlyle, Thomas, 3, 14, 15, 23, 25, 27, 28 n, 54, 64, 65, 73, 74, 92-94, 92 n, 100, 126, 144, 207
Cary, Phoebe, 139

[257]

Index

Catholic World, The, 232
Chadwick, J. W., 219, 239, 245-246
Channing, Walter, 108
Channing, Dr. W. E., 9, 11, 25, 31, 34, 39, 41, 74, 84, 85 n, 88, 92 n, 93, 117-118, 118 n, 145, 159, 167, 182, 195, 244, 247
Channing, W. E. (Of Concord), 95-96, 108, 110, 114, 124, 139, 165
Channing, W. F., 108, 142 n
Channing, W. H., 9, 18, 19 n, 29, 30, 31, 32, 48, 49, 54, 74, 80, chapter IV, 102, 106, 107, 108, 109, 110, 117-118, 128, chapter VI, 157, 165, 239
Cheney, Mrs. E. D., 222, 239, 240
Cincinnati Daily Gazette, The, 199 n
Child, Lydia M., 95, 96, 102, 117, 239
Chivers, T. H., 133 n
Christ, 50, 51, 99, 177, 190 n, 212, 217, 222 n, 232, 239, 241, 242, 248
Christian Examiner, The, 14, 17 n, 39, 44-45, 44 n, 51, 52, 53, 73, 80, 121, 159, 192 n, 195
Christian Register, The, 39, 115
Clapp, Otis, 107, 128
Clark, David H., 238
Clarke, James Freeman, 9, 13 n, 17, 18, 20, 24, 26, 28, 32, 34, 35, 61, 72, 108, 110, 115, 157, 201, 220-221, 242
Clough, A. H., 206
Cobbe, Frances P., 202, 220, 221, 239, 240
Coleridge, S. T., 3, 11, 19, 29, 54, 80, 100, 128, 144, 145, 165, 207, 212, 222, 224 n
Collyer, Robert, 219
Commonwealth, The (Boston), 15, 209, 249

Concord School of Philosophy, 12, 12 n, 13, 146, 242-243, 246, 253
Cone, C., 234
Confucius, 33, 190 n, 207
Constant, Benjamin, 3, 39, 40, 53, 70, 146, 203
Considerant, Victor, 94, 138
Conway, Moncure D., 9, chapter IX, 217, 229, 239, 240
Cook, Joseph, 228
Cooke, Joseph J., 109
Cooper, J. Fenimore, 6, 7, 116
Cooper, Thomas, 126
Cousin, Victor, 3, 5, 11, 19, 25, 38, 52, 53-58, 64, 65, 65 n, 70, 72-73, 80, 91-92, 100, 146, 195, 211 n
Cram, W. A., 226
Cranch, Christopher P., 5, 9, 15, 18, 18 n, 23, 24, 28 n, 29, 36, 96, 107, 108, 110, 114, 117, 119, 119 n, 239, 251
Cudworth, 11

Daily Chronotype, The (Boston), 107
Dall, Caroline, 204, 220, 226, 231
Dana, C. A., 95, 103, 105, 107, 108, 110, 113, 114, 115-117, 122-123, 124, 128, 128 n, 129
Dante, 256
Darwin, Charles, 202, 253
Davidson, Tom, 226
Democratic Review, The, 20, 21, 46, 71
Démocratie Pacifique, La, 125
Desor, Edouard, 167, 168, 169, 171, 202
De Wette, 34
Dial, The, 14 n, chapter II, 63, 64, 66, 73, 81, 85, 86 n, 89, 97, 110, 121-122, 157, 161, 200, 208
Dial, The (Cincinnati), chapter IX
Dickens, Charles, 6, 181

Dix, Dorothea, 96
Doherty, Hugh, 111, 126
Dorgan, J. A., 206
Drake, C. D., 19
Duganne, A. J. H., 108
Dwight, John S., 9, 29, 48, 49, 59, 103, 106, 107, 108, 109, 110, 111, 113, 114, 116, 116 n, 119, 122, 124, 129, 135, 141, 150, 170, 199
Dwight, Marianne, 104, 111 n
Dwight's Journal of Music, 199

Eclecticism, 45, 51, 52, 54, 64, 72, 80, 91
Edwards, Jonathan, 3, 11, 60, 78, 78 n, 98
Ellis, C. M., 4, 168, 172, 200
Eliot, William G., 17
Emerson, Charles C., 22, 207
Emerson, R. W., 4-5, 6, 9, 14-15, 19, 21, 22 ff., 25, 26, 27, 29, 34, 41, 42, 43, 49, 51, 55, 61, 62 n, 63, 65 n, 73-80, 83, 85, 92, 93, 96, 98, 116, 118 n, 120 n, 121, 122-127, 127 n, 128, 128 n, 131 n, 138, 144, 151, 152, 157, 158, 159, 160-161, 160 n, 161 n, 187, 192, 196, 197, 198, 201-202, 206, 206 n, 207, 208, 210, 211 n, 214, 220, 221-222, 223, 225 n, 231, 232, 235, 244-247, 252, 253
Espy, James, 202-203
Everett, Alexander H., 48, 54, 68
Everett, Edward, 154
Evolution, 12, 202, 253, 254

Fenelon, 100
Fichte, 5, 138
Finlay, George, 166, 170-171
Fishbough, W., 133 n
Flint, M. P., 19
Follen, Karl, 14 n, 212 n

Fosdick, W. W., 206
Foster, G. G., 108
Fourier, Charles, 13, 88, 89 n, 92, 94, 97, 100, 101-102, 103, 111, 111 n, 122, 122 n, 125 n, 128, 131, 131 n, 135, 136, 140, 142, 150, 150 n, 163
Fourierism, chapters IV, V, and VI (see *Fourier*)
Fox, George, 78
Francis, Convers, 7, 9, 31, 40, 78 n, 81, 223
Fredault, F., 203
Free Enquirer, The, 39
Free Religious Association, 229-233, 237, 238, 247, 249, 253
French Literature and Thought, 3, 11, chapter III, 94, 95, 100, 111, 125, 138-139, 146 n, 195, 202, 203, 227 (see *Cousin, Constant, Fourier*, etc.)
Friswell, J., 139
Frothingham, O. B., 9, 13, 47, 196, 205, 208, 219, 230, 237
Fuller, Margaret, 9, 29, 32, 36, 62-63, 68, 71, 71 n, 96, 122, 143-144, 146, 165, 197, 204, 208, 226, 242
Furness, W. H., 9, 11, 25, 31, 40, 93, 157, 186, 195, 203, 207, 219, 252

Gallagher, W. D., 19, 115
Garrison, William Lloyd, 84, 182, 225
Gerhardt, P., 175
German Literature and Thought, 3, 5, 27, 30, 30 n, 34-35, 39, 40, 51, 53, 54, 55, 56, 58, 63, 65, 78, 95, 100, 119-120, 119 n, 148, 161, 171, 174-176, 184, 195, 203-204, 206, 207, 217, 226-227, 242 (see *Goethe, Kant*, etc.)
Gilchrist, Anne, 225

Index

Giles, E., 109
Goddard, H. C., 31
Godwin, Parke, 43, 91, 94-95, 102, 105, 107, 108, 109, 111, 117, 130, 135, 151
Goethe, 19, 22, 34, 64, 74, 93, 163, 181, 184, 203, 227
Golden Age, The, 244
Goodnight, S. H., 35
Goodwin, J. M., 206
Gospel Advocate, The, 39
Grant, E. P., 108, 239
Greaves, J. P., 91
Greeley, Horace, 102, 107, 108
Greene, W. B., 138

Hale, J. P., 164, 165
Hallowell, R. P., 239
Harbinger, The, chapter V, 132, 133, 160
Hare, J. C., 207, 255-256
Harris, Thomas Lake, 136-137
Harte, Bret, 245
Harwood, P., 91
Hawthorne, N., 8, 20, 21, 71 n, 117, 144, 154, 165, 169, 187-188
Hecker, Isaac, 41
Hedge, F. H., 9, 42, 95, 108, 109, 114, 114 n, 146, 155, 170, 218-219, 221, 225, 231, 234, 237, 239, 247, 249, 253
Hegel, 65, 120, 120 n, 171, 207
Henry, C. S., 14 n, 54
Herder, 34, 100
Herndon, W. H., 240-241
Higginson, T. W., 9, 42, 95, 109, 114, 114 n, 146, 155, 170, 218-219, 221, 225, 231, 234, 237, 239, 247, 249, 253
Hildreth, Richard, 60 n, 166, 167, 168, 178, 192, 193
Hinton, R. L., 225
Hoar, G. F., 222

Holland, F. M., 219, 239
Holmes, O. W., 8, 20, 245
Holyoake, J., 240
Hooper, Ellen Sturgis, 155
Hotson, C. P., 151
Howe, Julia Ward, 168, 175, 225
Howe, Samuel G., 158, 160, 165, 167, 169, 170, 171 n, 193
Howells, William Dean, 194 n, 199-200
Howes, F., 168, 169
Huidekoper, H. J., 19 n
Hume, 38

Index, The, chapter IX
Ingalls, J. K., 136
Irving, Washington, 20
Ives, E., Jr., 109

James, Henry, Sr., 109, 118, 128, 130, 135, 167, 168, 188-189, 219, 239
Jefferson, Joseph, 226
Johnson, Samuel, 9, 216, 220-221, 226, 227, 229, 230, 236, 251-252, 253
Jouffroy, 53, 227
Journal of Speculative Philosophy, The, 15, 28 n
Judd, Sylvester, 140, 197

Kant, 3, 5, 29, 56, 57, 65, 120
Keats, 19, 35, 115, 168
Kelsey, A. W., 239
Kemble, Fanny, 95
Kennedy, W. S., 240
Kimball, W. H., 109
Kroeger, A. E., 227

Landor, W. S., 83, 165, 167, 186
Lane, Charles, 89-90, 138
Lazarus, Emma, 240
Lazarus, M. E., 108, 109, 112 n, 135, 203, 239

Index

Leibnitz, 164
Le Rousseau, J., 138
Leroux, P., 94, 100, 138
Lessing, 100
Lewis, I., 195
Lewis, T., 117
Liberator, The, 195
Linberg, H. G., 54
Lincoln, Abraham, 180, 241
Locke, David Ross, 234
Locke, John, 3, 5, 10, 38, 51, 54, 56, 57, 60, 62, 80, 152, 152 n
London Daily News, The, 139
London Phalanx, The, 94
Longfellow, H. W., 20, 96, 115, 116, 116 n, 211
Longfellow, Samuel, 9, 218, 227, 242, 250
Loring, G. B., 169, 172, 187
Lowell, J. R., 42, 96, 108, 109, 110, 114, 115, 117, 137, 137 n, 139, 167, 168, 169, 186, 192, 193, 245
Lynch, Anne C., 48, 115

Macaulay, 168
Macdaniel, Osborne, 102, 108, 109
Macomber, A. E., 234
Mann, Horace, 144
Marsh, James, 80
Martineau, Harriet, 21, 43 n
Martineau, James, 162, 211 n
Marvin, J. B., 214
Massachusetts Quarterly Review, The, 120, 121, 130, 135, chapter VIII
May, S. J., 170
Mayo, A. D., 168
Melville, Herman, 9, 116
Menu, 207
Middle-West, Literary Culture in, chapter II, 19-20, 23 n, 34, 36, chapter IX, 194 n
Mill, J. S., 138, 190

Mills, C. D. B., 219, 239, 249
Monthly Magazine, The (London), 92
Moore, Hannah, 29
More, Henry, 11, 67, 190 n
Morse, Sidney H., 214, 221, 226, 230, 238
Mott, Lucretia, 231, 238
Mueller, K. O., 153
Mueller, Max, 240, 248
Muller, W. H., 109
Muench, F., 161
Murdock, James, 9
Mysticism, 3, 33, 38, 45, 50, 53, 59-60, 62, 78, 79-80, 90, 111, 121, 124, 174, 176, 190, 190 n, 228, 243

National Liberal League, 236, 240
Neidhart, N., 109
New Jerusalem Magazine, The, 130, 130 n
New York Review, The, 42
New York Tribune, The, 88, 107, 115, 122
Newman, F. W., 240
North American Review, The, 54, 55, 121, 158, 159, 176
Norton, Charles Eliot, 98
Norton, Andrews, 24, 27 n, 59-62, 59 n, 62 n, 63, 64, 92

Ohio State Journal, The, 199
Oliphant, D. S., 108
Oliphant, Laurence, 137
Open Court, The, 235, 238
Oriental Literature and Religion, 33, 120, 140, 183-184, 190-191, 190 n, 206, 207, 227-228, 229-230, 231, 239
Orvis, John, 108, 109, 239
Osgood, Frances, 110, 143
Osgood, Samuel, 18, 22, 29
Owen, Robert D., 30, 41, 163, 231

Paine, Tom, 239, 241
Palfrey, J. G., 49
Palisse, J. M., 109
Parker, Theodore, 7, 9, 11, 31, 32, 42, 48, 60 n, 66, 67, 71, 72, 79, 80 n, 81-82, 118-119, 118 n, 144, chapter VIII, 195, 200, 201-202, 208, 210, 211, 213, 218, 219, 220, 221, 222-223, 227, 228, 241, 243-244, 248, 252
Parsons, Anna, 140-141
Patterson, H. S., 48
Patterson, J. S., 219, 226
Paulding, J. K., 152 n
Peabody, Elizabeth, 9, 15, 29, 32, 48, 71, chapter VII, 169, 183, 219, 239, 242, 247
Peabody, Ephraim, 17, 23 n, 29
Pease, M. S., 109
Perfectionist, The, 129
Perkins, J. H., 18, 18 n
Perkins, S. H., 154
Phalanx, The, 15, 87, 88, 89, 89 n, 102, 103, 121, 141
Philanthropist, The, 39
Phillips, Wendell, 168, 193, 201, 219, 224 n
Pierce, John, 7
Pioneer, The, 114
Plato, 3, 67, 117, 190 n, 207, 224, 232
Plotinus, 4, 224 n
Poe, E. A., 117, 119 n, 124, 143
Pope, A. R., 168
Pordage, John, 138
Potter, W. J., 219, 230, 237, 238, 246, 249, 252
Powell, W. B., 35
Powers, Hiram, 140, 166
Prescott, W. H., 167, 168, 177-178
Present, The, chapter IV
Price, Richard, 78
Prince, J. C., 91
Princeton Review, The, 55, 60 n, 64

Proudhon, P. J., 138
Pulte, J. H., 108
Puritans, 178-179, 218-219

Quakers, 11, 57, 78, 197, 239

Radical, The, chapter X, 230, 238
Radical Club, 213, 222
Radicals, 212 ff., 221
Redington, R., 162
Reed, Sampson, 151-152
Reid, Thomas, 38
Richter, J. P., 34, 203, 207
Ripley, George, 9, 11, 13, 29, 33, 34, 39, 40, 41, 44, 48, 49, 53, 58, 59 n, 65, 80, 80 n, 103-104, 105, 107, 108, 109, 110, 111, 111 n, 116, 118 n, 119, 119 n, 120, 120 n, 125, 132, 134, 165, 170, 176, 196 n, 210
Robbins, S. D., 48, 49, 50-51, 108, 115
Roelker, Bernard, 167, 171
Ruskin, 168, 169
Russell, J. L., 169, 173
Ryckman, L. W., 108

Saadi, 33, 207
Saint-Simon, 72
Sanborn, Frank, 205, 220, 231
Sand, George, 9, 112
Sargent, J. T., 213, 219
Saxton, J. A., 108, 110
Scheffler, J., 174
Schelling, 3, 65, 120
Scherb, E. V., 168, 171-172, 174-175
Schiller, 22, 34, 203, 207, 227
Schleiermacher, 25, 40, 120
Schlegel, A. W., 120 n
Sellers, J., 109, 110
Shackford, C. C., 227
Shaw, F. G., 108, 109, 111, 112
Shelley, 25, 25 n, 61, 140, 165

Index

Sill, E. R., 224-225
Simms, W. G., 116
Smith, Elizabeth O., 240
Socialism, chapters IV, V, and VI (see *Fourier*)
Southern Literary Messenger, The, 199
Southey, R., 165
Spencer, Herbert, 253
Spencer, W. H., 239
Spinoza, 63
Spirit of the Age, The, chapter VI
Stahlknecht, F. S., 95
Stallo, J. B., 119-120, 120 n, 169, 169 n, 195
Stanton, Elizabeth Cady, 226, 239
Starr, Eliza A., 109, 110
Stearns, G., 215
Sterling, George, 207, 255-256
Stevens, A. W., 238
Stewart, Dugald, 38
Stoddard, J. L., 239
Story, W. W., 108, 109, 113, 114, 117, 123
Sturgis, Caroline S., 30
Sue, Eugene, 139, 139 n
Sumner, Charles, 158, 159-160, 165
Sutcliffe, G., 151
Swedenborg, 3, 92, 92 n, 97, 100, 123-124, 125, 128-130, 128 n, 152, 167, 189-190, 189 n, 207, 207 n
Swedenborgianism, see *Swedenborg, Sampson Reed, Henry James, J. J. G. Wilkinson*
Swift, Lindsay, 88
Swinburne, 226

Taylor, Bayard, 115, 245
Tennyson, 124, 139, 169, 181, 186, 245
Thayer, G. A., 230
Thoreau, 31, 33, 35, 39-40, 40 n, 148, 154, 157 n, 158, 165, 168, 173, 186-187, 197, 205, 208, 220, 226, 229, 235, 242
Ticknor, George, 120 n
Tieck, L., 95
Toussenel, 203
Towne, E. C., 230
Transcendental Club, 12, 28, 40, 41, 157, 223
Transcendentalism, meaning and use of the term, 3, 4, 5, 6, 7, 9, 9 n, 10, 15-16, 19, 25, 40, 51, 55, 62, 64, 67, 70, 78, 124, 138, 145, 176, 178, 201, 211, 213, 232, 248, 249-250, 251; attitude toward problem of evil, 98, 113; connection with *belles lettres,* 15; controversy over, 14, 19 n, 23, 27 n, 45, 51, 59, 59 n, 60-62, 63, 64, 68, 74-75, 80, 92, 116, 129, 155, 204, 210, 211, 211 n, 220-221, 222-223, 228, 247, 248-253; effect of Civil War on, 12, 212; humorous aspects of, 7-8, 43, 68, 84, 90-91, 112 n, 138, 187, 198, 223; origin of, 3, 10-11, 49, 64, 145; outside of New England, chapters II and IX, 36; periodicals connected with, 14-15; scope of, 3, 15, 29, 49, 252; similarity to New Humanism, 10.
Transcendentalists, chief, 9-10, 11, 25, 41, 42, 122; concerted activity among, 13
Transon, Abel, 94
Traubel, Horace, 240
Tuckerman, J. F., 48
Tyler, Miss R. A., 48
Tweedy, E., 110

Uhland, 34, 175, 227
Underwood, B. F., 238, 239, 252-253
Underwood, Francis H., 192-193
Underwood, Sara A., 239, 243

Index

Unitarian, The, 39
Unitarians and Unitarianism, 9, 9 n, 10, 12, 17-19, 24, 28, 32, 84, 173, 183, .196, 201, 204, 208, 211, 212, 213, 219, 230, 231, 233-234, 235, 248
Univercoelum, The, 133, 133 n, 136

Very, Jones, 30, 33, 63, 115, 242
Voysey, C., 240

Walker, James, 73, 179
Ward, S. G., 149, 160, 166, 172, 172 n
Wasson, David A., 9, 216, 217, 231
Weiss, John, 9, 165, 168, 169, 216, 217, 224, 226, 227, 230, 231, 235
Western Messenger, The, chapter II, 61, 86 n, 115

Whipple, C. K., 217, 218
Whitman, Bernard, 39
Whitman, Sarah H., 48, 63
Whitman, Walt, 9, 9 n, 76, 99, 183, 221, 225
Whittier, J. G., 108, 114, 115, 139, 178 n, 226, 245
Wilkinson, J. J. G., 109, 110, 125-127, 127 n, 129, 135, 153
Wilson, W. D., 32
Winthrop, John, 210
Wollaston, W., 67
Woman's Journal, The, 225
Women's Rights, 47, 48, 143, 179, 204, 225-226, 233
Wordsworth, 21, 59, 165
Wright, Elizur, 239
Wright, Frances, 38, 39, 41

Zille, M., 168, 171

Printed in the United States
100008LV00003B/114/A